Royal
CHILDREN

Royal
CHILDREN

Ingrid Seward

St. Martin's Press
New York

For my mother

ROYAL CHILDREN. Copyright © 1993 by Ingrid Seward. All rights reserved. Printed in the United States of America. No part of this book may be used or reproduced in any manner whatsoever without written permission except in the case of brief quotations embodied in critical articles or reviews. For information, address St. Martin's Press, 175 Fifth Avenue, New York, N.Y. 10010.

Designed by Junie Lee

Library of Congress Cataloging-in-Publication Data

Seward, Ingrid.
    Royal children / Ingrid Seward.
      p.   cm.
    ISBN 0-312-10533-9
    1. Great Britain—Princes and princesses—Biography.
    2. Children—Great Britain—Biography.
    I. Title.
DA28.3.S47   1994
941'.009'92—dc20
[B]   93-37275
                                    CIP

First published in Great Britain by HarperCollins Publishers.

First U.S. Edition: January 1994
10 9 8 7 6 5 4 3 2 1

Contents

Royal
CHILDREN

Introduction

Family life has always been central to the British monarchy. It is what they have been there for – to stand as a symbol of continuity, a regal bulwark against the slippage of moral values and changing social mores.

As Prince Philip explained: 'If you are really going to have a monarchy, you have got to have a family, and the family has got to be in the public eye.'

The monarchy has been very much in the public eye, and the family, the *royal* family, has become a national obsession.

'We have a certain mystique which people look up to because they want to,' Prince Michael of Kent told me.

More than the adult members of the Royal Family, it was the children, in all their burnished innocence, in all their ordinariness, that provided the symbolic hope for the future – of the Royal Family, and of the nation it reigned over. From the moment of their birth, every detail of their development, no matter how mundane, how insignificant, was recorded in gushing tones. When a royal baby cut its first tooth, took its first step, or uttered its first word, the news was broadcast in tones of reverential excitement. The colour of its hair and eyes was discussed, the clothes it wore studied and copied. Even the names of its nannies, handmaidens to this live offering on the secular altar of Britain's national life, made front-page news.

But the foundations beneath the House of Windsor have shifted. The family, once so regal, so secure, finds itself on the defensive, its role the subject of a fundamental reappraisal. As first one, then *all*, of the marriages of the Queen's children came to their bitter ends, the methods by which they were raised – methods that seemed so right only a generation ago – came to be widely regarded as a woefully inadequate training for dealing with the demands and pressures of the modern age.

'Everyone has to have a sense of duty,' Prince Philip observed, 'a duty to society, to their family. If you haven't got a sense of duty you get the sort of community we have now.' But 'duty,' in the all-consuming royal sense which put the public performance before the needs of the individual, can exact its emotional toll. It did with Charles, Anne and Andrew – to the incomprehension of the Queen.

'And I thought I had brought them up so well,' she remarked sadly to her former private secretary, Lord Charteris, as she surveyed the marital ruptures in her children's lives in that '*annus horribilis*' of 1992 – which saw the Duke of York parted from his wife, Sarah, Princess Anne divorced and then remarried, and, most damaging of all, the official separation of the Prince and Princess of Wales. In the end duty wasn't enough to hold the family together, and each announcement stripped away another layer of that 'mystique' which George V believed was the Royal Family's greatest strength.

George V insisted that the dignity of their royal position had to be maintained at all times, and he carried this through into his family life. He summed up his attitude towards his offspring in a remark to the Earl of Derby: 'My father was frightened of his mother, I was frightened of my father, and I am damned well going to see that my children are frightened of me.'

He succeeded in his aim. His eldest son, David, later the

Duke of Windsor, wrote: 'We were, in fact, figuratively speaking, on parade, a fact that he would never allow us to forget.'

His children rarely saw him. When they did, they had to bow before they were first allowed to speak. From the viewpoint of the late-twentieth century, their letters home to their stern, intolerant father make poignant, pathetic reading. 'You must learn to behave like a boy and not like a little child,' he wrote to his ten-year-old son, the future Duke of Gloucester, who dutifully, fearfully replied, 'Dear Papa, Thank you very much for the nice letter you so kindly sent me . . .'

George VI, mindful of the unhappiness of his own childhood, tried to make amends with his own daughters, even going to the extent of bathing them himself – an almost unheard-of indulgence at the time. On matters educational, however, the old rule of benign neglect still applied. Elizabeth and Margaret's mother, now the Queen Mother, felt that the object of her daughters' education was to learn how to dance, draw, appreciate music, and to acquire good manners and 'lots of pleasant memories stored up against the days that might come and, later, happy marriage'.

It was left to the future Queen Elizabeth II and her forthright husband to bring the family into line with the modern world. The Royal Family still dwelt in their palaces, surrounded by courtiers. But they started to assimilate the new and decidedly more affectionate approach to childcare developed in the United States. Children were no longer to be seen and not heard.

The art of being royal, as the Queen pointed out, was a matter of practice. 'Training is the answer to a great many things,' she said. 'You can do a lot if you are properly trained – and I hope I have been.'

Prince Charles agreed. 'I've learnt the way a monkey learns – by watching its parents,' he remarked.

As Diana observed of her elder son, Prince William: 'I

always feel he will be all right because he was born to his royal role. He will get accustomed to it gradually.' His relations can give him specific advice, such as 'never cancel an engagement; if you have a headache take an aspirin' (Prince Philip); 'Never show emotion in public' (the Queen); and 'Never look at your feet' (the Queen Mother).

But if the deportment and decorum of royalty is there to be learnt by rote, there are other aspects that require more personal attention. 'What is much more difficult is bringing them up as people,' said Prince Philip. 'I've always tried to help them master at least one thing, because as soon as a child feels self-confidence in that area, it spills over into all others.'

He and Elizabeth tried to take a more caring interest in the development of their progeny. As part of their preparation for their royal role – a role that many had started to complain was in danger of becoming out of date, of losing its point – the Queen and Prince Philip invited a steering committee of educationalists to Buckingham Palace to discuss the best way of educating their children. It was a pointless exercise; Philip's mind was already made up. Tiring of the deliberations, he forcefully declared that his education had been good enough for him, and what was good enough for him was good enough for his children. Charles and Anne would be sent away to school.

As well-intentioned as it might have been, this insistence on 'normality' was never an easy objective for members of the Royal Family to achieve. They see their photographs in the newspapers almost every day. They observe the obsequious manner in which powerful people approach their parents. They are lavished with gifts.

'However hard you try, it's almost impossible to bring them up as ordinary children,' Prince Philip admitted.

The Princes William and Harry, so their father insists, 'are normal little boys'. But only up to a point. William, for example, received a £60,000 scaled-down Jaguar car for one birthday. His brother got a child-sized police motorcycle for his sixth birthday – and promptly asked what the Harrods van would be bringing him for Christmas. In 1992 Diana splashed out and bought them two £1,000 Go-Karts. When William got in an argument at school he threatened his adversary with his grandmother's soldiers. And after he was hit on the head with a golf club he wrote to a friend to report on his recovery – and warned him to lock the letter away so that it would not fall into the wrong hands.

As Prince Charles observed, everything they do creates 'an abnormal amount of attention'.

That, given the privileged position they enjoy, is inevitable. But the pressure the attention generates, as Princess Margaret has said, can be 'perfectly dreadful'. It has been exacerbated in recent years by the tide of unfavourable stories that has engulfed the Royal Family.

Referring to his own children, Prince Michael of Kent told me: 'They are obviously very unhappy when they read nasty things about any of us. We try not to let them see anything, but at school children talk.'

It was even worse for the heir to the throne, Prince William, and his younger brother, Prince Harry. There was no way, no matter how hard everyone tried, that they could be shielded from the catalogue of misfortunes that overwhelmed their parents.

The late Prince William of Gloucester remarked, 'It is almost impossible to describe what it is like being a member of the Royal Family. I suppose in essence it comes down to this: you can never be your real self. Just to know you are royal inhibits you. It wasn't that anyone ever said to me, "You are a royal prince and you must act like one." I simply knew that whether I liked it or not, I was automatically separated by my heritage from the rest of the world.'

'I think the younger members find the regimented side difficult,' the Queen conceded.

Forced to live under the ever-present scrutiny of telephoto lenses and the fear of unauthorized tape-recordings, the Royal Family has acquired something akin to a siege mentality. 'We have shown how to close ranks when the neighbours turn unfriendly,' the Queen said.

For the senior branch of the family, the isolation can be all but complete. It is reinforced by a protocol so rigid that even sons and daughters must bow and curtsey to their mother, the Queen. Only Princess Anne has managed to break free and bring her children up in a relaxed and truly normal way, and she could only achieve that by turning her back on her own royal inheritance. Anne refused to allow Peter and Zara Phillips to have a title, sent them to the local country school and insisted on looking after them herself for much of the time, rather than handing them over into the full-time care of nannies. In matters of the heart she has proved herself equally determined. She fell in love with Commander Tim Laurence, a former equerry to the Queen, and despite the hostility of several powerful voices in the royal Household who objected to her relationship with someone they regarded as a servant who had exceeded his duties, she went ahead and married him.

For her elder brother and future king, there was no such escape. He is a prisoner of his position. 'You can't understand what it is like to have your whole life mapped out for you a year in advance,' he once complained. 'It's so awful to be programmed . . . At times I get fed up with the whole idea.' But those constraints, inhibiting as they were, gave a comforting order to Prince Charles's life. When his marriage broke up, the pattern of his life was thrown into confusion and he descended into severe depression. He felt isolated and alone – and he was.

Prince Philip once stressed: 'The children soon discover that it is much safer to unburden yourself to a member of the family than just a friend. You see, you're never quite sure. A small indiscretion can lead to all sorts of difficulties.'

The greater indiscretion – allegedly of marital infidelity culminating in official separation – Charles had to face alone. His father, Philip, had suffered a severely disrupted childhood. Michael Parker, his first private secretary, said: 'When he needed a father there just wasn't anybody there.' His son felt the same. 'The last person Charles would have gone to for advice would be his father,' one courtier remarked. The royal system of family life had broken down.

The old routines of royalty are hard to break, however, and the outward structure is still in place. The family still comes together – at Balmoral and Sandringham – for their traditional holidays. The footmen still wear livery. And the nannies continue to underpin the system.

Throughout this century the royal children have been brought up, not by their parents, but by the spinster daughters of policemen and forestry workers. It is the working-class nannies, not the royal mothers, who have assumed the responsibility for what child psychologist Penelope Leach calls the 'nurturing and loving' so essential to the emotional development of any child. It is the nannies who have been responsible for making sure that the youngsters in their care learn how to sit still, to say 'Please' and 'Thank you', to curtail any bad habits (both the Queen and Princess Margaret bit their nails as children), for smacking them if they deserve it.

Most have been dedicated women who provided their royal charges with all the affection they required (though one was later revealed to be a sexual sadist). But however caring and competent they may have been, they could never completely compensate for the lack of parental affection.

Nor could they break the 'glass wall' that isolates and protects their charges from the rigours of the real world. In this closeted environment there has been little room for individuality – or for the tactile affection most 'ordinary' families take for granted. Royal children are taught how to behave in public. They are not taught how to deal with private problems. Instead of having to learn how to cope with emotional situations, they are able to retreat behind the protective panoply of their position.

When Prince Andrew met Koo Stark, for instance, he terminated his relationship with his previous girlfriend, a dancer with the Royal Ballet, Christina Parker, the following day. Overwhelmed by Koo but unwilling to come clean with Christina, he simply instructed the Buckingham Palace switchboard to stop putting through her telephone calls and never spoke to her again – exactly as his great-uncle, the Duke of Windsor, had done when he ended his liaison with Freda Dudley Ward.

However efficient that way may be when dealing with dispensable emotional jetsam, it is no method for dealing with the difficulties of married life, and it is noteworthy that the marriages of Princess Margaret and Princess Anne ended in divorce, that the Duke and Duchess of York separated after only five and a half years, and that the union between the Prince and Princess of Wales became marooned in the trough of incompatibility. To marry happily into the Royal Family, if one is not royal oneself, has proved an impossibility.

The attention that these failures attract is a fairly recent phenomenon. The cult of the Royal Family, with its attendant cast of children, uncles and aunts and distant cousins, is a Victorian invention. It was a sturdy, self-confident era and Britain was the richest nation in the world with an ever-expanding empire that embraced a quarter of the globe. Such power cried out for its own mythology, and to help provide it the concept of the 'Royal Family', which would symbolize all the inherent strengths of a nation at the zenith of its might, was conceived.

This natural development, engendered by chauvinistic national pride, was readily seized upon by the public, by the politicians and by the monarchy itself – Queen Victoria was delighted when her Prime Minister Benjamin Disraeli made her Empress of India, as he knew she would be. It was a temporal deity that drew its strength, not from any divinity (that notion had died on the block with Charles I), but from those stolid Victorian virtues of moral rectitude, thrift, good manners, and decorum which it came to represent. That certain members of the family should tumble from such an exalted pedestal was only to be expected.

'Like all the best families, we have our share of eccentricities, of impetuous and wayward youngsters and of family disagreements,' the Queen acknowledged. Those disagreements are sometimes so extreme that they spill over into physical violence.

Of greater remark, however, than the fact that some members of the Royal Family fail to live up to what is expected of them is that most of them have, repaying homage with duty, the trappings of their majesty with a commitment to hard work.

'If you have privilege, which in my case you were born with, you have no option,' Prince Michael of Kent said to me. 'You can't have all the perks without pulling your weight. You can't have it without some kind of obligation.'

It is an obligation, a sense of responsibility, that is bred into them – often at great personal cost, as we have now seen – from the day the guns sound to salute their births. And it is a way of royal life that is coming to an end, as the royal family faces up to the challenge of sustaining its existence into the next century.

Elizabeth

◆

*E*lizabeth was brought up, not to be Queen, not to shoulder responsibility, certainly not to get a job. She was brought up simply to enjoy a childhood which, as her governess observed, would provide her 'with lots of pleasant memories stored up against the days that might come and, later, happy marriage.'

The rigours of the three Rs were of secondary importance. Her mother had been taught to read the Bible and little else. That had been good enough for her. It was expected to be enough for her daughter and, later, her younger child, Margaret.

'I often had the feeling,' the governess, Marion Crawford recorded, 'that the Duke and Duchess, most happy in their own married life, were not over concerned with the higher education of their daughters.'

There was no apparent need for it, at least in their infancy. Elizabeth's father, Bertie, Duke of York, was a second son; a shy, unsure, frail man who was not destined for the throne and harboured no ambitions in that direction. He was a country man who had little interest in society, and was more than happy to let the sun of majesty shine on the blond head of his charismatic elder brother, David.

His wife was a woman of singular determination and great

11

spirit, as events would prove. But in 1926, when their daughter made her entrance by Caesarean section at 2.40 a.m. on the morning of 21 April, the horizon of parental ambition extended no further than the comfortable expectations of their class and the time.

Named Elizabeth Alexandra Mary—after her mother, great-grandmother and grandmother—she was the third grandchild and first granddaughter of George V and Queen Mary. The first General Strike in British history was only four weeks away, the barricades were being erected and there was talk of revolution. But such social upheavals made little indent on the secure world—of country houses and shooting parties and very occasional visits to Buckingham Palace—the young princess was born into. Her life was mapped out for her: a 'happy childhood' followed by a suitable marriage to a European princeling, or more probably, since the King had changed the ruling that members of his family could only marry royalty, a member of the aristocracy; then children of her own. Her royal connection was a fact of blood, not of responsibility. The baby Elizabeth was third in line to the throne—after her uncle and her father—but only, it was presumed, for the time being; only until David married and had children of his own, or until her own parents produced a son. And when that happened—and in 1926 everyone believed the 'when' was an inevitability—Elizabeth would slip hardly observed down the line of succession into upper-class obscurity.

To ensure that the little princess grew up into a young lady, Clara Knight, who had been nanny in turn to both the Duchess and her brother, David, and later to their elder sister Lady Elphinstone's children, was duly reemployed. She was a no-nonsense Hertfordshire woman who organized her young charge according to the same strict methods she had employed with the previous generation. Fashions in child-rearing may change in most circles, but the routine of the old-fashioned English nanny does not.

Known as Alah—the name was a childish derivation of her Christian name—she had unchallenged control of the nursery. She subscribed to the view that it was harmful to pamper children. Everything—feeding, baths—had its time, and if the child chose to raise a cry of protest she was left to get on with it.

The Duchess raised no objections to such methods and allowed Alah to do her job in her own way. She had no reason to wish it otherwise. Elizabeth Bowes Lyon and all her family had been brought up in exactly the same way. The era of 'bonding' and the associated belief in the importance of a mother's tactile love were several generations away in the future. In the homes of the well-to-do, children were seen only twice a day, once in the morning and then again before they went to bed at night.

The little princess was no less loved for that. The Duchess of York—she was twenty-five when her elder daughter was born—was an adoring mother. The Duke, constrained by his own childhood, always found it difficult to show affection (he found it embarrassing, Marion Crawford remembered, when his infant daughter, Margaret, wound her arms round his neck, nestled against him and cuddled and caressed him. 'He was not a demonstrative man'). But he did enjoy the sense of warm familial comfort his daughter's presence generated: he enjoyed bath-time and pillow fights and taught her how to play hopscotch.

Alah, too, for all her sternness (another of the Bowes Lyon family's nannies remembers her as 'quite easygoing', but given the constraints of the time the term is comparative) was very fond of her ward, and for that the little Elizabeth, when appraised of the unpleasant and sometimes violent misery a succession of unsuitable nannies had made of her father's childhood, would later have cause for gratitude.

Yet however much affection may have been showered on her, Elizabeth was still a personage of secondary importance in the grand scheme of things, and when she was only nine months old her parents left her for an extended six-month tour of Australia.

How attitudes towards a mother's responsibilities have changed. When the Duchess left her baby for six months in 1927 she was applauded for doing her wifely duty. When the next Duchess of York left her newborn child, Beatrice, for less than six weeks in 1988 to travel to Australia to see her husband, she was subjected to an outburst of public disapprobation from which she never recovered. But that is now; in 1927 it would have been considered strange, if not downright disloyal, had the Duchess allowed her royal husband to undertake such an 'arduous' trip alone.

It was the beginning of what for Elizabeth was going to have to be duty's lifelong victory over emotion, though, baby that she was, she was too young to remember the sound of those first salvos being fired. Hers was still a world of the most primal needs, and those were well taken care of, for as well as Nanny Alah, she also enjoyed the attentions of 22-year-old Margaret MacDonald, whom Elizabeth renamed Bobo, and who was in charge of the nursery kitchen, and her fourteen-year-old sister, Ruby, who acted as under-nurse.

Elizabeth had been born at 17 Bruton Street in Mayfair, the London home of her maternal grandfather, the 14th Earl of Strathmore, whose ancestor had acquired the family's title by marrying the daughter of Scotland's king, Robert II, and whose later forebear, the 9th Earl, had acquired a suitable fortune to go with it by marrying the daughter of a Durham mine-owner. With her parents gone, it was decided to remove the bairn and her nursery entourage to Strathmore's eighteenth-century mansion at St Paul's Walden Bury in Hertfordshire, where Alah had started work for the Bowes Lyons in 1901 at the age of seventeen. The house was little used at that time, and a bitterly cold winter forced a tactical withdrawal the following month back to London—not to Bruton Street, but to a speedily organized nursery at Buckingham Palace. They arrived on 10 February.

'Our sweet little grandchild arrived here yesterday and came to see us after tea,' George V recorded in his diary.

The King did not get on well with children of the male gender. His own sons had walked in fear of his louring temperament, and so did his grandsons, one of whom, George Lascelles, the future Earl of Harewood, remembers, 'The possibility of getting something wrong was, where grandfather was concerned, raised to the heights of extreme probability, and our visits to Windsor for Easter usually provided their quota of uneasy moments.'

Even a child's occasional ill-health elicited no sympathy from the King Emperor. One April, the then eight-year-old George Lascelles started to sneeze, 'either from the pollinated grass or sheer nerves, and no amount of assurance that I had hay fever could stop the shout of "Get that damn child away from me", which made a rather strong impression on an awakening imagination.'

The King, so unbending, so demanding with his male progeny, was more considerate towards the females. He had allowed his daughter Mary, whom he made Princess Royal, a licence he always denied her four brothers. And he doted, albeit in a gruff and frequently intimidating manner, on his eldest granddaughter. It was affection hard won. Neither Elizabeth nor her younger sister ever called him Grandpa England, as popular legend had it. As Princess Margaret would later recall: 'We were much too frightened of him to call him anything but Grandpapa.'

15

Elizabeth, however, always appeared to have his measure. He called her Lilibet, the nickname given her by her sister Margaret when she was too young to pronounce Elizabeth. She would play with his beard—it tickled—and the Archbishop of Canterbury, Dr Gordon Cosmo Lang, once observed her tugging him along by it across the floor, on his hands and knees.

There was another side to this grandparental equation, which came in the form of his imperious wife, Queen Mary. If the King could occasionally let, if not his hair, then his beard down, she was always as ramrod-straight in manner as her back was to look at. A visit to this stiff, imposing woman, Princess Margaret would remember, brought a 'hollow, empty feeling to the pit of the stomach.'

In a world where appearances counted for everything, Queen Mary had a mania for maintaining them. She had to, or so she thought, for this most royal of queens wasn't royal at all by the strict dictates of blood; or at least wasn't royal enough to be considered as the equal in rank to her British relations.

Queen Mary's grandfather, Duke Alexander of Württemberg, had ventured beyond his caste and married a Hungarian countess without a royal bloodline. Because their union was, according to the rules in force in the nineteenth century, a morganatic one, Francis, their son and Mary's father, was not allowed to succeed to the Württemburg throne. Queen Victoria, who was grand enough to make her own dynastic rules, wrote, 'I have always thought and do think it very wrong and very absurd that because his mother was not a Princess he is not to succeed in Württemberg', and Francis was duly allowed to marry Victoria's first cousin, Princess Mary Adelaide of Cambridge, who, like the Queen herself, was a granddaughter of George III.

This minor German princeling—who had been compensated for the loss of his inheritance with the title Prince

Teck—encountered little competition for the hand of his royal quarry, Princess Mary Adelaide. She was exceedingly large and, as the Foreign Secretary, Lord Clarendon, drolly remarked, 'Alas, no German prince will venture on *so vast an undertaking.*' The good-looking Francis had no such reservations, for as well as having no throne he had no money, and being married to a princess, even one whose own lady-in-waiting felt moved to describe as looking like a 'large plush purple pincushion', did have its compensations.

Their daughter Mary—who was born in May 1867, the year after her parents' marriage, and was thus nicknamed May by her mother who called her 'my May-flower'—was never anything more than a poor relation, however, and one who was getting poorer. Her parents were profligate with what little money they had and the lot they borrowed, and when their daughter was sixteen years old they were, as May observed, in Short Street. With creditors closing in and threatening writs, they debunked to Florence, where they remained for two years.

This background, coupled with her dubious pedigree, did not make her an enticing marriage prospect.

But again Queen Victoria intervened, and determined to marry her off. First she thought of one of her grandsons, the backward Albert Victor, Duke of Clarence, notorious because of his rumoured involvement in the Jack the Ripper case and the Cleveland Street Scandal which followed a police raid on a homosexual brothel. Then, when he died, she thought of his altogether more suitable brother, the future George V.

'So it came about,' Kenneth Rose wrote in his definitive biography, *George V*, 'that a young woman without a fortune, seemingly condemned to spinsterhood by a flawed pedigree, found herself destined to be Queen Consort of Great Britain. In that sense Princess May was indeed a Cinderella, and Queen Victoria a godmother of unbounded benevolence.'

The humiliations suffered in childhood, however, were to

govern the rest of her life. They would have a profound influence on the Royal Family, with effects which echo down to the present day.

Mary was well-educated, naturally intelligent, and far more cultured than her husband, since she had developed a learned interest in the history of art during her enforced stay in Italy. Those attributes, however, were well concealed. Her oldest friend, Mabell, Countess of Airlie, said of her; 'As a girl she had been shy and reserved, but now her shyness had so crystallized . . . The hard crust of inhibition which gradually closed over her, hiding the warmth and tenderness of her own personality, was already starting to form.'

The Royal Family have never been very adept at welcoming outsiders into their regal nest, and Mary was treated with ill-disguised contempt by her sisters-in-law. Princess Louise, disdainful of her morganatic lineage, would loudly say; 'Poor May! Poor May! With her Württemberg hands.' Princess Victoria once spitefully ordered a guest at Windsor; 'Now do try to talk to May at dinner, though one knows she is deadly dull.' It is hardly any wonder that this excruciatingly shy woman chose to retreat into herself. With her position as protection, she became alert to an almost disturbed degree to the nuances of protocol and status, unwilling and eventually unable to soften the defensive persona of intimidating formality she swathed herself in. She subjugated herself to her old-fashioned husband's will—the King did not approve of change, and Mary spent her life dressed in the styles of the Edwardian age he favoured—and expected her children to do the same.

'King George V and Queen Mary have often been depicted as stern unloving parents, but this they most certainly were not,' Mabell, Countess of Airlie wrote. 'I believe that they were more conscientious and more truly devoted to their children than the majority of parents in that era. The tragedy was that neither had any understanding of a child's mind.' Age would soften her only imperceptibly; the self-enforced habits of a lifetime are hard to change.

This, then, was the old lady into whose effective control the Duchess entrusted her young daughter during her six-month absence, and under whose orders Alah now came.

In any disagreement with the Duchess, Alah had the right of reply. The Queen, however, had to be obeyed without question. The Duchess, in her dealings with her former nanny, was by childish habit still a child, and Alah the surrogate mother. In the presence of the formidable May of Teck, however, the usually formidable Alah reverted to being a servant—highly regarded, one whose judgement and opinion were valued, but a servant nonetheless.

'Teach that child not to fidget!' she repeatedly commanded the nanny.

On the Queen's firm instructions, Elizabeth was taught to wave to the crowds on command, to pose for photographers, to control her bladder in return for the reward of a biscuit. To ensure that she didn't fidget, the pockets of her dress were sown up. All this before she was three years old.

The Duchess herself was a part of this system. Many women run into difficulties with their mothers-in-law. For a young woman obliged by protocol to open and close any conversation with her husband's mother from the humbling position of a formal curtsey, a certain tension was inevitable. The Duchess may have harboured misgivings and resentments about the situation—it would have been unusual if she hadn't—but this was one cross-generational battle Elizabeth Bowes Lyon was not going to win.

Duty, as Queen Mary impressed upon her daughter-in-law, had always to come before personal considerations. The 'family firm', as Bertie called it, had a business to run.

The Duchess, whose own childhood had been a happy and united one, was distressed by the separation and took leave of her baby in floods of tears. As George VI's official biographer, Sir John Wheeler-Bennett, noted, the car that took the Duke and Duchess to the station to catch the train to Portsmouth where they embarked on the battle cruiser HMS *Renown* 'had to be driven around until she was composed enough to face the crowds'.

The Duchess had reason to be upset. By being away for those six months during that formative period, by allowing her own nursery staff to fall under the direct order of the most 'royal' of this century's most formidable and caste-conscious royals, the Duchess had undermined her own maternal importance. Queen Mary had no desire to usurp the mother's role; unless the King happened to be in the room when Elizabeth was brought into her sitting room after tea, the visit would only last a few minutes before she was whisked back to the nursery. Displays of affection were not Queen Mary's style. Smothering order and system was, and the reference point had been established.

When the Duchess eventually returned, the baby, who had thwarted all Alah's efforts to get her to say 'Mother' or even 'Mama' (though she was quite able to say Alah and Bobo), refused to go into her arms. There were tears and much hanging on to Nanny's skirts before Lilibet could be persuaded to join her mother for the requisite family appearance on the Buckingham Palace balcony.

Putting that upsetting scene behind, the Duchess determined to build a happy home of her own for her husband and her daughter. The Yorks moved out of Bruton Street and into 145 Piccadilly, where the Intercontinental Hotel now stands, just a few yards away from where the queue starts for the Hard Rock Cafe. 'It might have been the home of any moderately well-to-do young couple starting married life,' Marion Crawford opined, with understatement. It was a bit more than that:

an imposing four-storey mansion situated at the genteel heart of an empire's capital, with commanding views from the back over the private Hamilton Gardens to Hyde Park and, from the front, across Green Park to Buckingham Palace. Elizabeth's nursery was on the top floor, 'comfortable, sunny rooms that opened on to a landing beneath a big dome'.

It was a self-contained world edged with loneliness. Elizabeth had no one to play with other than her cousins, and they were rare visitors. The birth of her sister, Margaret Rose, on 21st August, 1930, gave her a companion; but she was four years her junior and hardly a ready-made playmate.

'I shall call her Bud,' Lilibet declared.

'Why Bud?' Lady Cynthia Asquith enquired.

'Well, she's not a Rose yet, is she? She's only a Bud,' the elder princess is said to have replied.

The Duke of York, giving unconscious expression to their isolation, always referred to his family as 'us four'. The greater world was locked out, and Elizabeth and Margaret rarely mixed with other children. On their walks through Hyde Park they would see others of their age laughing and playing together, but they did not join in.

'Other children always had an enormous fascination, like mystic beings from a different world, and the little girls used to smile shyly at those they liked the look of,' Marion Crawford recalled. 'They would have loved to speak to them and make friends, but this was never encouraged. I often have thought it a pity. They seldom had other children to tea.' Destined, as it turned out, for society's pinnacle, they were always outside society.

Elizabeth's real friends were not people. They were the foot-high toy horses on wheels that she collected. Eventually there were some thirty of them, each with its own saddle and bridle, and they were carefully stabled around the dome on the landing. Before she went to bed, Elizabeth would unsaddle them, to groom and water them. It was 'a must-to-be-done chore' every night.

In the early thirties two books were published which allowed an unprecedented insight into the home life of members of the Royal Family. One was entitled *The Story of Princess Elizabeth* written by Anne Ring, a former secretary to the Duchess. The other was Lady Cynthia Asquith's *The Married Life of Her Royal Highness the Duchess of York*. Both were written with 'the personal approval of Her Royal Highness'. Both painted a cosy picture of domestic bliss: of bath nights with the Duke (itself an unusual occurrence in an age where fathers rarely ventured on to the nursery floor), with Alah begging him 'not to get Lilibet too excited'; of Elizabeth and Margaret Rose armed with the red brushes and dustpans 'with which every morning the little princesses sweep the thick pile carpet.'

But if it was cosy it was also strictly ordered, with little room for individual expression or the inquisitive vagaries of infancy.

Elizabeth got up at 7.30, breakfasted in the nursery, then joined her parents for fifteen minutes before starting her lessons—a ritual that lasted right up to the morning of her wedding day.

At 11 o'clock she broke for half an hour for a glass of orangeade and a biscuit. Lunch was at 1.15 which, when she was a little older, she ate with her parents if they happened to be at home. The afternoons were spent out of doors or, if it was raining, drawing, attempting to master knitting, which she was always very poor at, and studying music. Tea was at 4.45. Between 5.30 and 6.30 her mother came to play. Supper followed. Then, punctually at 7.15, she was sent to bed. It was an inflexible routine broken only by the trips north to Scotland in the autumn and weekends spent at Royal Lodge, the Yorks' country home in Windsor Great Park.

Marion Crawford arrived at 145 Piccadilly when Elizabeth

was five years old. 'Until I came she had never been allowed to get dirty,' she remembered. 'Life had consisted of drives in the park, or quiet ladylike games in Hamilton Gardens, keeping to the paths; or leisurely drives around London in an open carriage, waving graciously to people when Alah told her to do so.'

Relations between Marion Crawford and Alah started off on the cool side. The nanny regarded her rival for the children's affection with a mixture of what the new governess called 'reserve and apprehension'. The girls, susceptible as children are to moods, will have caught that initial atmosphere, though the two women eventually effected a stand-off of expedience. 'If on her side the neutrality was sometimes armed to the teeth, I was always very careful not to tread on her toes,' the governess recorded.

Marion Crawford, quickly dubbed Crawfie by Elizabeth, was a 22-year-old school teacher from Kilmarnock in Scotland who had worked with poor, undernourished, underdeveloped children in the slums of Edinburgh and, 'fired with a crusading spirit', had aspirations to become a child psychologist. Instead, a holiday job with the Earl and Countess of Elgin led to an introduction to Lady Rose Leveson-Gower and then to her sister, the Duchess of York. She was offered a job. The Duchess, determined to have her own way at least in her own home, insisted upon having a young governess, and after a month's probationary trial, Crawford gave up her ambition to work with the deprived and accepted the post in one of the most privileged households in the country.

It was, she recalled, a very *ordered* household, though, despite its royal master, an unpretentious one. She introduced her charges to games of Red Indians and hide-and-seek, and allowed Elizabeth, to her great delight, to get herself dirty (but only when Alah wasn't looking). But the high point of what in retrospect seems their rather dull routine was watching the brewer's dray drawn by two horses which passed by every day and drew up at the traffic lights below the nursery.

'The little girls, their faces pressed to the nursery window, would watch for them fondly, anxious if they were late,' Crawfie said. 'And many a weary little pony trotting home at the end of the day in its coster's cart little dreamed of the wealth of royal sympathy it roused from that upper window . . .

'No two children had a simpler outlook on life. Early to bed and very, few treats or outings, and those of an extremely unsophisticated nature.' A trip on a double-decker bus, sitting upstairs of course, one journey by underground to the YWCA at Tottenham Court Road, trips to Woolworth's to do their Christmas shopping, and one pantomime a year was the sum of their visits to 'the outside world of which they knew so little'.

Elizabeth was taught to ride and to fox hunt (her father wanted her 'blooded' with the Pytchley at the age of five but the fox got away that day), to swim, and to stalk stag in the Scottish Highlands. They were the kind of skills deemed necessary for well-born country women. While they certainly did the young Elizabeth no measurable harm—she was, her governess remarked, always an 'immensely interesting child' with a high IQ—it was hardly an upbringing designed to broaden her intellectual or social view-point. But that was not what was wanted. As Crawfie observed: 'Perhaps it was generally conceded in those days that the education of two not very important little girls did not matter a great deal.'

George V's only instruction to his granddaughters' governess was to make sure they learned how to write properly. 'I like a hand with some character in it,' he decreed.

The indomitable Queen Mary, on the other hand, had the most decided views on the education of the next generation of a dynasty which was not hers in name but was half hers by morganatic bloodline.

Crawfie had been in trepidation of her first meeting with the imperious May of Teck, and had spent the morning practising her curtsey before the oak tree in Hamilton Gardens. (Trees provide invaluable royal training. The last Kaiser's grandmother was the only member of the Prussian court who did not find the official receptions mind-numbing and exhausting, having been taught as a child to address a few well-chosen remarks to every tree she passed on her daily walks.) As it turned out, the old Queen and the young governess found common cause in first Elizabeth, then Margaret.

The Duchess was content to let Crawfie, as she had Alah, get on with her job as she saw fit. That troubled the governess, who 'worried a lot' at the responsibility so forced on her. In desperation she looked to Queen Mary for guidance. It was promptly given. The Queen became what Crawfie called a 'wonderful ally' as she battled to provide a practical educational foundation on which to build the Duchess's idealized notion of childhood, which was 'to spend as long as possible in the open air, to enjoy to the full the pleasure of the country, to be able to dance and appreciate music, to acquire good manners and perfect deportment, and to cultivate all the distinctly feminine graces.'

There were many times, Crawfie said, when she turned to the Queen when she was 'in trouble. She was always a rock of strength and wisdom to me, someone I could go to in moments of doubt and difficulty. There were to be plenty of both.' Less for Crawfie, as it happens, than for Queen Mary, who was having to face up to the consequences of the disturbingly irresponsible behaviour of her eldest son.

In the royal manner, nobody broke the code of discretion that cements their lips in silence and actually referred to the looming crisis. 'Maybe the general hope was that if nothing was said the whole business would blow over,' Crawfie said. It didn't. The Prince of Wales exchanged one married mistress for another, and then took up with the most undesirable one of all: Wallis Simpson. His wilful reluctance to find himself a suitable girlfriend who would make a suitable wife inevitably focused attention on the heiress presumptive, the little Princess Elizabeth.

It was vital, the old Queen ruled, that Elizabeth should study genealogy, that comedy of bloodlines running back to Queen Victoria which provided Europe with its royal houses.

History, too, was important, as was poetry ('wonderful memory training') and a knowledge of the geography of the British Empire.

But Maths? 'Was Arithmetic really more valuable,' the Queen wanted to know, 'than History?' Money is not a subject of practical concern to the Royal Family; Elizabeth, the Queen observed with telling foresight, would probably never have to do her own household accounts.

Crawfie took note. 'Queen Mary's practical suggestions were most welcome and I revised the schoolroom schedule for Princess Elizabeth accordingly.' Whether the Duchess ever knew about this, and if she did whether she cared, is not recorded. The answer in both cases is probably not. The Yorks, so determinedly bourgeois in all other things, simply did not consider education a matter of any great importance. 'No one ever had employers who interfered so little,' the governess noted.

What did concern the Yorks, just as much as it did Queen Mary, was the Prince of Wales's affair with Wallis Simpson. It was a liaison branded with the hallmark of catastrophe— for the country, for the Crown and, most particularly, for the Yorks themselves.

George V died on 20 January, 1936 (by the hand of his doctor, it transpired, who administered him a lethal injection of cocaine to ensure that the announcement of his death would make the next morning's edition of *The Times* and not the less respectable evening papers). David was now King Edward VIII. The Crown's hold on him, however, was less than Wallis Simpson's, and he would soon let go of his birthright 'for the woman I love'.

Bertie, afflicted with a bad stammer and frail of health, did not want to shoulder the responsibility of kingship. He did not believe he was up to it. He had not been trained for it, he complained. A number of senior government advisors agreed, and when it became clear that a new king was going to have to be found, there was a suggestion, recorded in 1947 'by gracious permission of His Majesty the King', by Dermot Morrah, Fellow of All Souls College, Oxford, that the Crown should go to his younger brother, the sexually adventurous Duke of Kent. It was, however, only a suggestion. As far as most people were concerned, the Crown could only go to Bertie.

'This is absolutely desperate,' he cried to his cousin, the future Earl Mountbatten of Burma. 'I've never even seen a State paper.' (Another cousin, Nicholas II, expressed the same sentiments when the imperial Crown of Russia came to him. 'What's going to happen to me?' the last czar wailed. 'I'm not prepared to be a czar. I never wanted to become one. I know nothing of the business of ruling. I have no idea of even how to talk to the ministers.')

The only real solution to the crisis threatening to engulf the Royal House of Windsor, however, was to pass the Crown to the next in line, however reluctant he might be to accept it. Some order had to be made of the chaos David's ill-considered affair had caused.

When the news was broken to Bertie by his mother that the uncrowned Edward VIII had done the unthinkable and abdicated the throne, passing his responsibilities to him, 'I broke down and sobbed like a child'. The Queen, needless to say, was highly embarrassed by this display of weakness in yet another of her sons. 'Really!' she was heard to complain in the middle of the abdication crisis. 'This might be Rumania.'

The Duchess had not been quite the support she might have been as events had moved towards their dénouement. As the abdication approached she retired to bed ill—'a not uncommon reaction, throughout her life, to moments of great stress,' as Robert Lacey has noted. Faced with a situation from which there was no retreat, however, the new Queen Consort showed her mettle. She had not wanted to be Queen, but when the role was thrust upon her she assumed its mantle with grace and natural poise.

There was a dark personal side to this apparently blossoming public face. Bertie, now transmogrified into George VI, had always been prone to tantrums, known to his family as 'gnashes'. The confusion and fear engendered by this dramatic change in his position and by the later worries caused by the war only served to exacerbate his unsteady and sometimes violent temperament.

His father, George V, had been subject to similar temper fits. His married life was less than blissful, and King and Queen found it so difficult to communicate that they had to write letters to each other instead. Late in his life, Edward VIII, then Duke of Windsor, told James Pope-Hennessy: 'Off the record, my father had a most horrible temper. He was foully rude to my mother. Why, I've seen her leave the table because he was so rude to her, and we children would all follow her out.' The Duke added, 'Not when staff are present, of course.' But staff have a way of always finding out about such things. George V's behaviour was well-discussed in the servant's quarters, as was George VI's: there are still people in the employ of the Royal Household who recall George VI's violent outbursts—who remember how on occasion he became so out-of-control that he actually struck his own wife.

Scenes of such private unhappiness and frustration were

never played out in public. Nor, as far as it was possible to contain them, were they allowed to intrude on to the nursery floor. 'We want our children to have a happy childhood which they can always look back on,' Queen Elizabeth would insist.

The happy family idyll, however, had been damaged. The family were forced to move out of 145 Piccadilly and into Buckingham Palace, a cold, impersonal building with endless corridors which could take a whole morning to navigate. Couldn't they build a tunnel back to Piccadilly, Elizabeth wistfully suggested? The real world, with its domestic upsets and feuds and subtleties of status and inexorable duty could not be locked out. The ritual of bath-time had to be changed because the Duke and Duchess, who before had spent most of their evenings at home, were now out almost every night at official functions.

The children, the older Elizabeth in particular, could not but be aware of the tensions—of the strain events had caused their father, of the way their mother, once so relaxed and easygoing, now looked drawn and older. There had also been a change in her own status. As a little girl, Elizabeth had been taught to curtsey to her grandparents whenever she visited them. The aura of majesty, in power even at home, had now fallen on her parents and she was instructed by Crawfie that henceforth they had to curstey to Papa and Mummy.

'Margaret too?' Elizabeth asked.

'Margaret also,' was the answer. 'And try not to topple over.'

The King and his Queen Consort quickly put a stop to that.

The ten-year-old princess was not in any doubt about what her position was, though—and hadn't been for some years. Elizabeth, Crawfie insisted, was a 'special' child; neat, courteous, conscientious, unusually well-behaved and 'very shy'. She was aware from the earliest age of just where she stood in the pecking order. Her parents wanted their daughter to feel herself a 'member of the community' but, as Crawfie remarked, 'just how difficult this is to achieve, if you live in a palace, is hard to explain. A glass curtain seems to come down between you and the outer world, between the hard realities of life and those who dwell in a court.' When she played in Hamilton Gardens, crowds of people would often gather to peer at her through the railings, as if they were contemplating some exotic creature at the zoo. When she went for walks through Hyde Park she was often recognized.

'Ignore them,' Alah ordered, following her own advice and striding purposefully past the gaping onlookers, looking neither to left nor right. With Alah as her trainer, Elizabeth's ability to completely disregard the stares of the inquisitive soon became second nature.

But she knew why they were looking.

When she was seven years old, Elizabeth was addressed by the Lord Chamberlain with a cheery, 'Good morning, little lady.'

'I'm not a little lady,' came the imperious reply. 'I'm Princess Elizabeth!'

This display of regal asperity proved too much for Queen Mary, who promptly marched her granddaughter into the Lord Chamberlain's office and said, 'This is Princess Elizabeth, who one day hopes to be a lady.'

But Princess she certainly was, and with her uncle gone and the likelihood of her parents producing a son and heir apparent receding with each passing year, a queen she was ever more likely to become. The impact of that impending burden only hardened her emotional restraint.

The death of George V had provoked no outward display of emotion, only the question whether it was right that she should continue playing with her toy horses (Crawfie said it was). After she was taken to see her grandfather lying in state in Westminster Hall, she remarked: 'Uncle David was there and he never moved at all. Not even an eyelid. It was wonderful. And everyone was so quiet. As if the King were asleep.'

'She was reserved and quiet about her feelings,' Crawfie noted.

'I've been trained since childhood never to show emotion in public,' Elizabeth once remarked.

When Uncle David abdicated and the Crown was placed upon the reluctant head of their father, Margaret turned to her sister in the nursery at 145 Piccadilly and asked, 'Does that mean you will have to be the next queen?'

'Yes, some day,' the ten-year-old Elizabeth gravely replied.

Back came the riposte: 'Poor you.'

The girls spent the day looking down the stairwell at the comings and goings of the Prime Minister and his ministers, and then rushing to the windows to stare at the thousands of people gathered outside. When a letter was delivered addressed to Her Majesty the Queen, Elizabeth turned to Lady Cynthia Asquith. ' "That's Mummy now," she said, with a tremor in her awestruck voice.'

Whatever awe she felt was offset by her inherent composure and her remarkable sense of responsibility. She was not worldly and has not become so. It was never intended that she should. The practice of keeping her emotions to herself in public was carried over by force of habit into her private life. She does not like being touched. She raises her voice rarely; anger and temperament have no part to play in her lifetime's exercise in self-control. Instead she shows her displeasure by icy silence. If that makes her incomplete as a person—and there is an element of the child in her inability to address the sometimes wayward behaviour of her own family—there is also a regality about her which is both reassuring and intimidating. It is an aura of majesty that comes naturally to her. It was as if she always knew she was destined to be Queen, and set about from the earliest age acquiring the necessary skills, always trying hard to do 'what she felt was expected of her'.

Elizabeth did not join Margaret in those practical jokes that are such a tradition in the Royal Family (as long ago as 1860, Lord Clarendon was saying that he never told the Royal Family his best jokes because pretending to pinch his finger in the door amused them more). When Margaret hid the gardener's rake or threatened to sound the bell at Windsor which brought out the guard, Elizabeth would hide with embarrassment.

Order always had to be maintained. She was, said Crawfie, 'neat and methodical beyond words.' She would sometimes get up in the middle of the night to make sure her shoes were neatly stowed.

Self-control was essential. At the Coronation of their father in Westminster Abbey, she said of her little sister, 'I do hope she won't disgrace us all by falling asleep in the middle.' And when their parents set sail for the propaganda tour of Canada and the United States just before the outbreak of the Second World War, and Margaret told her that she had her handkerchief ready, Elizabeth sternly warned her, 'To wave, not to cry.'

She was compassionate. During the war the two princesses were moved to the comparative safety of Windsor Castle. They were subjected to the occasional air raid but never to the full force of the Blitz. Even so, Elizabeth took a keen and caring interest in the welfare of those more directly affected by the carnage. When the battleship HMS *Royal Oak* was sunk she exclaimed, 'It can't be! All those nice sailors,' and that Christmas remarked, 'Perhaps we are too happy. I keep thinking of those sailors and what Christmas must have been like in their homes.' And when she read the name of someone she knew, usually an officer who had been briefly stationed at the Castle, she would write to the mother 'and give her a little picture of how much she had appreciated him at Windsor and what they had talked about,' said Crawfie. 'That was entirely her own idea.' More mundanely but very much in character, she would instruct her more rumbustious sister not to point and laugh at anyone wearing a 'funny hat'.

Elizabeth subscribed to Louis XIV's view that punctuality is the politeness of princes (and princesses) and was always on time. She was obedient—her only transgression of any note, apart from the occasional nursery scrap with her sister, was when she was seven or eight years old: she turned an ornamental ink pot over the head of the Mademoiselle employed to teach her French.

She was discreet. When the King flew to Italy in 1944 he told his daughter where he was going. His trip was classified as top secret and Elizabeth kept the information to herself and didn't even share it with those women—Alah, Bobo and Crawfie—she was so close to. She also acquired the Royal Family habit of banishing unpleasant thoughts and people from her mind. They simply ceased to exist. 'Uncle David was not dead,' Crawfie wrote. He might as well have been. The Duke of Windsor had been particularly fond of his niece. He had been a frequent visitor to the house in Piccadilly and took a childish delight in joining her in her games. Since the abdication he had ceased to exist for her.

'In the Palace and the Castle his name was never mentioned,' Crawfie noted.

Now that the Crown was all but certain to pass to her, her father, from the day he became George VI, started taking his daughter into his confidence, 'speaking to her as an equal'. By war's end she was attending council meetings, taking the counsel of Prime Minister Winston Churchill, and discussing the affairs of state with her father on a daily basis.

Queen Elizabeth also renewed her interest in her daughter's education, and it was on her instigation that she was sent to study Constitutional History under Sir Henry Marten, the Vice-Provost of Eton College, just across the River Thames from Windsor.

Yet for all her maturity she remained in many ways a child. Her polished manners and grown-up conversation concealed a wealth of inexperience. Throughout her childhood and almost all of her 'teens, she was dressed in the same clothes as her sister, who was all of four years her junior. She also shared her nursery classroom with Margaret. She never had to hone her talents on the grindstone of the competition of contemporaries of her own age.'

Isolated behind that 'glass curtain', she enjoyed little social life of her own. What little she did have she left to her mother to organize. It was not until a special Girl Guides troop was formed for her that her circle widened out to include children from beyond her own privileged background. A number of cockney evacuees from the East End joined the royal troop at Windsor and it was 'no doubt very instructive,' so Crawfie remarked, for Elizabeth to mix with youngsters who did not have a 'tendency to let them have an advantage, win a game, or be relieved of the more sordid tasks,' as the children of the court had. Now, said Crawfie, 'it was each for himself'. The princess was not comfortable in this competitive environment. She liked the security of the safe and simple routine of royal life. Ever since she was a little girl she had shared her bedroom with Bobo Macdonald, the Scotswoman twenty-two years her senior who became and remained her closest friend. She found the informal intimacy of a Guides camp difficult to deal with.

'She was getting older, and had been brought up so much alone, I could understand why she did not want to undress before a lot of children all of a sudden, and spend the night with them,' Crawfie said.

When it came to dealing with boys she was even more inhibited. Boys of any kind, Crawfie remarked, were strange creatures out of another world to the princess and her young sister. But whereas Margaret was instinctively flirtatious when in the company of the opposite sex, Elizabeth, fundamentally shy, was always much more reserved in their company.

'That unsophisticated air of hers has always been part of her charm,' her governess remarked.

When she was under the tutelage of Sir Henry Marten in his study at Eton, his regular pupils would sometimes look in but they, with typical Etonian insouciance, feigned not to know who she was, and after politely raising their top hats would speedily withdraw again. Elizabeth, for her part, pretended not to notice the interruptions.

At the age of almost eighteen she 'had not yet', her father's equerry, Group Captain Peter Townsend noted, 'attained the full allure of an adult. She was shy, occasionally to the point of gaucheness.'

No real attempt was made to put her more at ease with young men. Miss Betty Vacani, the London dancing mistress who would also teach the next royal generation their steps, was called out to Windsor during the war to organize dance classes for the princesses. By royal instruction they were for little girls only. 'The Princesses did not understand the antics of little boys, and this did not seem the moment to teach them,' Crawfie said.

There was one boy Elizabeth did notice, however. He was tall and blond, with 'Viking' good looks. His name was Prince Philip of Greece and she was dazzled by him from the first moment she saw him. She was thirteen at the time, he eighteen. They were married five years later. He was the only man she had ever known.

Elizabeth spent the night before she was married in her nursery bedroom. On the morning of her wedding she came out of the nursery, paused to say goodbye to the toy horses which had followed her from the house in Piccadilly and were now stabled in the corridor outside, and then spent a few minutes with her parents, as she had done every morning since she was a baby.

In a very literal sense Elizabeth Alexandra Mary, named after three queens and soon to be a queen herself, went straight from the nursery to the marital bed.

Philip

hilip's childhood was confused and rootless. It couldn't have got off to a more inauspicious start: he was born on 10 June 1921, on the island of Corfu, on the dining room table of a house called, most ironically, Mon Repos. His father, Prince Andrew of Greece, did not have any money and the house had no electricity, no gas, and no hot running water. But Philip could at least consider himself lucky to have a father.

Greece was at war with Turkey. Greek advance had turned into crushing Turkish victory, and by the autumn of 1922 the Greeks had been driven out of Asia Minor, so ending a presence there which dated back 2,500 years. Smyrna, the main Greek town on the Asian mainland, had been sacked, the young Aristotle Onassis had escaped and fled to Argentina to start his own meteoric social climb, and Prince Andrew had been arrested, charged with treason, and was facing death by firing squad.

'How many children do you have,' Greece's new military leader, General Pangalos, asked his royal prisoner.

'Five,' Andrew replied.

'Poor little orphans,' the general said.

The only advantage Andrew had at that time was that he was a relation of the British Royal Family, and that might have proved no advantage at all had George V not been consumed by the memory of what had happened to his other royal relations, the Romanovs, three years earlier.

Marion Crawford, governess of Philip's future wife, made a point of teaching history as 'the doings not of a lot of dusty lay figures in the past, but of real people with all their problems and bothers'. The dust of silence had deliberately been allowed to settle over certain incidents in the Royal Family's recent history, however, Crawfie certainly did not apprise the young Elizabeth of them—and certainly not of the fatal part her grandfather had played in their tragic outcome.

In 1917 Russia had fallen to the Bolsheviks and Czar Nicholas II had been deposed. He was the future George V's first cousin (their mothers were sisters). The two men knew each other well and were on friendly terms, sometimes meeting, frequently exchanging letters. They even looked alike. 'Exactly like a skinny Duke of York [the future George V]—the image of him,' one of Queen Victoria's ladies-in-waiting once observed of Nicholas. When Nicholas appealed to his cousin for asylum in Britain, however, George V made it his personal business to ensure that it was refused. Where would he stay, the King wanted to know? And who was going to pay for his upkeep?

The Prime Minister, David Lloyd George, had offered the Imperial family the sanctuary they sought. The King, however, aware of the social instability and the corresponding upsurge in republicanism the First World War had generated in Britain, was concerned that Nicholas would bring Russia's revolutionary chaos with him. Sacrificing family blood on the altar of expediency, he ordered his private secretary, Lord Stamfordham, to write to the Foreign Secretary, Lord Balfour, 'The residence in this country of the ex-Emperor and his Empress . . . would undoubtedly compromise the position of the King and Queen.'

The offer was duly withdrawn, and on 16 July, 1918, Nicholas, his wife Alexandra, their four daughters and their young son were shot and bayoneted to death in a cellar in Ekaterinburg in the Urals. There is no record of George V 'having expressed sorrow, much less contrition, at his own role in the tragedy'.

But now another royal relation—and one who also had a wife, four daughters and a young son—was facing execution. It was a matter the King could not ignore. Andrew, like the murdered Czar, was also a first cousin; his father, George I of Greece, was the brother of George and Nicholas's mothers. There were other connections. Andrew's wife was Alice of Battenberg, daughter of the former First Sea Lord, who changed his name to Mountbatten and became the first Marquis of Milford Haven. Once described as 'the prettiest princess in Europe', Alice was a great-granddaughter of Queen Victoria, the niece of Nicholas's murdered wife, Alex, and a first cousin once removed of George V himself.

Andrew—self-opinionated and with an eye for the ladies—had to accept a large part of the responsibility for the final disaster that seemed set to befall him and his family. He wasn't Greek at all. The family were Danish, if they were anything, though it would be more accurate to describe him as a member of the inter-related tribe of German princelings who had come to occupy all the thrones of Europe. But he was the grandson of the King of Greece and, more pertinently, he was an officer in the Greek army. At the outbreak of hostilities with Turkey in 1921, he was a major-general with command of a division stationed in Asia Minor. His troops, he declared, were 'riff-raff', his officers useless, the high command incapable. His assessment was accurate but hardly diplomatic. Nor was it the height of military professionalism to disobey the clear and direct order to advance and instead ask to be relieved of his command. When Symrna fell and his family were again ousted—a regular occurrence since they had first been invited on to the throne of Greece in 1863—Andrew provided the new military rulers with a made-to-measure scapegoat. He was arrested, tried and sentenced by a jury of junior officers who, said Princess Alice, 'had previously decided that he must be shot'.

George V had been prepared to leave the Romanovs to their fate, but the idea of allowing another batch of close relations to fall to the executioner's blade or bullet clearly proved too much even for a monarch as imperious as this to stomach. Following appeals by Princess Alice through her younger brother, Louis, the future Earl Mountbatten of Burma, the King personally ordered that his incautious relation was for saving.

Commander Gerald Talbot, Britain's former naval attaché in Athens, now employed as a secret agent in Geneva, was duly dispatched, in disguise and travelling under false papers, to open negotiations with Pangalos. They did not go well until the cruiser, HMS *Calypso*, sailed in, her guns raised, to help concentrate the military government's thoughts. Which it did: while Andrew's fellow-prisoners were being duly executed, he was driven to the harbour by Pangalos himself, and put aboard the *Calypso*, where his wife was waiting for him.

The warship then steamed to Corfu to pick up the eighteen-month-old Philip and his four sisters. The family seemed quite philosophical about being exiled, 'for they frequently are', as the *Calypso's* captain, Buchanan-Wollaston, drily observed.

Philip's sister, Princess Sophie, about eight at the time, was not so sanguine. 'It was a terrible business, absolute chaos,' she later recalled. The crossing to Brindisi in Italy was a rough one and the family, along with their Greek lady-in-waiting, their French governess and their English nanny, Mrs 'Roose' Nicholas, were all seasick.

Once ashore they took the train up from Brindisi to Rome

and then to Paris. Philip spent much of the journey crawling around on the floor, blackening himself from head to toe and even licking the window panes. His mother tried to restrain him but Mrs Nicholas—'A divine person, much nicer than all the other nannies, we adored her,' Princess Sophie recalled—kindly advised, 'Leave him alone.'

'He was,' says Sophie, 'very active.'

Philip's life until then had been one of distinctly unroyal disorder. Mon Repos, built by the British governor, Sir Frederick Ashton, in 1832 for his moustachioed Greek wife, was in 'wretched' decay, the staff (the English nanny, whom Philip called Roosie, always excepted) slovenly.

'They did not live like royals,' their housekeeper recalled. 'We had a few untrained peasant girls to help, and two unwashed footmen who were rough fellows.'

Nor could it be said that the squalor was offset by a happy atmosphere. His father had been arrested and dragged away in front of his weeping family to face trial and the threat of execution; his mother, meanwhile, was heading towards a nervous breakdown. But Mon Repos, for all its drawbacks, was at least a family home, and that was something that Philip would not experience again until he married the future Queen. Exiled, poor (they had to borrow the money for the train fare to Paris from the British ambassador to Italy, Sir Ronald Graham), forced to rely on the charity of relations, a few friends, and those still impressed enough by their royal status to pay for their company (the family didn't even have a proper surname), they were condemned to join the litter of dispossessed princelings which strewed Europe between the wars.

At the age of three months Philip had been taken to London for the funeral of his grandfather, the first Marquis of Milford Haven, where he had met his uncles, David and Louis, for the first time. But despite a proliferation of relations there,

England was not deemed a suitable place for their exile. Angry questions had been asked in the House of Commons about the use of a British warship in their rescue—an argument over who should shoulder the costs dragged on between the Treasury and the Admiralty for several years—and it was deemed 'undesirable' by both the King and the government that they should come to England 'at the present time'. Instead they set up camp in Paris, first in an apartment, then at St Cloud, the lodge in the grounds of the house owned by his uncle Prince George's wife, Princess Marie Bonaparte, great-granddaughter of Napoleon's brother, Lucien.

It was a foundering, fragmented existence. His parents drifted apart. His father spent his time in the cafés, plotting never-to-be-enacted coups to restore his family to the Greek throne, before he eventually drifted off to Monte Carlo and out of his son's life to set up home with a widowed actress. Then, when Philip was ten, his mother had her long-threatened nervous breakdown.

Deaf from birth, Princess Alice had overcome her physical handicap, had learned to lip-read in four languages, and had been a vivacious and enchanting young woman. The struggles of exile proved beyond her, however, and after several unsuccessful treatments in various Swiss sanatoriums, she re-emerged in nun's habit which she wore for the rest of her life. She founded her own order, the Christian Sisterhood of Martha and Mary, and all but withdrew from the world.

Philip saw little of her or his father; it was his older sisters and the indefatigable Nanny Roose who bore the responsibility for his upbringing, and Nanny who had the greatest influence. 'Nobody's allowed to spank me but my own nanny,' he informed a friend's nanny who was about to discipline him for breaking an expensive vase.

One of his closest friends was Hélène Foufounis, whose royalist grandfather was also in exile, and was rich enough to help the financially troubled Prince Andrew. Like Philip, she too eventually moved to Britain where, as Hélène Cordet, she became a London cabaret singer and nightclub owner, and remained one of his closest confidantes. She said, 'He was like an English boy rather than a Greek or German. He had an English nanny.'

When Philip was born Nanny Roose had ordered supplies of British soap, British baby food, and British woollies to be sent to Mon Repos. She taught him British nursery rhymes and, despite the lack of funds, insisted on dressing him in clothes sent over from London. And she made absolutely certain that he 'spoke English and was brought up with English customs'. Superficially, that is. For there was nothing 'English' about the lack of order or stability in Philip's childhood.

Holidays were spent rattling across Europe by train to stay with those relations who had managed to hang on to their possessions. To Rumania, for instance, where his aunt Missy was Queen (she wore a tiara at dinner every evening) and where Philip's cousin, Queen Alexandra of Yugoslavia, remembered 'our nannies all cheerfully sitting down to tea with bowls of caviar'. The young boy whose own means were so straitened was allowed no such extravagance. He was trained, Alexandra says, 'to save and economize better than other children, so much so that he even acquired a reputation for being mean.'

He had other advantages, though. He was handsome. 'Everyone adored him so much, particularly my mother, because he was so good looking,' Hélène Cordet recalled.

'He had such unbelievable charm,' said his sister, Sophie. 'He had a tremendous sense of humour.'

He was also a 'real boy' with an adventurous, outgoing personality, fond of climbing trees, forever testing himself against the elements and his playmates. 'It was always Philip,' Alexandra said, 'who ventured out of his depth' at the seaside, 'or who rounded up other boys encountered on the beach and organized intensive castle-building brigades.' He was given a box Brownie and took up photography, which remained a lifetime's hobby. He had a boy's interest in motor cars.

His humour was of a somewhat rumbustious kind. 'He was a great showoff, he would always stand on his head when visitors came,' one of his sisters remarked. On one occasion, when staying with another aunt, Queen Sophie of Greece, and her sister, the Landgravine of Hesse, Alexandra recalled him releasing a sty of pigs and stampeding them through the ladies' elegant garden tea party. (Philip himself has no recollection of that incident.)

He could be kind-hearted. When a rich cousin, who was very taken with Philip, once bought him a toy, she cruelly said to Hélène's nine-year-old sister Ria, who was stricken with a diseased hip, 'I didn't buy you anything because you can't play.'

'Philip went very red and ran out of the room,' Hélène said. 'He came back with an armful of his own toys, and the new one, thrust them on the bed and said, "These are for you." '

Later, at Salem school, he encountered the viciousness inherent in the new Nazi Germany. One boy, Philip remembered, 'so displeased the thugs that they caught him . . . and shaved his head. I lent him my Cheam 2nd XI cap and I hope he has got it still.'

Such engaging high points, as revealing as they are in isolation, should not be allowed to obscure the uncertainty that characterized his childhood as a whole. Or the fact that, for all his hearty high spirits, he was also sometimes rude and always academically lazy.

His early education was not notable for its classroom successes. At the age of six he was sent to an American school in Paris known as The Elms. Philip rode there on a bicycle he had bought himself with savings that had started with the £1 his uncle, the King of Sweden, sent him every year. His school report called him 'rugged, boisterous'.

At the age of eight, in educational confirmation of his 'Englishness', he was sent to Cheam preparatory school outside London. There he won the school diving competition, came equal first in the high jump, won the under-12 hurdles and became 'an improved cricketer'. But again he failed to shine academically. He did win the Form III French prize, but as his cousin, Alexandra, told him, so he should have, 'after all the years he had lived in Paris'. He had been sent to Cheam on the advice of his maternal uncle, George, the second Marquis of Milford Haven, who had been sent there in turn by his father who had been impressed by the good manners of two Cheam-educated midshipmen. Milford Haven's own son, David, who was two years older than Philip, also went there and the two became firm friends.

The fees to send him to these two expensive schools had been provided first by his paternal uncle George of Greece, then by his maternal uncle, the second Marquis of Milford Haven. Both men were married to women who formed an important part of his female support system, though given their sexual proclivities one can only imagine what kind of influence these benefactresses had on the young boy.

Marie Bonaparte, besides being the great-great-niece of Napoleon, was also the granddaughter of François Blanc, the founder of the Monte Carlo casino, who ended up as virtual owner of the principality and used his newly acquired wealth to buy his daughter a titled husband. His granddaughter had inherited not only a sizeable part of his Monte Carlo-made fortune but also a morality that went well with that Ruritania on the Riviera which Somerset Maugham called 'a sunny place for shady people'. She was notoriously promiscuous, had been subjected to blackmail, and numbered Aristide Briand, several times Prime Minister of France, amongst her lovers.

The Marchioness of Milford Haven was equally unconventional. The daughter of the Grand Duke Michael of Russia; Nadejda de Torbay, as she was, was a great-granddaughter of the poet Pushkin. Dark and beautiful, she was accused, in one of the most lurid trials of the 1930s, of being the lesbian lover of the heiress Gloria Vanderbilt. When Gloria went to court to fight for the custody of her daughter, the original 'poor little rich girl', also called Gloria, Mrs Vanderbilt's former maid took the stand to testify that she had seen the Marchioness embrace her employer 'like a lover'. Her husband, for his part, was an avid collector of pornography and early sexual aids.

Philip spent his holidays from Cheam at the Milford Havens' home, Lynden Manor, near Windsor.

Great emphasis is placed on Uncle 'Dickie' Mountbatten's role in Philip's upbringing. 'I don't think anybody thinks I had a father. Most people think that Dickie is my father anyway,' he said. In reality Mountbatten played no part until much later, and then rather less than he liked to make out. 'Mountbatten certainly had an influence on the course of my life, but not so much on my ideas and attitudes,' Philip informed the author Tim Heald. 'I suspect he tried too hard to make himself a son out of me.' It was in fact Louis's brother, George Milford Haven, who 'assumed the role of a surrogate father' to the young boy.

Indeed, at the time, the erotic Milford Havens were his only family, for between December 1930, when he was nine years old, and August 1931, shortly after he had turned ten, his four sisters, all members of the German aristocracy, left to start households of their own. The family dispersal which had started when they left Greece on the *Calypso* had turned into a diaspora which left the little ten-year-old without a home, a mother, or the protective affection of his sisters.

If this wasn't problematic enough, tragedy started to crowd in. In 1937 his third sister, Cecile, and her husband, George

Donatus of Hesse, flew to London for the wedding of his brother, Prince Louis, to Lord Geddes's daughter, Margaret. Over Ostend the plane hit a shimmy. Cecile, her husband, whom Philip had been particularly attached to, their two children, and the child Cecile was carrying were all killed. Their surviving daughter, who had been too young to make the flight, died of meningitis two years later.

In 1938, when Philip was seventeen, George Milford Haven died of cancer at the age of forty-six.

By now Philip no longer even had his nanny to turn to. His beloved Roosie, now well into her seventies, had contracted arthritis and had retired to the sunshine of South Africa.

Philip could have been forgiven for thinking that the fates were closing in on him, but he dismissed that notion. He was big and athletic and capable of looking after himself; his independence had been forged on the anvil of a harsh environment. His childhood, he insisted, was 'not necessarily particularly unhappy'. The disruption of exile, he maintains, did not concern him. 'I was barely a year old when the family went into exile so I don't think I suffered the same disorientation,' he said. And if his home life had been unsettled, so what. 'People talk about a normal upbringing. What is a normal upbringing?' he once gruffly demanded. The first thing Kurt Hahn, his headmaster at Gordonstoun, noted, was his 'undefeatable spirit'.

Some child psychologists would see such determined self-reliance in a different light. In *Child Development and Personality*, Mussen, Conger and Kagan described the overtly independent child thus: 'Because he has never experienced a continuous loving relationship or, more frequently, because the relationship he has had has been disrupted so severely, he has not only reached but remained in a phase of detachment. As a result he remains dead and so incapable of experiencing separation, anxiety, or grief. Lesser degrees of this condition are, of course, more common than the extreme degrees, and sometimes give the impression of unusually vigorous independence. Analysis, however, shows that the springs of love are frozen and their independence is hollow.'

Such academic theorizing would probably have been dismissed by the young Philip who was fond of saying that he was 'one of those ignorant bums who never went to university—and a fat lot of harm it did me!' He was not much given to self-analysis. He was what he was. But who exactly was he?

Hélène Cordet said: 'He was very aware of his position and we were too. You could not forget who he was. He had been brought up to realize he was a prince.'

There were moments, though, when Philip seemed determined to rid himself of his royal appellation. Hélène's mother, Anna, recalled how he hated being introduced as Prince Philip, grandson of the King of Greece. 'I'm just Philip. Just Philip, that's all!' he would shout.

His uncle, Louis Mountbatten, expended a great deal of his considerable energy inventing a magnificent pedigree for himself that traced his ancestry all the way back to Charlemagne, but disingenuously overlooked the fact that his grandmother was not royal at all, and that he was therefore the progeny of a morganatic union which had stripped his family of their royal A-rating. Whatever personal success Mountbatten achieved—and he enjoyed a glorious career: Supreme Allied Commander, South East Asia, during the Second World War; Viceroy of India; First Sea Lord; an earldom—did not exorcize his ancestral demons. Quite the contrary; it seemed to fuel his naked snobbery.

'We always took Dickie with a pinch of salt,' Queen Elizabeth the Queen Mother once witheringly remarked.

Philip took a more balanced view of his bloodline. Being royal, as he knew from his own experience, provided no guarantee of future employment. It could be a handicap as well as an advantage. It had given him a title and opened the palace doors of Europe to him. But it had also deprived him of a home and a stable family life.

Yet, despite his insistence that he be called Philip and not *Prince* Philip, royal he was. It was written into his family's genealogical past and future ambition. Even as an impecunious youngster in France he seemed to have an instinctive appreciation of where his destiny lay. 'Some day I'll be an important man—a king even!' he informed Hélène Cordet's brother, Jean.

He had no interest in returning to Greece. 'A grandfather assassinated and a father condemned to death does not endear me to the perpetrators.' Instead he looked to Britain, his mother's homeland, which he had become very attached to— at the end of one visit to her relations in England, Princess Alice had had to drag him out from under a bed and sedate him in order to get him on the train back to France.

After Cheam he had been sent to Salem, the school founded in 1920 by his sister Theodora's father-in-law, Prince Max of Baden, and formulated by his former secretary, Kurt Hahn. It was their attempt to rebuild a war-shattered Germany's manhood by educating them along British public school lines with a dollop of Plato thrown in. The early thirties were not the ideal time for a school whose ambition, as Prince Max put it, was to 'train soldiers who are at the same time lovers of peace'.

Prince Max had been the last chancellor of Imperial Germany and had arranged the Kaiser's abdication. But now a new chancellor was in power in the Reichstag and his name was Adolf Hitler. Philip, too 'international' as he describes himself, did not settle in well under this regime of muscular chauvinism. He found the Nazi salute hilarious. It reminded him, he said, of the gesture his Cheam classmates made when they wanted to be excused to go to the lavatory. He found the organized bullying of the party faithful offensive.

Some of his in-laws became high officials in the Nazi regime. The Badens did not. 'As none of that family was at all enthusiastic about them [the Nazis] it was thought best I should move out!' Philip explained in 1990.

In 1933 Hahn, a Jew as well as a radical thinker, was arrested. On his release he fled to Britain where he opened another school the following year. It was called Gordonstoun, and Philip was one of his first thirty pupils.

Hahn—Philip called him 'eccentric perhaps, innovator certainly, great beyond doubt'—believed in body over mind, in physical endeavour over the academic. It is not an educational system that suits everyone. The sensitive—Prince Charles, for instance—can sometimes find it hard to come to terms with the Teutonic austerity. But it suited Philip and he thrived in the tough, spartan environment Hahn created for his acolytes on the windswept coast of Scotland's Moray Firth. It developed and confirmed his sense of independence. He became, as one of his authorized biographers observed, 'his own man, anxious to learn and be advised but, in the end, taking his own decisions in his own way.'

It is a trait that can make him appear rude and sometimes arrogant, as someone who has little sympathy for those who may be less self-sufficient than he is.

It is also a characteristic that seems to need the fuel of competition. In his final judgement of his star pupil Hahn reported: 'His best is outstanding; but his second best is not good enough. Prince Philip will make his mark in any profession but will have to prove himself in a full trial of strength.'

The full trial of strength was contained at Gordonstoun, where the system is designed to make pupils compete, not with each other, but with themselves. He was taught to sail, for instance, and he thrived on the challenge.

'I was wet, cold, miserable, probably sick, and often scared stiff,' he would later recall, 'but I wouldn't have missed the experience for anything. In any case the discomfort was far outweighed by the moments of intense happiness and excitement. Poets and authors down the centuries have tried to describe those moments but their descriptions, however brilliant, will never compare with one's own experience.'

It was the air rather than the sea which most appealed to him as a career, however. 'I'd have gone into the Air Force without a doubt,' he said.

It was at this juncture that Lord Louis Mountbatten assumed a guiding role in his nephew's life. He persuaded him not to join the RAF, but to follow family tradition and enter the Royal Navy. And that set in motion the chain of events that would secure his future.

In July 1939, the Royal Yacht *Victoria and Albert* sailed up the Dart to visit the Royal Naval College at Dartmouth. Aboard were George VI, his Queen, Elizabeth, and their two daughters, Elizabeth and Margaret. Mountbatten was in attendance. Waiting to greet them was the young cadet, Philip of Greece.

The College was afflicted with an outbreak of mumps and the King ruled that the two princesses should not be allowed to mix with cadets. On Mountbatten's instigation, Philip was delegated to look after them. They played together with a clockwork train-set laid out in the Captain's house; then, when the eighteen-year-old Philip tired of that, went to the tennis courts where he impressed the thirteen-year-old Elizabeth by jumping over the nets.

"How good he is, Crawfie. How high he can jump,' Elizabeth whispered to her governess.

When the Royal Yacht set sail that evening a number of the cadets rowed out after it. Philip—Crawfie described him as a 'rather bumptious boy'—rowed further and longer than anyone else. Eventually the King shouted, 'The young fool. He must go back, otherwise we will have to heave to and send him back.'

Philip was good-looking, 'rather like a Viking,' Crawfie gushed, 'though rather offhand in his manner.' He would employ those looks to some effect over the next few years. He had, said his cousin Alexandra, a sailor's eye for a pretty face: 'Blondes, brunettes and redhead charmers, Philip gallantly and I think quite impartially squired them all.'

The dynastic die had already been cast, however, that summer's afternoon in Dartmouth. Mountbatten undoubtedly played his part, but it would have been to no avail had Philip—talented, determined but poor—not played his.

Early in 1940 Philip was posted to the battleship *Ramillies*, which was working as an escort vessel in the Mediterranean under the command of Vice-Admiral Harold Tom Baillie-Grohman. According to one account Baillie-Grohman pointed out to him that unless he became a British subject he would not be allowed to advance very far in rank in the Royal Navy. Did he want to get on in the Navy, Baillie-Grohman asked.

'Yes,' was the emphatic rejoinder. Philip then added: 'My uncle Dickie has ideas for me; he thinks I could marry Princess Elizabeth . . . I write to her every week.'

In 1941 his cousin Alexandra remembers him writing a letter. 'Who's it to?' she asked.

'Lilibet, Princess Elizabeth in England.'

'But she's only a baby,' his cousin exclaimed.

'But perhaps I'm going to marry her,' Philip replied.

Philip would later insist that the question of marriage did not enter his mind before 1946 when he went to stay at Balmoral. 'I suppose one thing led to another. It was sort of fixed up.'

Sir Henry 'Chips' Channon, the American who married

into the Guinness family, became an MP and kept a copious diary, believed it was 'fixed up' long before that.

Channon was in Athens in January 1941 when Philip, aged nineteen, happened to be there on shore leave. Channon was a society butterfly who made it his business to know everyone. After a chat with Philip's aunt, Helen, the wife of Prince Nicholas of Greece, he recorded in his diary: 'He is to be our Prince Consort, and that is why he is serving in our Navy.'

George VI, his court and his government had their doubts. As Margaret observed, 'He's not English.'

Nevertheless, on 20 August 1947, and despite the initial and in part extreme reservations of those involved, the handsome, worldly sailor married the shy, ingenuous princess. Philip dropped his Greek title, which he had never been attached to, and became the Duke of Edinburgh and, eventually, a British prince.

After twenty-six years of rootless wandering, the exile who entered the world on a dining-room table had become a fully-fledged member of the grandest royal family of all.

Margaret

❧

Princess Margaret was born in the middle of a rain storm. It was a symbolic début to a turbulent life.

Where Elizabeth was well-behaved and dutiful, Margaret was always mischievous and set on her own individual course.

In the argument over whether environment or genetic inheritance plays the greater part in the formation of character, recent evidence has come down substantially on the side of the latter. This would certainly appear to be borne out in the lives of the princesses Margaret and Elizabeth.

Their parents, who wished to show no favouritism, made a point of treating their daughters alike. Despite the four years' difference in their ages, they were dressed in the same clothes, almost to the moment Elizabeth left the nursery to be married. They attended lessons at the same time and frequently in the same subjects. Treats were always shared. They got up at the same time, went to bed at the same time (in the rarest concession to Elizabeth's older status, she was allowed to read for an extra half hour), listened to the same radio programmes, went on the same outings, mixed with exactly the same people. Yet, right from the outset, Elizabeth and Margaret were very different, both in their interests and their talents.

Where the elder sister was indifferent to the vagaries of

fashion, the younger was fascinated by them. Where the girl who would become Queen was always polite and considerate of others, the one who was destined to remain a princess could be cutting and sharp with her observations.

Elizabeth was always 'dear, sweet Elizabeth'. Margaret, as their grandmother, Queen Mary, observed, was always an '*espiègle*', a little rogue. And for all their togetherness, there was always an element of competition between the two. 'Margaret always wants what I want!' the young Elizabeth once complained.

The Duke and Duchess of York's younger daughter and last child arrived in the summer of 1930. Elizabeth had been born at the London home of her maternal grandfather, the Earl of Strathmore. The Earl offered to provide his home for this second birth, but this time the Duchess, intensely proud of her Caledonian heritage, insisted that the delivery should be made at Glamis Castle, her family's ancestral seat in Scotland.

Glamis has a romantic and often bloody history. Shakespeare used it as the setting for Macbeth's murder of King Duncan. A number of Ogilvys, ancient enemies of the Bowes Lyons, were imprisoned in the 'Room of Skulls' and, after devouring their own flesh in hunger, starved to death. It has its own ghost, a tongueless, hideous old woman with a 'fiendish face'. It also had a monster: one of the children of the Duchess's great-grandmother, Charlotte, was grotesquely deformed and is said to have been kept locked away in one of the castle's rooms for the seventy piteous years of his life.

The Duchess, however, had only the happiest of memories of her childhood home. It was there that she had spent part of her honeymoon, and it was there she retired to, after obtaining special permission from her father-in-law, George V, for her confinement.

The baby was duly delivered (without the need of a Caesarean) in the middle of a rainstorm on the night of 21 August.

Margaret insists it was not a thunderstorm, as modern legend would have us believe. The Home Secretary, J.R. Clynes, was in attendance, as required by an edict dating back to the reign of the Stuarts, to ensure that the infant was not switched at birth. (George VI abolished that archaic law just before the birth of his grandson, Charles.)

After the rains had abated, bonfires were lit and Lord Strathmore provided barrels of free beer for the crowds of well-wishers who gathered before the castle gates to cheer the new arrival. King George and his queen, Mary, informed of the news, immediately set off from Sandringham to travel north to see their latest grandchild.

Her birth was registered in the village shop at Glamis. She would be christened Margaret Rose and not Margaret Ann, as her mother wished, because George V did not like the name Ann. Her godparents were her uncle, the future Duke of Windsor, her great-aunt, George V's sister, Princess Victoria, the future Queen Ingrid of Sweden, and her maternal uncle and aunt, Lady Rose Leveson-Gower, and David Bowes Lyon.

Elizabeth's reaction, when taken in by her nanny Alah to see her new sister, was one of initial disappointment. The tiny child in her mother's arms was hardly the ready-made playmate the young and rather lonely princess had been hoping for. But that is what she soon became.

An age difference of four years is a gap too broad for most young children to bridge. In the isolated world of the Royal Family, however, Elizabeth was given little alternative in her choice of companions. For all her governess Marion Crawford's claims that the Duke and Duchess of York were keen that their daughters should be treated like any other children, the system they were born into made certain that they weren't. They were kept cocooned in environmental cotton wool, never exposed to the competitive hurly-burly of school or playground, to the pleasures of making new friends, the challenge of dealing with different circumstances, the problems of coming to terms with other people's emotions and dislikes.

This, according to the unspoken belief of the court, was the way royal children should be trained for the job of being royal. Regal isolation was enforced on them, and from an early age they were forced to look to their own family for companionship.

Elizabeth fitted easily into this system. Margaret did not. Reserved and bookish, Elizabeth appeared content with the small world her parents had constructed for her. Margaret was always more outgoing, more gregarious, with an impish sense of humour.

As an infant she was prone to 'stoutness'. When the sisters were being taught to swim at the old Bath Club next door to Claridge's hotel in Mayfair, she looked, 'everyone owned, like a plumb navy-blue fish'. She could be 'tiresome' on occasion. She was also much naughtier than her extremely well-disciplined sister. When she was a Girl Guide and camping out in the grounds of Windsor, 'she was a menace to the Guides officer in charge,' Crawfie recalled. Ignoring the order to go to sleep, she would stay awake chatting to the other girls in her tent. 'The Guides officer would appear, say a few well-chosen words, and retreat. The ensuing silence would reign for a minute or two, then a fresh outburst probably meant Margaret was giving her companions an imitation of the Guides officer's lecture.'

There was an engaging charm about her behaviour, however, and she was always fun to be with. When the family played charades, a game that still entrances them, 'there was never any doubt about Margaret's efforts!' Crawfie remembered. 'They were unmistakable' and kept everyone 'in fits of laughter. The gift of fun-poking—and very clever fun-poking—Margaret had from an early age in a very large quantity.'

Sometimes her rather prissy sister became the brunt of her

humour; it was Margaret's ability to do imitations that ridiculed Elizabeth out of her obsessive habit of getting out of bed to make sure that her shoes were straight.

According to Crawfie, however, who was somewhat biased, she was no match for Elizabeth. She possessed a 'bright quickness of mind', had a talent for art and was very good at music. But when it came to the schoolroom Elizabeth was always ahead, and not just in years. Margaret, Crawfie said in summation, 'did not make such rapid progress as Lilibet'.

Indeed, a story was abroad at one point that she was backward—and deaf and dumb as well. Crawfie blamed Alah for the rumours—and for the pampering which in later life would lead to her being labelled spoilt.

'Alah, like all fond nannies,' the governess crisply remarked, 'longed to keep one baby in the nursery, and as no new one was forthcoming, clung on to Margaret so that the long-suffering child was penned in her pram long after she pined to run about with us in the gardens, and was fed by hand when in reality she had done with such childish things.'

It wasn't until Margaret took matters into her own diminutive hands and actually climbed out of the pram that her babyhood was allowed to come to its belated end. It was high time, for Margaret was always a precocious child. When she was nine months old and being carried down stairs by Lady Strathmore, she started to hum the waltz from *The Merry Widow*. 'I was so astounded I almost dropped her,' her maternal grandmother recalled.

She also showed an early talent for drawing which enabled her to give expression to her fascination with clothes. It is royalty's obsession to be interested in what they wear, as much for reasons of status as out of personal vanity. As Cornell University professor Alison Lurie observed in her book, *The Language of Clothes*, 'Just as the oldest languages are full of elaborate titles and forms of address, so for thousands of years certain modes have indicated high or royal rank.'

George V was engrossed by the subject and was forever berating his sons, and the flashy David in particular, for being 'incorrectly dressed'. George VI was almost as finicky. Elizabeth inherited her mother's disregard for the subject. Margaret, however, was her father's daughter when it came to dress: before the Coronation she created a scene when she discovered that her sister's mantle was longer than hers. She was a great admirer of her uncle Prince George of Kent's stylish wife and would declare, 'When I grow up I shall dress like Aunt Marina does.'

When she was young Margaret was dressed exactly as her sister—in plain tweed coats, cardigans, cotton frocks, usually blue with a floral pattern, business-like berets and stout walking shoes. Elizabeth 'never cared a fig', Crawfie said, and wore what she was told without argument. Margaret, on the other hand, was always interested in how she looked and in that she was encouraged by Alah. As it turned out, those austere, practical clothes set a fashion amongst upper-middle-class children which is only now in retreat. Alah, however, did not approve of her mistress's choice of wardrobe for her daughters. She believed that—'little princesses should be little princesses always'—and that included dressing the part.

Margaret did just that, if only in her imagination. From a young age she would spend hours drawing sketches of beautifully dressed ladies 'and pictures of frocks she would have liked to have had herself. Excellent designs some of them were, too.' And much better than Elizabeth could ever manage.

Margaret was also the one who left the instant impression. Sir James (J.M.) Barrie, the creator of *Peter Pan*, frequently came to tea and entertained the girls with tales from his imagination. He was, Elizabeth observed, 'the most wonderful storyteller'. Barrie attended Margaret's fifth birthday party, and remarked on her presents. They were inexpensive, 'simple things that might have come from the sixpenny shops,' he said, 'but she was in a frenzy of glee over them, especially one to which she had given place of honour by her plate.'

'Is that really your very own?' Barrie kindly remarked.

'It is yours *and* mine,' Margaret replied.

Barrie used the line in his play, *The Boy David*, and paid her a penny for every time it was used. When he died in 1937 his secretary, Lady Cynthia Asquith, went to Buckingham Palace and gave the seven-year-old Margaret her royalties out of a bag.

In the steady pace of growing up, Margaret was always several steps behind her sister, partly because of her age but also because of the difference in their positions in heredity's pecking order.

'I'm three and you're four,' Elizabeth grandly informed her sister one day.

'No, you're not. *I'm* three and you're seven,' Margaret replied, confusing age with their relative positions in the line of succession.

She resented being cast in the role of 'younger sister' and the nursery, first at 145 Piccadilly, later at Buckingham Palace, would resound to her furious shouts of 'Wait for me, Lilibet,' and, on occasion, the less than princess-like cries as the two girls battled over some toy or other ('I never won,' Margaret ruefully recalled, which is hardly surprising, considering that she was giving away four years). When Elizabeth was taught to shoot red deer on the Balmoral estate 'she felt very left out and again resentful' and 'conveniently' decided that shooting was an unwomanly pursuit. At no time, though, did Margaret ever indicate that she would like their positions to have been reversed. Rather the contrary.

'Isn't it lucky that Lilibet is the eldest,' she once remarked. The restraint of always having to do what was expected of her did not fit easily into her spontaneous character. She was a 'born comic' who also took great delight in entertaining her parents' occasional visitors to light-hearted renditions at the piano, something she still does. Upon learning that her father was to be king, she asked, 'Will he have to sing "God Save My Gracious Me?" ' She was, Queen Mary observed, 'so outrageously amusing that one can't help encouraging her'.

Margaret took a more acerbic view of her own behaviour. 'I was probably thought a horrid child', she recently observed. Yet for all her bounce, there were moments of insecurity.

The princesses received half an hour's religious instruction every Monday morning. That did not satisfy Queen Mary, but it left a deep impression on Margaret, who has often sought comfort in prayer from a very early age. A conjuror was hired for her sixth birthday party and she prayed that he wouldn't call her up on to the stage. He didn't. 'That childish experience gave me confidence in the power of prayer which I have believed in ever since,' she remarked.

During the War Elizabeth and Margaret were evacuated to what was officially called 'a house in the country' and was in fact Windsor Castle, that thousand-roomed symbol of monarchy which has been in continuous use as a royal residence for over 900 years. In between watching the German bombers flying overhead and playing practical jokes on the gardeners, Margaret also persuaded Crawfie to allow them to stage several pantomimes.

'She talked pantomime constantly, and it was a great deal to do with her persistence that in the end we began to think very seriously about it,' Crawfie recalled. 'Margaret knows what she wants, and she never lets go.'

They started with a nativity play in 1940, in which Elizabeth wore a golden crown, and Margaret sang 'Gentle Jesus, Meek and Mild', much to the pleasure of her father, who wrote in his diary, 'I wept through most of it.'

The next year they performed *Cinderella*, the year after that *Sleeping Beauty*. In 1943 it was *Aladdin*—Prince Philip came to see his future wife in that one—and in 1944 they staged *Old Mother Red Riding Boots*.

Margaret enjoyed her moments on stage and being the centre of attention, but only once she was there. On the morning of the performance she would turn 'absolutely pea-green', and couldn't be roused from her bed until ten minutes before she was due on stage at two o'clock.

Giving speeches brought on even more violent attacks of nerves. She made her first speech at the age of thirteen at a school in Windsor. She was, she recalled, 'dreadfully sick' with apprehension. She never overcame those feelings and, where possible, has avoided public speaking ever since.

But whatever reservations she harboured about putting herself on public display, and so subjecting herself to the kind of scrutiny her upbringing had been designed to shelter her from, she quickly acquired a well-developed sense of the potency of her royal position and its drawing power. The audiences were charged for the privilege of seeing the princesses perform in pantomime. One year Elizabeth objected to the proposed seven shillings and sixpence entrance fee.

'No one will pay that to look at *us*!' Elizabeth said.

'Nonsense!' Margaret replied. 'They'll pay anything to see us.' She was right, of course: the pantomimes were always a sell-out and raised the princely sum of almost £900 for their mother's wartime Wool Fund.

The war, for all the strain it put on their father, does not appear to have unduly affected the princesses' carefully structured routine. There were fire drills and nights spent in the hastily constructed bomb shelter in the Castle's cellars.

(Alah, firm in her belief that her charges should always be correctly turned out, even in the middle of an air raid, took so long getting them dressed after the siren had gone that Crawfie had to run up and order her down, which would not have eased relations between the two women.) But there was also the excitement of the Guides, which gave the sociable Margaret the chance to meet people of her own age.

Food was occasionally short, but Margaret did enjoy the treat of kippers which she was introduced to by the castle's housekeeper, Mrs Alice Bruce. Walking along one of the Castle's seemingly endless corridors with her sister, she was entranced by the smell coming from Mrs Bruce's own kitchen. They followed the aroma, knocked politely at the door and were invited in for their first taste of that traditional Scottish breakfast dish of smoked herring. Mrs Bruce then showed her how to fry them in the traditional manner and the recipe remains a firm favourite.

She was taught to drive by Elizabeth, who had passed her test during her training with the Auxiliary Territorial Service, and when the war was won she was allowed out with her sister to mingle with the crowds that gathered outside Buckingham Palace on VE night, accompanied by a group of suitable officers and their uncle, David Bowes Lyon, who knocked a policeman's helmet off—the princesses 'ran off, just in case we were caught,' Margaret recalled.

Margaret, as Crawfie observed, was allowed more freedom than Elizabeth ever was at the same age. Her parents' views on child rearing had been modified by practical experience, as parents' views usually are. Even so, adolescence proved difficult for Margaret and for the people charged with her upbringing. The greater freedom only seemed to encourage her to take even greater liberties, and her exuberance did not sell well in the tightly structured formality that royal life still was.

Thwarted and frustrated, she started chafing against the

restrictions imposed on her. Her sister had acted as a restraining influence, but as soon as she was married and Margaret was left as the only princess in the Palace, she started breaking away. 'She loved breaking the rules,' a contemporary remarked. She painted her fingernails bright red and wore lipstick to match. When Queen Mary objected to her smoking in public, 'she replied by being photographed with longer and longer cigarette holders'. She acquired a set of late-night friends, led by Sharman Douglas, daughter of the American ambassador and, according to Prince Philip's former Private Secretary Mike Parker's ex-wife, Eileen, 'an ambitious girl, determined to break into the highest, fastest circles in London'. They went out to restaurants and stayed out at nightclubs.

The press, quick to seize on her activities, dubbed the group the Margaret Set. 'They were Sharman's friends first so, if anything, it was *her* set, not mine,' the princess insisted. 'There never was a Margaret Set.' The sight of a princess enjoying her youth in a modern manner was too good a story for the newspapers to ignore, however, and the Margaret Set it remained.

Her mother took an indulgent view of her younger daughter's lifestyle. 'We want her to have a good time,' she would say.

The king, by now unwell, also took a lenient view. 'It was clear for all to see how he doted on her,' Eileen Parker remarked.

Those still charged with the responsibility for her education were not so understanding. Margaret, they felt, was setting a bad example to the nation's young. There was no 'crossing' Margaret, however. When Crawfie raised the subject of her late nights and said, 'Other girls have work to do. They can't stay late in bed. They have got to get up in the morning . . . They probably have to get their own breakfast,' Margaret replied that even if she wanted to cook her own breakfast, she couldn't 'because there's nothing here to cook on'.

Crawfie observed resignedly, 'She turns it all into a joke,' adding presciently that her 'doings' sometimes seemed to lack the 'wisdom and discretion expected of those who live at court'.

There were some indiscretions that had to be taken seriously sooner or later, however. In 1944 Group Captain Peter Townsend was appointed equerry to George VI. He was handsome in a clean cut, English way. He was brave: a Hurricane pilot, he had flown over five hundred sorties during the war and had been awarded the Distinguished Service Order and the Distinguished Flying Cross and bar. Margaret quickly developed a crush on him. He, in turn, noticed that her eyes were the blue of a 'deep tropical sea'. He was sixteen years her senior. He was also married.

Eileen Parker recalled; 'Rosemary Townsend and I were both married to men frequently lured from us by the lustre of glittering prizes. But it was slightly easier for me then. At least, to the very best of my knowledge, Mike was not having an affair and creating public humiliation. Rosemary as a wife and mother had to stand to one side while Princess Margaret, hardly out of ankle socks, entertained her husband. Understandably, she had every cause to sound bitter sometimes.'

The Townsends were divorced on 19 December, 1952, on the grounds of her affair with royal portrait painter Philip de Laslo's son, John. According to Eileen Parker 'Peter lost much respect' over the way he handled the breakdown of his marriage. Rosemary, 'in her frustration, became involved with another man. Despite the fact that all in the Household were fully aware of what was going on, Townsend reacted to Rosemary's own affair with the stung indignation of a true cuckold. He sued for divorce on the uncontested grounds of adultery.'

There was no happy ending to that sad episode. However

independent and unshackled Margaret may have thought herself to be as she ventured forth into the post-war world, she was never going to break free from the reins of royal convention. She was gifted enough, so her governess believed, to have made a name for herself as an artist or a singer or a dancer. That was out of the question. Whether she ever had the artistic 'genius' Crawfie attributed to her is irrelevant. No daughter of the king was ever going to be allowed to follow a career in the theatre or anywhere else for that matter. She had been brought up to be 'royal' and that was considered career enough.

Nor, when it came to it, would she be allowed to marry the man she loved. When Townsend broached the subject with the Queen's Private Secretary, Sir Alan Lascelles replied, 'You must be either mad or bad.'

By then Lilibet was Queen Elizabeth II. On the advice of her private secretary and her ministers she had to inform her younger sister that she could not marry a divorced man. Margaret was faced with the distressing choice of giving up either Townsend or her titles and position in the Royal Family.

'Princess Margaret didn't know from one week to the next whether she wanted to be treated as the Little Princess or Cinderella,' Eileen Parker observed.

She chose to remain what she had been trained from royal birth to be. A princess.

Charles

~

P rince Charles celebrated his fourth birthday with a party in the white and gold Music Room at Buckingham Palace. Fourteen children were invited and the corridor outside was cleared of its impedimenta of chairs and tables and busts so that the prince and his guests could run up and down.

In the forecourt below the band of the Grenadier Guards entertained the youthful revellers with a selection of nursery rhymes and then, as a special treat, with a rendition of Charles's favourite song, 'The Teddy Bears' Picnic'.

There were two cakes. One was shaped as a galleon in full sail with marzipan masts and sweets in the hold; the other, a present from the Queen Mother, was made in the form of Hansel and Gretel's cottage. His presents included a pedal car.

It was, so one observer recounted, 'the lightest-hearted party given at Buckingham Palace since the period of the Crimean War when Queen Victoria still had children young enough to romp in the same spirit'.

It was also notable for something more contemporaneous. For this was the first time Prince Philip had been present at one of his son's birthdays.

Charles had seen little of his father in his first formative years. He would soon see less of his mother, though for different reasons.

Elizabeth had looked forward to motherhood. 'After all, it's what we're made for,' she said.

As a child she had declared that she wanted to marry a farmer, live in the country, have lots of animals and four children, two boys and two girls. She had married a sailor instead, but she had the animals and the country estates and their farming interests and she would eventually fulfil the last ambition.

Her greatest wish, she said, was for her children to be brought up to be 'normal'. She would often confide to Eileen Parker, whose husband was equerry-in-waiting to the princess and her husband and later Prince Philip's Private Secretary, 'I would like them to live ordinary lives. I wish I could be more like you, Eileen.'

Her confidante was not entirely convinced. Elizabeth may have harboured doubts about her own upbringing—about its formality and protocol. 'But, I pondered, how much of a price would a princess truly be willing to pay in order to bring her children up like "ordinary people"?' When it came to the routine of child rearing, not very much, it seemed.

Elizabeth suffered the discomforts of morning sickness during the early part of pregnancy. Charles, like his mother, was born by Caesarean section; at Buckingham Palace on the evening of 14 November, 1948. Philip, a typically nervous expectant father, played a game of squash with Michael Parker to occupy himself during the waiting time and then went for a swim in the Palace pool. He was just drying himself when a footman hurried in with the news that the princess had given birth.

Hair still wet, Philip rushed up to the drawing room where the king and queen were already receiving congratulations. Leaving his equerry to hand round the champagne, he went in to see his wife and new-born son. She was still under the anaesthetic. When she came round Philip presented her with a bouquet of red roses and carnations Parker had had the foresight to have ready.

Like all mothers, Elizabeth examined the baby's features, looking for family resemblances. She was struck by his hands. 'They are rather large, but fine with long fingers—quite unlike mine and certainly unlike his father's,' she wrote. 'It will be interesting to see what they will become. I still find it difficult to believe that I have a baby of my own.'

Philip's opinion was typically blunt. Asked what his new-born son reminded him of he replied, 'A plum pudding.'

The boy was christened Charles Philip Arthur George in the Music Room where four years later he would host his first proper party. His godparents were George VI; his great-grandmother, Queen Mary; his aunt, Princess Margaret; his paternal great-grandmother, Victoria, Marchioness of Milford Haven; his great-uncle, David Bowes Lyon; Earl Mountbatten's daughter, Lady Brabourne; and his great-uncles, Prince George of Greece, and King Haakon of Norway, who had chosen not to spend his wartime's exile in England with his British relations whom he held to be responsible for the death of his cousin, Czar Nicholas of Russia.

Elizabeth breast-fed her young son for the first few weeks and Charles spent the first month of his life in a round wicker basket in the dressing room adjoining his mother's bedroom. Then, according to the dictates of circumstance and tradition, he was taken away from his mother and handed into the care of Nanny Helen Lightbody and the nursery maid, Mabel Anderson. Two world wars had delivered a hammer blow to the cosy, upper-class world of servants and nurseries. The Royal Family, however, secure in their time warp, had weathered the changes and Charles soon fell into the routine that had been so much part of Elizabeth's own childhood. He was taken to see his mother every morning at nine, just as she had been taken to see her parents. And in the evenings, engagements permitting, she would join him for bath time, which he came to love (he thoroughly enjoyed playing with his plastic yellow ducks and a toy submarine). But that was just about the extent of it. After the first flush of involvement, the mundane chores of motherhood, like nappy-changing, were usually left to the nursery staff.

'To my knowledge she never bathed the children,' Mrs Parker said. 'Nanny did all that.'

'Woman's paramount duty is to the home,' the Queen once opined. 'It is there she finds her truest fulfilment.' But as the eldest daughter, Elizabeth was forced to assume more and more of her ailing father's public duties, and that inevitably left less time for her son and his sister, Anne, who was born twenty-one months later.

The situation could only get worse once she had ascended the throne and her children's upbringing, as her own had been, was left in the care of the nursery staff. It was therefore to his nannies that Charles, who soon revealed himself to be a shy and sensitive child, turned for the affection he needed. Both Nanny Lightbody, who had been recommended to the Edinburghs, as they were then known, by Princess Marina, and Miss Anderson were Scottish. Mabel, Eileen Parker remembered, 'was prim and proper' while Helen 'was an awfully kind person and terribly fair. Prince Charles adored her.' One of them, though no one knows who, serviced him with his earliest memory—of being pushed through either Green or St James's Park in a pram, him at one end, his nanny's hands at the other, and wondering at the prodigious length of his carriage. It was Nanny Lightbody—Charles called her Nana—who got him up in the morning and dressed him, just as Alah had dressed Elizabeth. Nanny also slept in the same room as him and comforted him when he woke during the night.

As Charles's step-grandmother-in-law Dame Barbara Cartland observed, much of his early life was lived 'behind the green baize door . . . Mummy a remote and glamorous figure who came to kiss you goodnight, smelling of lavender and dressed for dinner. Prince Charles worshipped his mother, but from afar.' The habits Elizabeth had acquired in her own childhood were proving hard to break and, undemonstrative by nature, she always found it difficult to hug or kiss her son, preferring to leave such important tactile displays of emotion to the nannies. Indeed, Charles does not remember his mother kissing him at all after the age of eight. He wistfully told a girlfriend that his nanny meant more to him emotionally than his mother ever did.

Elizabeth became even more distant as a mother when George VI died and she became monarch. Godfrey Talbot, the BBC's Court Correspondent at the time, recalled: 'She had been trained since the cradle by her father that duty came before everything, including her family. She reluctantly had to abandon her family and they virtually didn't see their parents for months on end. It was very upsetting and bewildering for a little boy.'

In 1953 the new Queen and her consort left on a long-delayed tour of the Commonwealth. They were away for six months. Like her mother before her, Elizabeth cried at the parting. And as her mother had discovered after her six-month trip to Australia in 1927, the long absence exacted its inevitable toll. When they were eventually reunited, the Queen recalled her children 'were terribly polite. I don't think they really knew who we were.'

In Philip's case that was understandable. He had managed to spend Charles's first Christmas with his wife and son, but that would prove to be the last time for several years that they managed to be together for what is usually considered a time for family celebration. Charles's mother chose to leave her son at Sandringham with his grandparents and went to join her husband in Malta where he was serving in the Royal Navy. On Charles's third birthday both his parents were away on a tour of North America.

Eileen Parker had known Philip for several years before he married the future Queen. From the very first, she said, 'He was a real loner. He was very good looking; tall, with that blond hair and those piercing blue eyes. You would turn and say, "Who's that?" "Oh, that's Prince Philip of Greece, but he never has anything to do with anybody." '

Marriage had not mellowed him. He was a man of his time and background, just as his wife was a woman of hers. Very much a man's man, he enjoyed drinking and jesting with his cronies and continued to keep to a bachelor routine. On one occasion he and Mike Parker were so late home to Clarence House, where he and his wife had established their first home, that he found the gates locked. He had to climb in over them. 'Serves them both right,' his wife commented, drily.

He was soon surrounded by a group of like-minded people his wife referred to as 'Philip's funny friends'. Eileen Parker called them 'distinctly odd'.

The Palace old guard did not approve. They were most concerned at what Mrs Parker saw as 'his apparent desire to continue bachelor friendships' with people of somewhat dubious reputation. Their attitude, rather than reining him back, only seemed to spur Philip on. Independent and single-minded, he disliked the constraints imposed by his membership of the Royal Family.

In 1951 the ill-health of his father-in-law the King forced him to give up his active career in the Navy where he had excelled. When his wife succeeded her father on the throne, he found himself outmanoeuvred by the Palace old guard who excluded him from having any say in his wife's affairs of state. Even learning to fly a helicopter proved difficult. When the

Prime Minister, Winston Churchill, learned that Philip had taken to the air, he summoned Mike Parker to Downing Street, kept him standing in silence for several minutes while he carried on working at his desk, then gave him 'a long accusing stare' and coldly asked, 'Is your objective the destruction of the whole of the Royal Family?'

Naturally irascible, these impositions only served to heighten Philip's irritation, as did the government's firm ruling, which had the backing of Queen Mary, that his children were not to be called Mountbatten, the name he had assumed, but Windsor, as George V had decreed. He felt, he complained, like a 'bloody amoeba'.

He had little time to devote to his son as he struggled to find a role for himself in these frustrating circumstances. Nor did he show any inclination to be a hands-on, nappy-changing kind of father. Charles, as everyone noted, was an 'exceptionally sweet-natured little boy' who was always thoughtful—of others and the world around him. He learned to walk with the help of a blue elephant on wheels called Jumbo, was soon fond of pedalling his white tricycle around Richmond Park and down the corridors at Sandringham shouting 'Fire! Fire!' to the amusement of his grandparents, and was very attached to a stuffed rabbit, which he took to bed with him, and a teddy bear, which would eventually follow him to school.

George VI, in his dying days, remarked, 'Charles is too sweet, stumping around the room.'

He was neither aggressive nor sporting, however. His little sister soon came to dominate him physically. He was not mechanically-minded like his father. He suffered from knock-knees like both his grandfather, George VI, and great-grandfather, George V. He had flat feet and had to wear a special pair of orthopaedic shoes. He was prone to chest complaints and a constant succession of coughs and throat ailments.

'Philip tolerated Charles but I don't think he was a loving

father,' Eileen Parker observed. 'He would pick up Charles but his manner was cold. He had more fun with Anne. 'I think Charles was frightened of him.'

It is frequently stated and generally believed that Earl Mountbatten's overwhelming drive to succeed was motivated by his need to expunge the humiliation suffered by his father, whose German ancestry and accent forced his resignation as First Sea Lord at the outset of the First World War. In a similar way, Philip also appeared to be compensating, if only subconsciously, for the failings of *his* father. Prince Andrew had been accused of cowardice and condemned for treason. His son was a ruthlessly efficient naval officer who would certainly have risen to very high rank had he been allowed to pursue his career. Those who knew Andrew during his exile in Paris remember him as an effeminate whinger. Philip, conversely, was overtly masculine and spoke his mind without apology. He set himself manly tasks and expected others to follow his example.

Philip believed in corporal punishment and Charles was summarily spanked if he was rude or obstreperous, though his father usually left the administration of such discipline to the nannies. His remarks, however, could be more wounding.

'He could be incredibly cutting, not only to his children, but to other people,' Mrs Parker recalled. 'He always had to fight for himself from the very beginning. The Queen adored him but she didn't rough it. He did rough it and I've heard him say some awful remarks.'

The women charged with looking after the little boy did not always approve of Philip's brusque methods. Just before the Queen and Philip embarked on their six-month tour, Catherine Peebles, another capable Scots-woman, was employed as governess. Charles, she recalled, was a reticent, reflective child. 'He liked being amused rather than amusing himself. He was very responsive to kindness but if you shouted at him he would draw back into his shell and you would be able to do nothing with him.' Philip's manner did not draw the best out of his son.

Nanny Lightbody also had her reservations. 'She never said she didn't like him but I don't think she saw eye to eye with him one bit,' said Mrs Parker. Philip's way of teaching his son to swim was to jump into the Buckingham Palace pool and loudly order the often terrified Charles in after him. One Saturday morning Charles was 'slightly chesty'. Nana did not want to let him into the water but Philip insisted. The little boy ended up with a bad cold. Nana was furious. 'I was very cross with his father,' she said later, 'but the trouble is I can only say so much.' Philip, still the naval officer at heart, did not tolerate his decisions being questioned.

There were occasions when his manner would soften. And Mabel Anderson publicly insisted, 'He was a marvellous father. When the children were younger he always set aside time to read to them or help them put together those little model toys.'

There were none the less moments when his exasperation got the upper hand. He tried to teach his son to sail, without noticeable success. Charles was often seasick and did not respond well to the hearty discipline of boat-board life. He later recalled: 'I remember one disastrous day when we went racing and my father was, as usual, shouting. We wound the winch harder and the sail split in half with a sickening crack. Father was not pleased.

'Not long after that I was banned from the boat after an incident while cruising in Scotland. There was no wind and I was amusing myself taking pot shots at beer cans floating around the boat. The only gust of wind of the day blew the jib in front of my rifle just as I fired. I wasn't invited back on board.'

The difference in their personalities opened a gulf between

father and son. 'I didn't listen to advice from my father until I was in my late teens,' Charles said. He was more at ease in the company of his grandmother, who now bore the title Queen Elizabeth, The Queen Mother.

As a mother she had been warm and loving but frequently distracted. Being a grandmother, however, suited her and she brought more affection to the role than Queen Mary had ever been capable of. In her dying days the old Queen unbent a little, allowing her great-grandson to play with her collection of jade objects, a pleasure she had sternly denied her grand-daughters, Elizabeth and Margaret. But despite the mellowing sadness of old age (she lived to see her husband and three of her sons die and another exiled), she never lost her intimidating air of haughty majesty, even with her own family.

The new Queen Mother, by contrast, was gentle and welcoming. She remembered her grandson as 'a very gentle boy with a very kind heart, which I think is the essence of everything'. The feeling was reciprocated. On the occasion of her eightieth birthday Charles said: 'Ever since I can remember, my grandmother has been the most wonderful example of fun, laughter, infinite security and, above all else, exquisite taste.

'For me, she has always been one of those extraordinarily rare people whose touch can turn everything into gold—whether it be putting people at their ease, turning something dull into something amusing, bringing happiness and comfort to people in her presence, or making any house she lives in a unique haven of cosiness and character. She belongs to that priceless brand of human beings whose greatest gift is to enhance life for others through her own effervescent enthusiasm for life.'

The other grandmother was Philip's mother, Princess Alice, who had now retired into a nun's habit (the costume did not inhibit her chain-smoking consumption of noxious untipped Greek cigarettes or her taste for strong, caffeine-loaded coffee, or sherry). She made occasional visits to England from her convent retreat in Greece, then spent the last years of her life living at Buckingham Palace, where she died in 1969. She took particular delight in Charles's company, though Charles found her a rather alarming figure.

'She was very severe,' Eileen Parker remembered. 'She always sat bolt upright and had an almost overpowering personality. The room filled with smoke when she was around.' She spoke broken English in a thick; guttural accent. Because of her deafness she was hard to make conversation with. 'She had to be near you so that she could look at you and lip read what you were saying,' Mrs Parker remembered. 'The Queen Mother was completely different. Very natural; she had the gift of putting you at your ease and making you feel as if you were the only person in the room.'

The Queen Mother once observed, 'I'm not as nice as you think I am.' Charles did not agree. She offered him a sanctuary from the 'near-Teutonic' demands of his father and a kindly embrace during the unavoidable absences of his mother.

'He turned to Granny for a shoulder to cry on,' Godfrey Talbot said. 'During the first years of the Queen's reign the Queen Mother was both mother and father.'

It was the nursery staff, though, who had the most direct influence on his young life. They taught him his manners. Particular emphasis was placed on politeness and he was taught from an early age to address people as 'Mr' and not to poke his tongue out or pull faces. Nanny Lightbody was forever saying, 'Have you said thank you?' and he was made to go and thank the engine driver whenever he took a train ride. They protected him as best they could from his aggressive younger sister. They disciplined him when he was naughty, which was rarely. They made a home for him in the nursery and filled it with a menagerie of animals; as well as the corgis there were a pair of South American love-birds named David and Annie

(Mabel Anderson called them 'horrid, vicious creatures'), a hamster named Chi-Chi, and a rabbit called Harvey. The animals were a 'dominant passion' and Charles, taught to clean his own teeth, used to try and brush Harvey's.

He developed an early interest in cooking and what went on in the Palace kitchens and was forever popping in to help the chefs weight out the ingredients, fetch the pots, and give warning when the saucepans and kettles were coming to the boil.

Not all his culinary efforts were successful. He was once sent to the Palace store-room by a chef named Aubrey—and dropped the tray loaded with butter, baking powder, two dozen eggs, and sultanas on the floor on the way back. His attempts at making ice lollies were equally fraught. Mabel Anderson kept turning up the temperature of the nursery fridge because her sibling's milk was getting too cold. Charles kept turning it down again because his lollies wouldn't freeze. Whether it was the milk or the lollies that came out right depended on who had last been at the fridge. Not surprisingly, his presence did not always meet with the approval of the kitchen staff who would complain that he got in the way.

He enjoyed ballroom and Scottish dancing and was taught, as his mother had been, by Miss Vacani who came to the Palace to give him lessons with a few other children belonging to members of the Household. Miss Peebles said he had a strong sense of rhythm and Eileen Parker agreed and said, 'He was a very good dancer even at that young age and could keep time very well.' The Queen sometimes looked in to see how he was progressing.

The reserve he has never managed to overcome manifested itself from early on. As a little boy he found it difficult to mix with other children. He was very friendly with the Parkers' daughter Julie, but as her mother recalled, 'If there were other children there he would cling to Nanny Lightbody.' When he was nervous, Mrs Parker noted, his mouth would twitch to one side in the manner later seized on by comic impersonators.

That shyness carried through into his studies. Miss Catherine Peebles, who was promptly named Mispy as in Miss P, set up a schoolroom at Buckingham Palace, but instead of other children being invited to join him in his studies, as had then become the convention for children who were privately educated, Charles was taught on his own. Even his sister, Anne, was not allowed in when he was working. As the Arundel Herald Extraordinary, Dermot Morrah, wrote in 1968 in his 'privileged account' of Charles's childhood 'written with the approval of HM The Queen,' his mother 'saw that Charles was likely to get more embarrassment than encouragement from working as one of a group [looking back today he is certain that her assessment was right], and she consequently decided that, at least while he was with Miss Peebles, he should have lessons alone.

'A good deal of what was important in his life was lived internally, within the bounds of his own imagination. Miss Peebles discovered that she had to deal with a vague child, or, perhaps more accurately, a child who still had only a vague relationship to the external world.' The doughty Mispy found herself dealing with a 'plodder' who was good at art but took rather a long time learning to read, found it hard to concentrate on written subjects, and was incapable of understanding the 'language' of mathematics.

Like his mother before him, Charles was also taught to ride and swim (by the age of six) and was taken on educational visits to the museums and, of greater interest, to Madame Tussaud's waxworks where he gazed at the effigies of the parents he saw less of than he would have wished. He also visited the London Planetarium, which fed his interest in the stars, an interest he shares with his mother, who is a 'country person' like himself.

To ensure that these outings went off with the minimum of disruption, the Queen's press secretary, the later knighted Sir Richard Colville, sent a letter to the editors of the Fleet Street newspapers asking them to allow him to enjoy himself 'without the embarrassment of constant publicity'. It was a vain appeal. Attitudes towards the Royal Family had changed since the days when his mother could go for open carriage rides around London waving politely to the people Alah told her to. In the still ordered society of the 1930s royalty was treated with respectful deference. Twenty years later public interest in this grand family, with its palaces and panoplies, had sharpened. Royal-watching was becoming a national sport. The popular newspapers had started pandering to their readers' interests, and when they discovered that Charles had started attending Hill House, a 'pre-prep' school five minutes' drive from Buckingham Palace in Knightsbridge, an army of photographers and reporters descended.

The decision to break with royal tradition and send her son to a proper school illustrated the Queen's determination to give him a 'normal' childhood. This, she believed, was the best way to equip him for his future role as king, and in that she was encouraged by her husband.

'The Queen and I want Charles to go to school with other boys of his generation and learn to live with other children, and to absorb from childhood the discipline imposed by education with others,' Philip declared. The academic side was deemed to be of secondary importance. As Philip told his son, 'Look, I'm only going to bother if you're permanently bottom. I really couldn't care less where you are. Just stay in the middle, that's all I ask.' The middle was more or less where Charles stayed for the whole of his school life, except for mathematics where he was permanently rooted near the bottom. That did not particularly concern his father. It was 'character' that he was interested in, and while it was the Queen who authorized this experiment in royal education, it was Philip who had the deciding say in which schools he would attend.

Hill House set the course. It was founded by Colonel Henry Townsend, a believer in the educational properties of sport and competition. His school tried to instill in its pupils, as its manifesto declared, 'a sense of rivalry . . . and the urge to win.' Both were new to the young prince, surrounded as he had been by affectionate women—nannies, governess, his grandmother, his aunt Margaret—and with only his sister to contend with.

Hill House was only a day school and every evening he retreated to the security of the Palace. At the age of eight, however, the boy who, as one of his biographers observed, 'had never been shopping . . . never been on a bus . . . had never been lost in a crowd . . . had never had to fend for himself', was marched out of this supportive environment to follow in his father's footsteps, first to Cheam, then up to the remote coastal plain of Morayshire to Gordonstoun. He found the transition excruciatingly painful.

His first few days as a boarder at Cheam, he would later recall, were the most miserable of his life, and his mother recalled how he 'shuddered' with apprehension as he journeyed there for his first day.

'He dreaded going away to school,' Mabel Anderson recalled. 'He felt family separation very deeply.'

He would write to Mispy every day, Princess Anne recalled. 'He was heartbroken. He used to cry into his letters and say, "I miss you." ' The governess was equally distressed by the absence of the little boy she had come to love. She stayed on to teach Anne and then Andrew, but her real interest was always Charles and they corresponded regularly for the rest of her life. (Catherine Peebles died in the impersonal vastness of Buckingham Palace in 1968. She retired to her rooms one Friday night. No one missed her and her body was not found until forty-eight hours later. Charles, his family remembered, was 'inconsolable' when he was told the news.)

Charles eventually settled in as best he could, but he did not have a particularly happy time there. He was too difficult, too shy to make friends easily or to stand out and up for himself in the rough and tumble. He still carried his puppy fat, and during one game of rugby was upset to hear the shout directed at him from somewhere below, 'Oh, get *off* me, Fatty!'

It was the same at Gordonstoun. Philip had thrived there. It did not suit his son. The hearty outdoor life, if never as Spartan as legend made out (there were always hot showers to go with the cold and the early morning runs were little more than fifty-yard trots up the road and then never when it was raining), was still tougher than he would have wished.

'I hated the institution, just as I hated leaving home,' he would later say. 'I did not enjoy school as much as I might have, but this was because I am happier at home than anywhere else.'

The American psychiatrist M. Scott Peck maintains that there is a 'pattern for children leaving home. Those who grew up in warm, nurturing, loving homes usually had relatively little difficulty in leaving those homes, while children who grew up in homes filled with back-biting, hostility, coldness, and viciousness often had a great deal of trouble leaving.'

Peck's book, *The Road Less Traveled*, has sold over four million copies. It continues to sell over 500,000 a year, making him one of the best selling authors in history. He continues: 'We tend to project onto the world what our childhood home is like. Children who grow up in nurturing homes tend to see the world as a warm and loving place and say, "Hey, let me at it." Children who grow up in a home filled with hostility and viciousness tend to see the world as a cold, hostile and dangerous place.'

Charles could certainly sense the hostility his regal position generated. He saw less of his mother than he would have liked and there were moments of tension with his father. And royal courts, even in a modern age, are breeding grounds for just the kind of backbiting hostilities Peck refers to. But whatever the flaws in his home life, he still enjoyed a full support system of nannies and female relations to service him with the necessary emotional succour which, had his temperament been of a different kind, might well have been enough to see him through. Anne confronted the outside world with vigorous self-confidence. Her brother did not.

'I had a dream,' he once recalled, 'that I was going to escape and hide in the forest, in a place where no one could find me, so I wouldn't have to go back to school.' More than anything he wanted to be with his grandmother, and Gordonstoun certainly stood in rugged contrast to that comforting, female-dominated world.

He was put into Windmill Lodge, whose housemaster, Robert Whitby, made a habit of appearing to be always angry and shouted a great deal. Another housemaster of that time described the school thus: 'Good for the very clever, good for the laird's idiot son, but not so good for the average boy.' And in matters academic and athletic Charles was never other than average. He only managed to pass O-level mathematics at the third attempt. His history, for all his stated view that 'I honestly believe that the only way one can hope to understand and cope with the present is by knowing and being able to interpret what happened in the past', was something of a struggle. On one well-reported occasion his tutor, Robin Birley, shouted at him in front of the whole class, 'Come on, Charles, you can do better than this—after all, this is the history of your family we're dealing with!' He was disappointing at rugby and cricket.

Where he did excel was in music and acting. He was taught to play the cello by an old German woman who had been at the school since Philip's day. And his ability on the stage was quickly noted by Dr Eric Anderson, who would go on to become headmaster of Eton. Anderson cast him in the role of Macbeth and he turned in a memorable performance. His art work, and pottery in particular, was also of a high standard.

These were never more than very minor interests at a school that placed such emphasis on the physical, however, and Charles often seemed out of step with his classmates. He had few friends amongst the school's four hundred other boys. He usually walked the half-mile from Windmill Lodge to lessons in the complex of huts around the main school building by himself. Those who tried to strike up a conversation with him had to endure a gauntlet of snide comments from their contemporaries, who would loudly accuse them of 'sucking up'.

The Queen Mother, aware of her grandson's introverted nature, had argued that he would be better served at Eton College, on the other side of the Thames from Windsor Castle, with its six hundred years' experience of accommodating the wide-ranging interests of its pupils. A number of the Queen's advisors agreed with her. But Philip was not to be swayed and Gordonstoun it was. 'In effect the decision meant an attempt to mould him in his father's image, to which . . . he did not naturally approximate,' Dermot Morrah wrote.

This did not prevent him becoming Guardian, as Gordonstoun's headboy is called, as his father had been. The whole point of Charles's education was to train him to accept responsibility, a responsibility that was his by birthright and one which was not to be evaded.

'I didn't suddenly wake up in my pram one day and say, "Yippee",' he said, referring to the prospect of kingship. 'It just dawns on you slowly that people are interested . . . and slowly you get the idea that you have a certain duty and responsibility. It's one of those things you grow up in.'

His parents had tried to shield him from his fate for as long as possible. When he was three, for instance, a courtier passed him in one of the Buckingham Palace corridors. 'Where are you going?' the prince asked.

'I'm going to see the Queen,' the courtier answered.

'Who's she?' Charles enquired.

In another break from tradition, he was not obliged to bow to his mother once she became Queen. Reality could not be locked out for long, however, and he was soon well aware of his position. Soldiers presented arms when he passed them in the Palace courtyard. Crowds cheered him when he passed. And how many little boys have the band of the Grenadier Guards on call to play 'The Teddy Bears' Picnic' for them on their fourth birthday?

'You always felt he knew his destiny even at that age,' said Eileen Parker.

He was surrounded by reminders of who he was and what lay ahead. His mother's face was on the stamps he stuck on the letters to Mispy and on the coins he bought his chocolate with in his school tuck-shop—a fact that his schoolmates were not slow to point out. Brought up amongst the sons of the privileged, he was always more privileged. A private detective accompanied him to Gordonstoun. Whereas everyone else had to see each term at Gordonstoun through without the benefit of a break (there was no half-term holiday at the school when he was there), he was allowed out to join his parents on various state occasions.

He was spared the anxiety of choosing a career: he was going to Cambridge. Then, and despite his seasickness, he was going into the Navy. His great-uncle, Earl Mountbatten, spelt it out: 'Trinity College like his grandfather, Dartmouth like his father and grandfather; and then to sea in the Royal Navy, ending up with a command of his own.' A suitable marriage would follow.

In 1987, in a cry of frustration, he declared; 'You can't understand what it's like to have your whole life mapped out for you a year in advance. It's so awful to be programmed. I know what I'll be doing next week, next month, even next year. At times I get so fed up with the whole idea.'

As a youth he had to bear it even if he couldn't grin. And no matter how definite the plan, it provided no protection against the bruisings he received along the way. Rather the contrary.

At Cheam he watched his mother on television announce that she was going to make him Prince of Wales. 'I remember being acutely embarrassed,' he recalled. 'I think for a little boy of nine it was rather bewildering. All the others turned and looked at me in amazement.'

He was faced with similar moments throughout his schooldays. His photograph was often in the newspapers, and if the accompanying stories owed more to imagination than fact, that was no consolation to Charles as he struggled and usually failed to live up to the image the press were determined to create for him. One small example was an article that appeared in the *Daily Express* when he was at Gordonstoun. The William Hickey column boldly predicted that the 'Action Man' prince would make the rugby 1st AV. That caused considerable mirth amongst pupils and sports masters alike, for Charles never even made the 4th, the lowest team fielded by the school.

Such incidents left their mark. He could be gracious and charming. When faced with situations over which he had no control, however, he would withdraw deep into himself. Fearful of confrontation, desperate to avoid ridicule, he constructed a wall of regal reserve to protect the sensitivity which had been his most notable characteristic as a child.

Anne

rincess Anne once observed that she should have been a boy. There are those who are close to the Royal Family who believe that she should not only have been born a boy, but that she should also have been the eldest. Prince Philip was one who held that view.

She is gutsy, sensible, and pragmatic. She does not talk to plants. She is not given to bouts of introspection. She is single-minded and believes in deeds, not words. She is sporty and brave. She is unimpressed by rank or title, is unafraid of controversy and cares little for the opinion of others. And if she can be disconcertingly 'royal' when the mood takes her ('I'm not your "love", I'm your Royal Highness', she once admonished an over-familiar photographer), she is someone who has no qualms about letting her hair down and mucking in when the occasion so demands.

In other words, she is very much her father's daughter—in a way that Charles could never be his father's son. Of all his children, Anne is the only one who merits a photograph in his private office at Buckingham Palace.

'He always had more fun with Anne,' Eileen Parker observed. 'Charles is more like the Queen while Anne is very like Prince Philip.'

Philip himself would later admit: 'Perhaps I did spoil her at times.'

Anne was born on 15 August 1950. 'It's the sweetest girl,' Philip remarked ('With quite a definite nose for one so young,' photographer Cecil Beaton remarked cattily). She was twenty-one months younger and, at 6 lbs, one pound and six ounces lighter than her elder brother. What she gave away in weight and age she soon made up for in temper and physical determination.

'Anne would boss Charles; she would take command of things,' recalled Mrs Parker. 'If she saw a toy she wanted, she would grab it. She also grabbed everything that Charles wanted—and everything he had she wanted.'

Charles had a blue pedal-car he was particularly fond of. He was often unceremoniously bundled out of it by his more aggressive sister. It was the same with the tricycle they shared. If Charles was riding it, Anne was sure to want it.

'There were terrible scenes,' said Mrs Parker, who used to entertain the royal siblings at her home in Kensington's Launceston Place. 'Nanny Lightbody would say, "Now stop this!" '

There was no stopping Anne, however. When their father presented them each with a pair of boxing gloves and tried to instruct them in the art of self-defense they set about each other with such fury that he had to take them away again.

Once, when they were staying at Balmoral, Lady Adeane, the wife of the Queen's private secretary, gave them a paper bag full of mushrooms she had just picked. A row quickly ensued over who was going to present them to their mother. They started tugging at the bag, which burst open, spilling its contents over the gravel drive—at which point Anne, who had just returned from a riding lesson, set about her brother with her riding crop. Charles burst into tears just as the Queen opened the door. In exasperation, she shouted 'Why can't you behave yourselves!' and boxed them both around the ears.

As the Princess herself admitted: 'We fought like cats and dogs.' And 'No' was not a word she readily responded to.

'When she got really worked up she would start throwing things at him,' Mrs Parker said. 'She was very strong-willed, a real menace.'

She was forever ignoring her nanny's instructions not to take too many toys out, but instead emptying the entire cupboard on to the floor and, in those days of coal fires in every room, making herself 'filthy in the process'.

If she didn't get her way 'she had the most frightful fit of temper, lying on the floor and kicking with sheer temper'.

Charles was surprisingly nice to his boisterous little sister ('perhaps too nice,' Mrs Parker observed), always inviting her to join in his games, taking a concerned and conciliatory attitude towards her excesses. And for all their squabbles, the two got on reasonably well together. They had to. For like their mother and her sister before them, Charles and Anne spent more of their infancy in the company of adults—servants, courtiers, family members—than they did with children of their own age and it was to each other that they turned for playful companionship.

That happened to suit Charles, who did not mix easily. Anne was 'always very confident', as Mrs Parker remarked. At Madame Vacani's dance classes, for example, Charles would hang back, clutching on to nanny and watching as Anne 'would go off with the other children'. And while Charles was often too shy to talk, 'Anne talked non-stop'.

She was also much naughtier than her compliant brother. She was the one who kicked the corgis. During her days as a Brownie she set off a major alarm when she disappeared into a bush in the Palace grounds and started frantically blowing her whistle. That brought a posse of policemen, uniformed and plain-clothed, courtiers, gardeners, and Guards running to the scene—much to her mischievous delight.

And it was Anne who teased the Guards on duty at Buckingham Palace. As soon as she discovered that they presented arms when she walked past them, she started doing just that, much to the anger of Nanny Lightbody. Charles was never so daring; he had confined himself to imitating their march.

But if Anne was more than her brother's equal on the parade ground of the Palace forecourt or the battlefield of the nursery, it was Charles who commanded the greatest attention, no matter what their father might have thought about his abilities. He was born to be king and that fact was subtly drummed into him and his sister from earliest memory.

By her own account she 'always accepted the role of being second in everything from quite an early age. You adopt that position as part of your experience. You start off in life very much a tail-end Charlie, at the back of the line.' And however much she might kick and scream, there, by genetic accident and the law of primogeniture, she was destined to remain.

She would be grateful for that in years to come. She developed a healthy view of her position in the royal hierarchy. 'I'm the Queen's daughter and as a daughter I get less involved than the boys,' she said. That allowed her to develop her own interests, in her own way, without the pressures of a centre-stage royal role that so inhibited Charles.

'I'm me, I'm a person, I'm an individual, and I think it's better for everybody that I shouldn't pretend to be anything that I'm not,' she once remarked. If the public really wanted a 'fairy Princess' to fill 'a void', then the Princess of Wales was much better suited to the part, she caustically observed.

She was not quite so self-effacing as a youngster. As her authorized biographer, Brian Hoey, observed: 'Perhaps it was this feeling of being second all the time that subconsciously prompted her as a young child to push her way to the front whenever she and Prince Charles were together. If he held back when she appeared in public, Princess Anne would be first out of the car or train, determined that no one would miss her.'

There was no place for her, though, at the great occasion of the Coronation of her mother. She was too young to witness that pivotal transition not just from one reign to the next, but from one era to another—from an age where the monarchy was secure in its position to one in which it would be thrown into stark relief and, within forty years, see its value and continued existence called into question.

George VI died at his beloved Sandringham on 6 February, 1952. Of equal moment was the death thirteen months later of his mother, Queen Mary. Grand and imperious, she had insisted on her due respect right up to the end, and Charles and Anne were ordered to bow and curtsey when they came into her presence.

But if she was the 'epitome of patrician rectitude', she was also a 'sad figure burdened by longevity'—a Queen whose Empire was in terminal decline and whose heirs would come to shed, through force of circumstance but also through vagaries of temperament, much of the awesome majesty she had stoutly believed was essential to the monarchy. Anne often stubbornly refused to curtsey to her great-grandmother.

Queen Mary's death should have delayed the Coronation. By the old-fashioned protocol of which she was the ultimate symbol, the court should still have been in mourning when Elizabeth was crowned in Westminster Abbey on 2 June 1953. But in a last gesture to the formality that had governed her life, she insisted that the Coronation should go ahead as scheduled and it did—with all the succulent pomp and gorgeous ceremony that her great-grandfather, Edward VII, and his advisors had been able to devise. Indeed, so recent was the pageantry that when the procedure for the Queen's accession was discussed, Crown Equerry Sir Norman Gwatkin said, 'Let's look at an old copy of the *Illustrated London News* and see what they did last time.'

Charles, aged four and a half and technically senior Royal Duke and head of the peerage, was taken in at the last minute to see his mother crowned. He was brought in at the back to stand between the Queen Mother and Princess Margaret. He was dressed in a white satin suit. His nanny said, 'I just hope everything goes all right, as you know what children are.'

Midway through the ceremony he wiped his hair and then put his hands to his nose—Nanny Lightbody had combed his hair down with brilliantine and he wanted to smell it.

Anne, not quite three, remained at Buckingham Palace, suffering 'the normal sisterly fury at being left behind'. There was a party for all the children in the Madame Vacani dancing class. They watched the ceremony on a flickering black and white television set. It was also the day that the news came through that Sir Edmund Hillary had conquered Everest.

'My husband and Prince Philip were more interested in watching that than going to the ceremony,' Eileen Parker recalled.

Anne's memories of the day itself are inevitably vague. What she does remember is being taken out on to the balcony afterwards with the rest of the family and being told to 'wave to the people'. It was a public lesson in the demands that came with being a princess. There was no escape from being royal. As she would later say, 'The idea of opting out is a non-starter.'

In the 1950s there were none the less long periods when the Royal Family were able to enjoy the privilege of comparative anonymity and her childhood, she recalled, was mercifully spared the unremitting attention that befell the next generation.

'The pattern of my life from birth until I went to boarding school, at the age of thirteen, was living in London during the week and at Windsor at the weekends,' she wrote. 'The holidays were divided between Christmas and the New Year at Sandringham, Easter at Windsor and most of the summer holidays at Balmoral.'

She settled into the time-honoured routine of country life. School work would occasionally intrude, and to help improve their French a tutor, a certain Mademoiselle de Roujoux, was employed. But football seemed to play as important a part in the curriculum as irregular verbs.

'The Queen is always goalkeeper and Prince Philip, Princess Margaret and the children join in,' Mademoiselle de Roujoux recalled. 'Charles and Anne were real little devils and never stopped playing tricks on me. The last words they shouted at me as I left for the train back home were "*Café au lait, au lit*" which I had taught them and which they had found most amusing. It means, coffee with milk in bed.'

It was a pastorale of advantaged youth. Anne learned to ride on a strawberry roan pony named William. She had the pleasure of threshing the corn and watching the corgis' 'inefficient attempts to kill rats that ran out from the shrinking stacks', and watching the slow passage of the seasons in an age before advancements in agricultural machinery and methods changed the countryside for ever.

In Scotland there was 'the magic of the views of Lochnagar and the Dee valley, the beautiful autumn colours of the rowans and silver birches, the majesty of the Caledonian Forest and the animals and birds that live in these relatively unspoilt wild places.' At Sandringham there was 'the best riding country' across the miles of flat stubble fields of the family estate.

'In the early fifties, when I was growing up, there were still lots of people working and living in the countryside,' she recalled. 'Information was passed from parents to children, knowledge was absorbed rather than taught. My "knowledge" of ponies, horses and riding was largely acquired that way, by absorption.'

The Queen took an active interest in Charles and Anne's equestrian progress and would go out with them 'when she could . . . I really don't know how she put up with the noise and aggravation that almost always seemed unavoidable whenever my brother and I did anything together.'

It was her father, however, who really encouraged her riding. When he saw just how good she was—and how much better than her brother—he contacted Sir John Miller, the then head of the Royal Mews at Buckingham Palace, and told him to 'get on with it'.

'Not being nearly as brave as my sister—which very often happens—I rather got put off,' Charles recalled. When he was still at the end of a leading rein, Anne was off jumping and galloping before she had properly learned how to trot. Philip had no reservations about letting his daughter expose herself to the dangers inherent in equestrian sport.

'It was almost as if he treated her as a son,' one observer recalled.

Philip was not the most attentive of fathers. He had been promoted to the rank of Lieutenant-Commander in the Royal Navy on the day Anne was born and given command of his own ship, the frigate HMS *Magpie*. He had helped choose her names and Anne, which George V had overruled in the case of Princess Margaret, finally made it into the royal nomenclature. He had registered her with the Westminister Food Office and obtained for her the ration book, number MAPM/36, which the little princess, like the rest of the population in the austere post-war years, still required in order to obtain her allowance of meat, eggs, butter, bread, sugar, milk, and, for a growing child, a weekly bottle each of orange juice and cod liver oil. He flew home from Malta where he was stationed for the christening which was held in the Music Room of Buckingham Palace (the godparents were the baby's grandmothers, the Queen Mother and Princess Andrew of Greece; Philip's eldest sister, Princess Margarita von Hohenlohe-Langenburg; the Queen's cousin, Andrew Elphinstone; and Philip's uncle, Earl Mountbatten).

After that he very much went his own way. Even when he had to give up his naval career to devote his considerable energy to the mounting royal duties, he was as likely to spend his evenings out with his cronies as at home with his family. (One of his friends at the time was Prince Alfonso von Hohenlohe, the founder of the Marbella Club, who would scandalize European society by marrying Princess Ira von Fürstenberg, an heiress to the Agnelli car fortune, who was only fifteen at the time.)

He did find the time, though, to introduce his daughter to sailing on the waters of Loch Muick near Balmoral with considerably more success than he had with Charles, and Anne soon became a proficient yachtswoman.

He would also take them camping on the windblown Highland hills. They would cook their bacon, sausages, eggs, milk and tea and then spend the night in sleeping bags in a bothy built in Victoria's day as a picnic hut. Again it was Anne rather than her altogether more delicate brother who derived the greater pleasure from these Spartan escapades. But that, given their physical differences, was inevitable. Charles was a poor athlete; Anne became a first-class tennis and lacrosse player, and, most notably, an Olympic three-day-event rider.

The contrast was reflected in their relationships with their parents. Charles gravitated towards his mother who provided him with a sympathetic ear; Anne was close to Philip. Charles sometimes gave the impression of being 'terrified' of his father, who had little understanding of his son's fears and inhibitions and was inclined to laugh at them. He laughed at Anne too, but she could deal with that, cheerfully braving his ridicule, saying anything she wanted to him, and laughing back at him and with him, as she did when they were playing a game involving car number-plates.

To keep his children amused on long car journeys Philip would call out the registrations of passing vehicles and ask them to make a sentence out of the letters. One car had the number plate PMD.

'That's easy,' Anne said. 'Philip's my dad!'

In the comparison with Anne, Charles did not even have the compensation of a shining academic lead. Anne was intelligent and capable of passing her exams with ease. Her eventual A-level grades in History and Geography would have been sufficient to secure her a university place if she had wanted one, which she didn't.

'I think it's an overrated pastime,' she said, articulating her family's anti-intellectual bias.

Neither the Queen nor Prince Philip took a particular interest in Anne's academic progress. Before she was sent away to Benenden, a very Establishment girls' boarding school in Kent, she had been educated privately at Buckingham Palace under the tutelage of Miss Peebles. The schoolroom was in the old nursery wing. The Queen's rooms were close by on the floor directly below. Yet Anne does not recall her mother paying even one visit to her classroom to see how she was progressing.

It was left to Princess Margaret to monitor her niece's work and she did so with enthusiasm, going into the schoolroom to speak with the governess and even conducting oral examinations of her own. It was the foundation of a relationship between aunt and niece that matured into adult friendship, even though the results of these impromptu tests were not always as satisfactory as 'Charlie's Aunt', as Margaret called herself, would have wished.

Miss Peebles was a competent enough teacher but Charles

had been her favorite, and when he left to go to Cheam she 'virtually lost interest', as Anne recollected. She didn't go to any lengths to hide her belief that after Charles everyone else was 'second best'. There was never any overt estrangement between the governess and her pupil, but when Mispy died Anne did not share her brother's sense of bereavement. In fact, she felt no emotion at all except guilt—and that, she said, was only brought on precisely because she *didn't* feel any sense of loss.

Anne had been as upset as Miss Peebles when Charles had left for his first boarding school. Despite their arguments, brother and sister were always close. It was to offset her sense of loneliness that two girls of her own age were invited to join her for lessons at Buckingham Palace. They were Susan Babington-Smith, granddaughter of an admiral who had been equerry to George V, and Caroline Hamilton, granddaughter of the Dean of Windsor.

According to Susan, who married John Hemming, director and secretary of the National Geographic Society, all three were treated in exactly the same way. If there was any favouritism it worked against Anne. 'There was the odd time when Miss Peebles would be stricter with her than she was with us,' she recalled.

There was never any doubt, though, about who was royal. 'Not by anything she consciously did or said,' Mrs Hemming said. 'It was simply something about her that made us realize that she was different.'

They could hardly fail to miss the clues. Their classroom was in Buckingham Palace. At 11.30 every morning the military band in the forecourt would strike up for the Changing of the Guard. Celebrity guests like Soviet cosmonaut Yuri Gagarin called by. And if there was still any doubt, on state occasions the governess would break off lessons and take the three girls to a window to watch the carriages depart. The

Queen, in crown and full regalia, would look up and give a wave. Philip, in his uniform of Admiral of the Fleet (a promotion directly related to his marriage) would blow them a kiss.

There were also Anne's own outings to emphasize the difference in their status. She was a bridesmaid at the weddings of Earl Mountbatten's daughter, Lady Pamela, to interior designer David Hicks; Princess Margaret to the photographer Antony Armstrong-Jones; and the Duke of Kent to Katharine Worsley. When her brother Andrew was born, as well as pushing him around the garden in his pram, she also appeared in the official photographs. And when her two friends were invited to join their royal friend at Wimbledon, they watched the tennis from the royal box.

It was an idealized, hugely privileged style of education, and in any previous generation it would have continued to its conclusion. Philip had other ideas. As with Charles, he wanted Anne to experience life on the other side of the Palace walls. It was, he argued, a vital preparation for dealing with the exigencies of the modern world. Benenden, a traditional establishment for 'young ladies', was duly chosen, and at the age of thirteen Anne became, not the first princess (that honour belongs to her cousin, Princess Alexandra), but the only daughter of a reigning sovereign ever to be sent away to school.

Like Charles, she was stricken with nerves on her first day and was physically sick on her way to the school. Unlike Charles, she soon settled in and did well. Her first impression of school was 'the continuous noise and the fact that everywhere you turned there were so many people'. But whatever adjustment problems she may have had she kept to herself. She was not, so her contemporaries noted, a 'whiner' and the headmistress only found out about her bout of nausea en route to the school by chance, and then not until several weeks later.

She was put in the Magnolia dormitory with three other girls, and had drummed into her the oldest rule of the British public school system, which is that to learn how to command one first has to learn how to serve. She waited on table, and was made to give up her comfortable seat to girls her senior, and follow the routines and traditions of an establishment of which she was a very small part.

She learned how to handle money, a commodity the Royal Family have very little practical experience of. 'We had £2 a term and as I had been brought up by a careful Scots nanny to appreciate the value of money, I simply didn't spend my allotment. I've always been mean with money and as far as I know, I was the only girl in the school who had any left by the end of term.'

She was encouraged to pursue her riding at the nearby Moat House equestrian school which was run by Mrs Hatton-Hall, who, as Cherry Kendall, had been a top class three-day-eventer.

Anne eventually rose to be a prefect and captain of her house. She was, the headmistress Miss Elizabeth Clarke noted, 'able to exert her authority in a natural manner without being aggressive'. She then added the criticism that would always be levelled against her most famous pupil: 'If there was any failing at all it was possibly her impatience. She was extremely quick to grasp things herself and couldn't understand anyone else not being able to do so.'

Anne's own memories of her time at Benenden are pleasant ones. 'I enjoyed my time at school, and no doubt my riding experiences helped,' she wrote. Her willingness not to stand on royal ceremony had certainly helped. She was, as she said, determined to be herself and be judged by that criterion. Children, she later observed, 'accept people for what they are rather quicker than adults do. They have no preconceived ideas.' Charles, who was never allowed to forget who he was, would not have agreed, but then he was very different in character from his sister, who had the independence of mind to stand up for herself and even went so far as to admit that 'As a child and up to my teens, I don't think I went along with the family bit.'

Yet however determined she was to go her own way, she was never allowed to forget her royal status. As a concession to her position she was allowed out to attend certain state ceremonies though they were severely rationed because, as Elizabeth Clarke observed, 'The creation of precedents has to be watched in school life'.

There were other, more insidious reminders of who she was and what was expected of her. As a child, her parents had 'warned me that some people would want to make friends because of who you are. And I think that was fair comment, and it was important to know that.'

Even those children who, as Anne would have it, accepted her for what and not who she was were kept at arms' length. When Anne left for Benenden, all contact with Susan Babington-Smith and Caroline Hamilton ended.

'We never wrote to each other after leaving the Palace,' Susan said. 'We didn't even have a farewell party. There was no contact. It was just the end of one part of one's life and the beginning of the next.'

Susan believed that that unnatural parting was part of an official policy. 'I'm sure it was laid down by the Queen and her advisors that we should split up,' she said.

The Queen and Prince Philip had broken with tradition by sending Charles and Anne away to school. The change was only intended to go so far. They were still 'royal', the glass wall still in place. Charles would retreat behind it. When it came to raising a family of her own, Anne, like her aunt Margaret, would do what she could to shatter it.

Andrew and Edward

Nanny Mabel Anderson used to say no nursery could hold two Prince Andrews. But however naughty he was—and he could be very naughty indeed—Mabel loved him dearly. Enough to pick up the telephone twenty years later and tearfully ask him if what she had just heard on the radio was really true—that he and his Duchess were about to separate?

When Andrew heard his old nanny's voice he covered the receiver, turned to his wife and asked with a trembling voice, 'What shall we say to Mabel?'

Fergie, faced with her own problems and depressed by what she regarded as Andrew's inability to measure up as a husband, replied: 'Tell her what you want.'

Mabel Anderson was distraught to think of her beloved Andrew's unhappiness. Rejection was not something he had been trained to deal with. The cosy nursery world his nanny had created for him thirty-two years before had in no way prepared him for the emotional upheaval he was now experiencing. Mabel, by then in her late sixties, was aware of this and she was worried. So was Andrew.

It was all a long way from the Buckingham Palace days, which Mabel remembered so fondly.

Andrew was born on the afternoon of 19 February 1960,

first child to be born to a reigning British monarch in 103 years. The Queen and Prince Philip had been married for twelve and a half years.

The unplanned pregnancy came on the eve of a Canadian tour which was scheduled to cover 16,000 miles in nine weeks. It was a wearing journey for a woman in the early stages of pregnancy, but the Queen refused any advice. Unlike her sister, Margaret, she seldom drank, had never smoked and was, she insisted, in the best of health.

The strain of the intervening years had taken their toll, however, and the hormonal changes the Queen was experiencing left her very tired. She refused to give in and rest and, stubborn to the last, she came home from the tour exhausted and was immediately ordered to bed by her gynaecologist Lord Evans. Five days later she had recovered sufficiently to journey to Balmoral for the summer.

The beginning of the sixties was a time of great change, not least for the monarchy. Recent years had seen rumours as to the state of Elizabeth and Philip's marriage, and during 1959 the Royal Family had come under bitter attack, as their relevance began to be questioned for the first time in a debate started by Lord Altrincham, the writer John Grigg who later renounced his peerage.

The announcement of the 7lb 3oz infant prince's arrival, however, was greeted with the usual patriotic fervour the British reserved for royal births. There was much rejoicing amongst the crowd in the Mall, who were treated to a fly-past of thirty-six Hunter jets over Buckingham Palace and the traditional 21-gun salute.

Inside the Palace Prince Philip was in his study, far away from the bathroom of the Belgian suite on the ground floor which had been converted into a delivery room. His wife had made it clear she didn't want him hanging around—and certainly not at her side for the birth. That idea was distasteful to her. She was far happier to be in the care of her medical team, headed by Lord Evans, John Peel—later Sir John, who had spent the night in a nearby room—and midwife Sister Rowe.

It was Lord Evans who told the Duke that the waiting was over, that his wife had given birth to a son. As soon as Philip heard the news he ran out of his study, taking the stairs two at a time, and burst into the bedroom of the Belgian suite. He took his newborn gingerly from the nurse and held him in his arms. On his wife's previous instructions his first call was to the Queen Mother and Princess Margaret. He then bounded upstairs again to the nursery to tell Princess Anne she had a baby brother. 'It's a boy!' he shouted excitedly to the nursery staff.

The birth of a new baby is a cause for some celebration amongst the Palace staff. By tradition a bottle of fine vintage port is sent to each department of the Household 'to drink a toast with Her Majesty'. In some departments the port is raffled, and one lucky footman won a special bottle after the births of both Prince Andrew and Prince Edward. The port had been a gift to the Queen from the President of Portugal.

Andrew asserted himself from the moment of his birth, crying lustily when he was hungry until he got some attention. On the advice of her doctors the Queen was encouraged to breastfeed the baby for the first weeks before switching to the bottle. She was helped by Sister Rowe, who, acting as a maternity nurse, was on call to bring the baby from his canopied cot in the nursery to his mother's bedroom.

The Queen and Sister Rowe were great believers in the benefits of fresh air, and unless it was foggy or raining, Andrew would sleep outside in the Buckingham Palace garden for a couple of hours each day in a large Silver Cross pram. Sometimes the Queen would push the pram around the gardens herself when she took the corgis for their afternoon walk. She was determined to enjoy motherhood to what she considered its fullest extent, which was not very much by ordinary standards, but more than she had been able to give to either Charles or Anne. This did not run to changing nappies and nightly bathing of the baby, but it did mean she allotted him as much time as her role as monarch allowed.

In her typically orderly way, she pencilled into her leather-bound appointment book the times she would be with Andrew. And during that time, nothing short of a crisis would prevent her from being with her baby. It was a lesson she had learnt when, as a young monarch with two small children, the affairs of state had had to take precedence.

A few days before Andrew's birth, a decree was issued by Buckingham Palace declaring that henceforth the Queen's children would use the surname Mountbatten-Windsor, a combination of Philip's adopted name of Mountbatten and hers of Windsor. It was in clear defiance of the promise she had given in council in 1952, but the Queen was now eight years into her reign, and experienced and confident enough to do things her way. So when Andrew Albert Christian Edward was christened in the Music Room of Buckingham Palace on 8 April 1960, he became the first royal child to hold the new family name from the moment of his birth.

He was also the first royal child not to have any official christening photographs. Instead his father snapped away with his own Hasselblad as the godparents (or sponsors as they are known in royal circles) stood around the silver lily font. The late Duke of Gloucester, Princess Alexandra, Lord Elphinstone, the Earl of Euston and Mrs Harold Phillips were the honoured friends and relatives chosen.

Both Prince Philip and the Queen were of the opinion that Charles and Anne had suffered unnecessarily from over-zealous media attention during their formative years—especially Charles, who was painfully shy. They decided the best way of avoiding a repetition of the situation was to keep the baby, who was second in line to the throne, away from public places. Instead of going to the park, Nanny would restrict walks to the gardens of Buckingham Palace or Windsor Castle, a discreet distance from any public highway. That way the Palace could control the amount of coverage the baby received.

The first photographs to be released of Prince Andrew were those taken by Cecil Beaton, when the baby was already one month old. Beaton's diaries give a revealing and acerbic account of the event, which the late photographer did not enjoy one bit.

'We were set for action when my friend Sister Rowe arrived with the baby and the two young children,' he recalled. 'I was surprised and said "Oh well I suppose we'd better start photographing right away if it will be alright." Whereupon Princess Anne in a high fog horn voice said, "Well I don't know that it will be. I don't really think it will be."

'I just started to organize a photograph when Martin [now Lord Charteris, then the Queen's Private Secretary] nodded that the Queen was due to appear. To my surprise she was accompanied by Prince Philip, who had just got out of a bed of flu. He looked pale and drawn. When I asked after his health he dismissed one unpleasant topic for another—the photographs—Well where do you want us?'

Andrew was kept quiet with a bottle. 'I got very impatient and felt that the odds were ganging up against me,' Beaton noted. 'The Queen's face was real white—with not a trace of mascara on her lashes—her cheeks untouched by rouge and only a vague rubbing of lipstick on her mouth. Her dress of brilliant red—better than most of hers—was simple and without drapery.'

The family, stiff and unfriendly, settled into conventional poses. 'No good—I moved around—but the lights were arranged the other side of the screen for the Queen's pictures. I felt as if I were being chased in a nightmare when one's legs sink into the mire.

'The family stood to attention. I said something to make them smile so clicked. I clicked like mad at anything that seemed even passable. The baby, thank God, behaved itself and did not cry or spew. It sometimes opened its eyes. But even so I felt the odds tremendously against me. The weight of the Palace crushed me. The opposition of this hearty naval type must be contended with, and due deference to the Queen. She seemed affable enough but showed no signs of real interest in anything . . . Not one word of conversation—only a little well bred amusement at the way I gave my instructions in a stream of asides [to his assistant].

'P. Philip in that maddening Royal way kept suggesting I should use a ladder—take it from here—why not there—once I told him why not and quite firmly.'

Much to Beaton's relief, Philip started taking some photographs of his own 'with a camera that had a lens three times the size of mine'.

With Philip distracted, Beaton carried on trying to get a suitable picture. 'The baby was good. Sister Rowe was good—and I felt that the poor little Prince Charles was good . . . [He has] a perpetually hunched effect of the shoulders and a wrinkled forehead and pained look in his eyes as if awaiting a clout from behind, or for his father to tweak his ear or pull the tuft of hair at the crown of his head . . . I realized soon that he was nice and kind and sensitive—but he has to be hearty—to be in a perpetual rugger scrum because that's what Papa expects of him. Somehow from his bright blue eyes—and sweet smile, I got more sympathy from him than any of the others. Princess Anne continued her shrewishness—but almost unnoticed for I relegated her to the edges of the pictures and knew I could cut off her Minnie Mouse feet in the finished picture . . .

'As it was it was Prince Philip who called the whole thing off. As he loaded his camera anew he kept saying over his shoulder "surely we've had enough—if he's not got what he wants by now he's an even worse photographer than I think he is!" Ha! Hah! that sort of joke is admirable for the Mess or an official review—but oh the boredom of today.'

That extract clearly reveals the photographer's dislike of Prince Philip, his contempt for Princess Anne, and the Queen's painful shyness. Even holding her new baby and sur-rounded by her family she felt uncomfortable in the presence of strangers even though she had known Beaton since the 1940s when he first photographed her and Princess Margaret.

Being photographed is not something the Royal Family ever enjoys. Prince Philip behaved in exactly the same dismissive way to Beaton's nineties equivalent, Terry O'Neill, at the christening of Prince Andrew's youngest daughter, Princess Eugenie, in December 1990. When Terry, who works very quickly with just one assistant, was snapping the christening group at Sandringham, Prince Philip kept saying, 'Come on, come on, haven't we done enough.' Then he added what is known as his photographer's phrase: 'If he hasn't got what he wants by now, he's an even worse photographer than I thought!'

As Andrew, who became a keen photographer himself, later observed, 'My family always cringe when they hear the sound of a motor-drive, even if it's mine.'

It was always Philip who set the abrasive tone. Once he and the Queen had left the room, however, when Beaton was photographing baby Prince Andrew, he relaxed and with the help of Sister Rowe managed to prop baby Andrew up against an embroidered cushion for some more pictures. The good-natured baby allowed himself to be surrounded by the flowers Beaton had brought with him.

'The baby looked like a Spanish Christ as it waved its strong little arms in a baby's hallucination and opened . . . eyes to the skies. The pictures would be the best I knew.'

The Queen and her husband did not agree with the photographer's judgement and refused to allow the pictures of Andrew sitting alone to be published, although the others were duly doled out to the newspapers and magazines. The Queen's private secretary, Martin Charteris, decided no further photographs would be released until the Queen Mother's sixtieth birthday on 4 August, and then only because the Queen Mother herself suggested that it might be nice to have the baby in the pictures too.

The lack of any real news or meaningful pictures of the royal baby had its inevitable consequence. One of the duties of the Royal Family is to be seen. When Andrew wasn't, the rumour started that there might be something wrong with the baby and it wasn't long before a French newspaper ran a story claiming that the baby was malformed.

Prince Philip was furious, the Queen upset, and Buckingham Palace defeated. Then as now, the Palace are reluctant to give way to media pressure, but in the light of this kind of speculation it was clearly self-defeating to keep Andrew hidden any longer. So at sixteen months old he made his first public debut on the Buckingham Palace balcony for the Queen's Official Birthday Parade. When the crowd spotted the baby dressed in his best embroidered romper suit bobbing up and down in his mother's arms, a huge cheer went up.

This was what the public wanted to see and they were reassured to learn that, far from having anything wrong with him, Andrew was the picture of health. He was heavier than Charles at the same age and had the endearing habit of smiling at everyone he saw. When Sister Rowe gave her six-month progress report she called him 'a baby full of smiles. He's simply wonderful in every respect,' she cooed.

Both Charles and Anne agreed. They were delighted with

their baby brother. He seldom cried and quickly established himself as something of a character. His arrival offset the loneliness Anne had felt when Charles was sent to Cheam, and at ten she was old enough to enjoy playing mother and helping with the baby. His arrival brightened the atmosphere in the second-floor nursery suite where they all slept. In fact his arrival brightened the atmosphere throughout the entire Palace and gave Mabel, who had taken over from Helen Lightbody who had just left royal service, the fresh interest of a new charge to look after.

Mabel's routine had varied little in the twenty-seven years she worked at the Palace. Her father, a Liverpudlian policeman, had been killed in an air raid during the Second World War, leaving her and her Scottish mother looking for employment Mabel, who was not a trained nursery nurse, gained her experience from working with several Scottish families before coming South. When the family she worked for moved to South America at the end of the war, they wanted Mabel to go with them, but the idea did not appeal to the tall Scottish lass.

Instead she advertised her services in the situations wanted section of a nursing magazine. The advertisement was spotted by royal nanny Helen Lightbody, who, on the instructions of her employer, was looking for an assistant. So at the age of twenty-four, with no formal training, Mabel Anderson found herself working for Princess Elizabeth.

Until 1980 the nursery was on the second floor above the Privy Purse entrance. Its long windows looking out over the forecourt provided an excellent vantage point for watching the sentries and Changing the Guard. An old-fashioned lift serviced the suite of nursery rooms which proved useful when nanny's legs got too tired and Andrew got too heavy to be carried to the Queen's private rooms on the Principal floor below. The main sitting room or play room was large and high-ceilinged with pale green walls and an open fireplace. There was a fire and a brass fire-guard on which the children's clothes were dried. A large chintz-covered sofa dominated one part of the room, while scaled-down chairs and tables including a miniature high-backed chair occupied another. On both sides of the fire were glass-fronted cupboards which were filled with toys and books from Charles and Anne's childhood. The rocking-horse in the corner had originally belonged to the Queen, as had some of the toys, including the silver rattle Andrew liked throwing out of his pram.

Off the nursery to one side was a large bathroom with a large enamel bath fitted with old-fashioned chrome taps. To the other side were the bedrooms. When Princess Anne was born, a nursery kitchen was installed; until then all the meals had to be brought up from the kitchens and left on a hot-plate.

Mabel, who was thirty-four when Prince Andrew was born, ran the nursery in the traditional royal manner, unchallenged, unopposed, almost as a private fiefdom. She had the assistance of a nursery footman and an under-nanny, June Waller, who helped her in much the way she herself had helped Helen Lightbody with Charles and Anne. Royal nannies do not have to clean, cook or do the laundry. Their job is purely to see to the children's wellbeing, though Mabel did insist on Andrew's delicate baby clothes being washed by hand and dried in front of the fire as they always had been. She also insisted on the toys being tidily stacked away after use.

It was an unswerving routine, with Mabel as the pivot, and Philip and the Queen, for all her good intentions, rather remote figures.

Child psychologists argue that the love children receive in their infancy is important in the development of their ability to form adult relationships. A child that is not cuddled a great deal as a baby, they maintain, is unlikely to be able to show affection easily, whereas one who is given a lot of love will probably develop into a more tactile and emotionally expressive adult.

Given the long absences of their parents, it was from their nannies that the Queen's children learned how to relate to other people and, as kind and caring as they were, it was affection that could only be given according to strict routine. That continuity gave them stability and confidence, but it did little to prepare them for the harsher realities of the outside world.

The day started at 8.15 a.m. when the children would troop in, kiss their nanny and then help themselves to a breakfast of kedgeree, scrambled eggs, tomatoes and bacon laid out on the hot-plate, with either coffee or tea served in white china bearing the gold ER cypher. Even after she was married Annie never missed the nursery breakfast if she was staying at the Palace, and if Mark Phillips happened to be in town, he would come too.

Mabel's Roberts wireless would be turned to BBC Radio 2, the newspapers were read, and once the plates had been cleared, Nanny would settle down to do the *Daily Telegraph* crossword. If the Queen chanced to look in, they would sometimes compare clues and Nanny would usually discover that she had gone completely wrong.

At 9.30 sharp she would take the nursery lift to the Principal floor below where the Queen and Prince Philip have their private apartments. She would leave the baby there. But not for long. After half an hour she would return to take him back upstairs. The affairs of state could not be kept waiting, and when she was in residence at Buckingham Palace the Queen had appointments every twenty minutes throughout the morning.

When Charles and Anne were younger the Queen seldom had the time to see them during the day. She would sometimes pop into the ballroom where they had their weekly dancing lessons with Madame Vacani, but that was all. With Andrew it was slightly more relaxed, in his infancy at least, and on the occasional morning she would say, 'Leave him with me, Mabel', and Andrew would play on the floor of her study while she worked at her desk.

That was before he could walk. When he grew older he was too impish to be left to his own devices and was banished to the nursery floor. He continually tried to invade her sitting room, however, often with some success, slipping past the duty page. On one occasion the page running after him failed to notice a ball Andrew had been playing with, put his foot on top of it, and skidded to a halt just in front of the Queen. Hiding her amusement she told Andrew off and sent him to put his toys away.

If the time he spent with his mother was short, it was still long enough for him to observe and practise the royal wave, which he did from an early age, much to the amusement of the Palace staff who nicknamed him Andy Pandy after the popular children's television programme of the time.

Imitation and identification are important in a child's development and Andrew soon learned that waving brought the rewarding response of people waving back and smiling. As Charles observed, the world was 'a wonderful place because everyone was always smiling'.

It was soon to be the royal wave goodbye, however, for a month before Andrew's first birthday the Queen and the Duke of Edinburgh left for a seven-week tour of India, Pakistan and Nepal.

During the tour Prince Philip, President of the World Wildlife Fund, shot a tiger, for which he was duly criticized. Back home Andrew celebrated his first birthday with a few wobbly steps under the watchful eye of GanGan, the Queen Mother, who enjoyed her role. 'Half the fun of being a grandmother,' she said, 'is being able to spoil your grandchildren.'

Perhaps because he was older, perhaps because he had finally found a niche for himself, Philip found fatherhood the third time around more enjoyable. He liked doing things with Andrew, took no exception when his son put his sticky fingers down his dress shirt just before he went out to dinner, and was far more patient with him than he had been with Charles or even Anne.

His appearance in the nursery filled Mabel with apprehension, however, as it had Nanny Lightbody before her. It was usually a prelude to tears, as Andrew often became overexcited when playing with his father, who had a habit of rushing away quickly to an appointment, leaving Nanny to sort out the tears—though not before once collecting a black eye in the rough and tumble.

Conventional discipline did not work with Andrew, so Mabel simply dried his tears and calmed him down with a story. He adored 'Mamba' as he called her, but took a sly delight in playing her up.

The Queen communicated with her staff by memos and as soon as Andrew was old enough to realize the chaos he could cause by hiding them, he did precisely that. Even Mabel wasn't exempt from his mischief-making. On one occasion the Queen sent her page running up to the nursery demanding to know where Andrew was, which was when Mabel discovered her 'darling' had moved the memo requesting her to bring him downstairs to meet the luncheon guests. She was not pleased.

When he deserved it he was spanked or slapped, but, in his boisterous way, he soon forgot about it. The one thing that made his parents and nanny extremely angry, though, was when he was rude to others, since as he was the little Prince the 'others' were not in a position to answer back. Then the slaps really did hurt.

Once Andrew started to talk there was no stopping him, and when he was two and a half the Queen was already giving him simple lessons. She had a small blackboard, which included a clock-face and a counting frame, installed in her green dining room and after breakfast, when Mabel brought him down from the nursery, would assume the role of teacher, telling him the time and encouraging him to learn his ABC. It was in the days before videos and morning television, and children's entertainment was comparatively limited. Andrew responded well for the first few minutes, but after that his concentration would wander, usually to the corgis at his mother's feet, which he would sometimes try to kick.

'A pliant and intelligent youngster with a vital and happy disposition and full of quicksilver activity,' was how photographer Lisa Sheridan described him when she visited Buckingham Palace for a photograph session with the young prince. He was certainly full of quicksilver activity as he kicked a football or pedalled furiously up and down the long red-carpeted corridors of Buckingham Palace on his pedal bike. The royal children had the use of a huge amount of space and on rainy days the corridors became a playground where they would play cricket and hide-and-seek or football.

Andrew remembered: 'I've always played in the top passageway where we live—we used to play football along the passageway and every now and then a pane of glass got broken, but I don't think we ever broke a piece of Meissen or anything like that!'

Like his sister Anne, he was prone to toddler tantrums and would lie on the floor screaming with rage. He was not popular with the Buckingham Palace staff, who regarded him as an unholy nuisance and felt that 'Mamba' was unable to control him when he was in one of his mischievous moods. He tormented everyone from the nursery corgis to the scarlet-coated sentries at the door in their tall bearskins with bayonets fixed to their rifles. He too used to walk up and down in front of them, forcing them, as protocol demanded, to present arms.

From a very early age Andrew had what came to be seen as an arrogant disregard for the Palace staff. He would treat them like servants, and no effort by Mabel could modify his attitude. He used to thump the footman from behind with a clenched little fist, then run along the corridor shouting 'Get me! Get me!' Mabel, in exasperation, would give his chubby bottom a slap, but it made no difference. He took a little more notice of his mother, who would slap him around the back of the legs, reducing him to tears and the yells of hurt pride.

In a behavioral study of New York toddlers, ninety-five percent had 'stubborn attention-seeking behaviour'. Andrew was just naughtier than most, a genetic inheritance from his father. Other studies have shown that some children are born with a difficult temperament and Andrew, as the Palace staff remarked, was a chip off the old block. He even looked like Philip as a child. Princess Alice, Philip's eccentric deaf mother, who by the time Andrew was born was living at Buckingham Palace, thought Andrew was just like her only son. She noticed him hunching his shoulders about his ears when anything excited or amused him, just as Philip had.

Sculptor Franta Belsky disagreed. She was commissioned by the Queen Mother to fashion a bronze of the then three-year-old Andrew before he lost his baby looks, and studied him with an artist's eye over the eight sittings. He had the Queen Mother's brow, the Windsor (not Mountbatten) mouth and nose, but his father's colouring and shape of head, she concluded. Franta kept Andrew amused with picture books, toys and chocolate money during the sittings, but by far the most successful ploy was to give him some clay of his own to mould into shapes.

'I have never seen such sustained concentration and excitement of discovery in a child,' she said later.

This early concentration didn't always follow him into the schoolroom; only if something really interested him would Andrew give his full attention. As she had done with Anne, the Queen arranged for some children of a similar age to join Andrew for his lessons with Miss Peebles. There were two boys, Justin Beaumont and James Steel, and two girls, Katie Seymour and Victoria Butler, the daughter of Lord Dunboyne.

The arrival of Prince Edward on Tuesday 10 March 1964 was a surprise to Andrew, who had been told he was getting a playmate, not a delicate little baby who looked like a doll. It was something of a surprise to everyone else for other reasons. The Queen was not expecting the baby for another week and was startled when her contractions began five days earlier than anticipated.

At 8.20 p.m. the Queen gave birth to a 5lb 7oz baby boy in the Belgian suite of Buckingham Palace, where once again the large bathroom had been converted into a delivery room. The medical team, again headed by her surgeon gynaecologist John Peel, had thought the baby would be a girl because of its size. The Queen thought so too. Indeed, so convinced was she that she had only discussed girls' names with her husband, and it was not for several days after the birth that the infant prince's names were finalized.

On Saturday 2 May the six-week-old Prince was christened Edward Antony Richard Louis in the private chapel at Windsor Castle. Because of the confusion over the baby's sex and subsequent disagreements over his name, the Queen and Philip decided to choose the godparents first and use them as the child's middle names; Antony after Antony Armstrong-Jones, Richard after the Duke of Gloucester and Louis after Prince Louis of Hesse. The godmothers were Prince Philip's sister, Princess Sophie, and the Duchess of Kent, who had just given birth to a baby boy herself and was unable to come. Her mother-in-law, Princess Marina, stood proxy for her.

The birth of Edward did little to alter the unswerving routine of the nursery. While Mabel Anderson looked after the baby with the help of a maternity nurse, Andrew and his friends carried on with their lessons in the schoolroom. Every morning at eleven o'clock everything stopped and Miss Peebles, Mabel, the nurse and any other nursery staff would have a cup of tea together. The children were allowed orange juice or Ribena—Andrew once spilt his glass of the blackcurrant juice over the Queen Mother—and a biscuit. If they had been good, they were allowed 'just one' boiled sweet before starting work again. Andrew always rummaged for a black one (as does his daughter Eugenie thirty years later). The Queen didn't eat many sweets or approve of her children doing so, but if they were going on a long journey, Nanny would always carry a bag of boiled sweets and bars of Kit-Kat chocolate wafers.

It was as normal an existence as the Queen could hope for, but by any standards it was extremely protected. The only children Andrew mixed with apart from his family were his little school friends. Attempts were made for him to integrate with children from less well-to-do backgrounds, but they failed. He joined the local cub pack, but because of worries about security it was deemed wiser if the cubs came to him, so once a week a minibus carrying the other cubs arrived for a meeting at Buckingham Palace. Andrew was indifferent. He enjoyed their company, but because the meetings were held in his back garden, it hardly provided him with the excitement it did the other boys.

It was the same when he went to a private gymnasium for lessons in physical training. It was the same when he was taken secretly to the Brigade of Guards sports ground to learn to kick a football or given tennis lessons by former Wimbledon champion Dan Maskell. It was the same when he went skating at Wimbledon stadium where he was tutored by the professional, Ron Lee. When the little prince appeared, the other skaters were ordered off the rink. And later, when he wanted to learn cricket and was taken to Lord's cricket ground, he was taught by professional cricketer Len Muncer.

It was a young life filled with special privilege. His mother's desire for him to lead a normal existence was becoming less and less likely to be fulfilled. However, his lively personality obliterated all traces of shyness when dealing with strangers, as Cecil Beaton observed when he went back to Buckingham palace on 22 May 1964.

'As we were leaving a lively scene of perambulators, children and dogs presented itself,' he recorded in his diary. 'The new born, trundled like a Georges de La Tour infant, was being brought in from the rain, Andrew was driving his tricycle in the hall, to be greeted with loving amusement by his girl-eyed father. The Duke looked—in spite of the Cyclops effect and yellow complexion—at his most human. The children with their nonchalant nannies and nurses give the Palace a sense of reality that necessarily it lacks. I asked Andrew if he minded my taking photographs of him tomorrow. He smiled and said "No I don't mind." A welcome contrast to a reply I might have got from Princess Anne.'

The following day Beaton returned for the session itself. 'I waited in the picture gallery looking at some of the rather boring pictures, including a dull Vermeer. 'There he is,' said the Queen in a loud little girl's voice—and Andrew ran towards me—Cheerful, polite and willing to please. At the end of the gallery . . . was the Queen accompanied by her new born in the arms of a nurse. My heart lifted as I noticed the Queen was wearing rather a beautiful color—a Thai silk dress—almost as light in tone as I would have wished . . . The mouth when smiling is delightfully generous . . . that was the saving feature of the photograph sitting: that mouth and Prince Andrew.

'He is a boy with a quality that shines out with his niceness, and goodness and good spirits. He is trained to behave well, to be polite and amenable—but he has the right instinct. Whatever test one puts him through he comes out well. (May I take some more or would you be bored? I'd like some more).

'The infant showed bonhomie and an interest in the activity that was going on. His adult behavior pleased the Queen who was in a happy and contented and calm mood—and not only smiled at my instructions but with amusement at the activities and fast developing character of the new born. Andrew was determined to be in every picture and behaved like a professional, adding the quality of charm of the too young to know what it is all about.

'The Queen's grin dominated the picture and other felicitous elements were provided by Andrew's wistful little boy's eyes—and the infant's holding its own, by being alert and curious and already a character . . . The minimum of gurgles, or sticky mouth and each time I asked the Queen if she had had enough—was just willing to continue a little longer. It's twenty past and those poor dressmakers are waiting! Look his eyelashes are all tangled! She said, it's most unfortunate that all my sons have such long eyelashes while my daughter hasn't any at all.'

With Charles and Anne both away at boarding school, Andrew and Edward should have been able to enjoy the undivided attention of their parents, but the reins of the monarchy were always pulling. Even during the weekends at Windsor Castle she was busy with the affairs of State and surrounded by members of her Household. When the Queen and Prince Philip did join their children, it was for tea in the nursery.

They never arrived unannounced and the staff always knew

when either one of them was coming. Mabel would fuss around putting toys away and making sure everything was in place and the children were clean and tidy. Sometimes on Mabel's day off or when she went to her evening pottery classes, the Queen would come and babysit with the two children. It was still very formal, however, and she would bring her own page and footman, who would serve her supper in front of the large nursery television. If the children awoke she would soothe them back to sleep. She relished those rare private moments with her children, and in later years she admitted that she felt guilty about not spending more time with them.

But if there was no escaping the royal merry-go-round of engagements the Queen and Philip would never go out to dinner without saying goodnight to their children. If they were going out on an official function such as a film première, Miss P or Nanny would take them out into the corridor so they would wave goodbye. Before she got into the car wearing her tiara and long dress the Queen would always look up to the nursery floor and, seeing their anxious little faces pressed against the glass, give them a wave. Philip would blow a kiss. Always.

Charles also took an interest. When Philip was away and the Queen otherwise engaged, he would make a point of going into the nursery to play with his brothers and read them stories. One summer while they were cruising around the Western Isles of Scotland aboard HMY *Britannia*, he wrote a story for nine-year-old Andrew and five-year-old Edward and called it, 'The Old Man of Lochnagar'.

Like most parents the Queen's and Philip's theories about bringing up children had been tempered by experience. As Philip explained: 'It's no good saying, do this, do that, don't do this, don't do that,' he has said. 'It's very easy when children want to do something to say no immediately. I think it's quite important not to give an unequivocal answer at once. Much

Queen Mary, seen here with Princess Elizabeth in 1927. *Marcus Adams, Camera Press*

Below: Princess Elizabeth, photographed with her parents in July 1929 in the nursery of 145 Piccadilly, pouring tea for her cosmopolitan collection of dolls. The Duke of York often appeared for photographic sittings, as he hated to miss out on the fun. *Marcus Adams, Camera Press*

Princess Elizabeth at the age of five already has perfect manners. Here she is talking to Lady Airlie at Glamis Castle, Scotland, in the summer of 1931. *Press Association*

The Queen with her daughters, Princess Elizabeth, aged fourteen, and Princess Margaret, almost ten, in April 1940 at Windsor Castle, where they spent the war. Later that year Princess Elizabeth made her first BBC broadcast for *Children's Hour*. Margaret remained silent until the end when she said shyly, 'Goodnight, Children.' *Marcus Adams, Camera Press*

Prince Philip, aged seven, riding on the sands at Maimaia near Constanza with his cousin, King Michael of Rumania. *Press Association*

Princess Margaret peeks over the side of the carriage as she goes for a ride with her sister, Princess Elizabeth and Mrs. Knight (Alah), in March 1933. *Press Association*

Princess Anne with her arms round her mother in March 1960. Anne was not Beaton's favourite— he found her 'shrewishness' difficult— but despite this and the Queen's lack of conversation that day, he managed to get some excellent shots. *Cecil Beaton, Camera Press*

Princess Margaret and her sister playing with one of their many dogs in the grounds of the Royal Lodge, Windsor, their family home in 1936. Despite their age difference, the sisters were always dressed identically. Their appearance impressed Wallis Simpson, who was staying with 'Uncle David' at nearby Fort Belvedere. By the winter of that year Uncle David had abdicated in favour of their father. *Camera Press*

Above: Prince Andrew, always mischievous, loved playing hide-and-seek in the Palace nursery.
Camera Press / Studio Lisa

Right: A rare shot of three-year-old Prince Charles laughing in his pram. Baron captured the toddler prince's delight as he reached out to grab some flowers. Twenty years earlier his pram had been used by the Queen.
Baron, Camera Press

Eleven-year-old Prince Charles bends down to hold his newborn brother's hand in March 1960. During the photo session Beaton placed the flowers around Prince Andrew's crib claiming the baby, who was very 'good natured', looked like 'a Spanish Christ'. *Cecil Beaton, Camera Press*

Right: The new governess, Miss Lavinia Keppel, teaching Lady Sarah Armstrong-Jones and Edward in the Buckingham Palace school room. They were joined by James Ogilvy and various children from the Royal Household. *Camera Press*

Above: Prince Edward with pinwheel.
Camera Press

Right: Prince Andrew and Prince Edward in the garden at Buckingham Palace in the autumn of 1968: Andrew lost no time in burying his little brother in the leaves.
Camera Press / Studio Lisa

Diana, aged thirteen, with a Shetland pony,
Soufflé, at her mother's home on the isle of
Seil, south of Oban, in the summer of 1974.
After her parents' bitter divorce it was nice
for Diana and her brother to spend carefree
days with their mother and stepfather,
Peter Shand Kydd. *Press Association*

Right: A month before the death of
her father in a flying accident in
August 1942, Princess Alexandra is
photographed with one of her
favourite toys in the garden at
Coppins. *Baron, Camera Press*

Above: The handsome Prince George of Kent with Prince Edward, Princess Alexandra, and their pet chow at Coppins in the late thirties. *Baron, Camera Press*

Right: Lady Diana Spencer in 1964 at the age of three, at Park House, Sandringham. *Press Association*

Freddie and Ella photographed in their Kensington Palace nursery playing with Lego. *Private Collection*

Right: Lord Edward Downpatrick, who was born on 2 December 1988. Here the two-year-old is being thrown into the air by his father, the Earl of St. Andrews. This delightful picture was taken in the small back garden of their Cambridge home.
Tom Hustler

Left: Princess Michael of Kent with her adored son Freddie in the Kensington Palace attic nursery. *Camera Press*

Above: Lord Nicholas Windsor aged about four with a favourite teddy bear. This angelic child was later to come in contact with the law when he was caught smoking pot. *Tom Hustler*

At Badminton in 1972, David and Sarah watch the horse trials with their cousin Prince Edward (far left) and their parents. *Alpha*

Zara Phillips squeals with delight as she watches an equestrian event with her father, Captain Mark Phillips. *Alpha*

Peter and Zara at the Windsor Horse Trials in 1985. Both their parents believed in keeping them out of the limelight and they were usually only photographed at horse shows. *Alpha*

Right: Peter aged five and Zara aged eighteen months, photographed by Norman Parkinson. *Norman Parkinson, Camera Press*

Prince Harry gives his mother a kiss on the cheek at Highgrove in 1990. Both the boys are extremely affectionate. *Patrick Demarchelier, Camera Press*

Prince William with his pet rabbit. William has developed into a serious child and has become something of a loner since the troubles with his parents' marriage. *Patrick Demarchelier, Camera Press*

Prince William and his mother at Wimbledon in 1991. William is close to his mother and worries about her. Despite her efforts, the guilt of his parents' separation falls heavily on his shoulders. *Alpha*

Right: Prince Harry in 1989 thoughtfully sucking his finger. He is dressed in his best Turnbull and Asser blazer and shirt for an official engagement with his father and brother. *Alpha*

Left: Three-year-old Princess Beatrice and twenty-one-month-old Princess Eugenie enjoying themselves at Chessington Zoo in the autumn of 1991. *Private Collection*

Above: Sarah holds baby Beatrice close to her as she says goodbye to her sailor husband on the quayside in Scotland in April 1989. *Alpha*

Left: Quite a little lady. Princess Beatrice in the school uniform of Upton House in the summer of 1992. *Daily Express*

Right: At a party in 1993, Princess Beatrice puts a loving arm around her younger sister. Both girls love dressing up in matching hairbands and party frocks. These are made by Sarah's step-mother, Susan Ferguson. *Private Collection*

better to think it over. Then, if you eventually say no, I think they really accept it.'

Perhaps there weren't enough 'no's' in Andrew's young life. Andrew bullied everybody and would constantly swipe his younger brother. If he saw Edward going for a particular cake, Andrew would try and grab it first. He tried to provoke him, but Edward wasn't going to be provoked.

When the Queen wasn't around, Philip took charge of the children, but he became easily distracted and often let them wander off. One weekend when he was five, Andrew made his way to the bottom yard of the Royal Mews at Windsor while his father was out carriage-driving. The coachmen and grooms who worked there had little time for the prince, whom they had frequently seen taunting the dogs and aiming sly kicks at a helpless guardsman. Sensing their studied indifference and in order to attract attention, he started beating the ground with a large stick.

No one took any notice, so Andrew doubled his efforts and beat the ground even harder, taking a sideways swipe at the legs of the horses. When he refused to stop, a couple of the grooms swooped on him, picked him up and threw him into a dung heap and shovelled manure all over him.

Andrew was too shocked to cry. The impact of his humiliation soon hit him, however, and when at last he managed to extricate himself from the foul-smelling mess, he ran as fast as his legs could carry him up the hill to the Castle shouting, 'I'll tell my mummy! I'll tell my mummy on you!'

No one knows if he ever did. But there were certainly no repercussions.

Nor were there on another occasion when his taunting so annoyed a young footman that he took a swipe at Andrew that deposited him on the floor and left him with a glistening black eye. Fearing for his job, the footman confessed what had happened and offered his resignation. When the Queen came to hear of it she refused to accept it. She said her son had obviously deserved it and that the footman was on no account to be punished for Andrew's bad behavior.

Edward by contrast was the 'quiet one'. He was a 'sweet' child, whose delicate good looks and permanently flushed cheeks endeared him to the Palace staff (and still do, especially to the gay fraternity that constitutes a large portion of the Royal Household).

While Andrew was almost permanently bored as an adolescent at Buckingham Palace, Edward enjoyed the solitude and spent his time reading and listening to the radio. They all loved the radio and always listened to Radio 2 until Terry Wogan went off the air. Then Edward moved to Capital Radio, Anne to Radio 1 and Charles to Radio 4. Andrew preferred cassettes. Edward enjoyed the radio so much he had a special wooden case made so that he could take his Roberts everywhere with him. If it were forgotten or mislaid, footmen were sent scurrying to look for it.

As a child he loved books and as soon as he learnt to read he devoured everything, from the popular classics to detective thrillers. He also liked the French cartoon books *Asterix*, which he would read in French. 'He was extremely bright,' a member of the Household staff remembers. The Swedish pop group Abba were his favourite listening. His great enjoyment was riding and as soon as he was old enough to sit on a pony, his riding lessons became the high point of his day.

Unlike Andrew, who developed hay-fever around horses and no longer rides because, he explained, he fell off 'too many times when I was small', Edward became an accomplished horseman. His first pony was a Shetland pony called Valkyrie—the name which the Royal Family later applied to Princess Michael of Kent—which he shared with his older brother. But whereas Andrew liked grooming the pony and putting on its tack, Edward liked sitting on its back. It sounded a perfect solution, but as soon as Andrew realized his little brother was going to ride the pony away he would try and lead Valkyrie back to her stable to take her harness off.

Between the ages of four and eight Andrew had been educated in the security of the Buckingham Palace schoolroom by Miss Peebles, and it was assumed that Edward would follow in his educational footsteps. But just before he was due to start his formal education in September 1968, 'dear Miss P' was found dead in her room at Buckingham Palace. She had ruled the schoolroom for fifteen years. Now suddenly a replacement had to be found.

The Queen's Lady-in-Waiting, Lady Susan Hussey, sportingly offered her own governess, Miss Adèle Grigg, who ran a small class from her Chelsea home. Edward was taught by her for a couple of months until a new governess, Miss Lavinia Keppel, was engaged.

Miss Keppel was a relation of the famous Alice Keppel, for many years the mistress of Edward VII—intriguing proof that there are many different ways to serve the Royal Family. She had first taught at Lady Eden's school in Kensington and had a more modern outlook on education, but still followed Miss P's basic pattern of lessons. The day always began with prayers and a Bible story and included some kind of physical activity. The Queen, still pursuing the grail of integration, was anxious for Edward to mix with other children, and the schoolroom always had at least three other little pupils in it. Lady Sarah Armstrong-Jones, James Ogilvy and Princess Tanya of Hanover, granddaughter of Philip's sister, were the regulars and they were sometimes joined by the children of members of the Household. It proved a successful experiment for both Andrew and Edward.

Both Anne and Charles had dreaded their first day at boarding school. Anne had been physically sick and Charles so frightened that he shook. This was not the case with Andrew, who at the age of eight and a half was sent to Heatherdown, near Ascot, conveniently close to Windsor Castle, or with Edward, who followed him there two years later after a spell at Gibbs pre-preparatory school in Kensington.

In the holidays Mabel transported the familiar atmosphere of the nursery to whatever they were. At Balmoral the nursery quarters were in a small corner turret. Prince Edward had a tiny bedroom next to Mabel's, but the routine was the same. Lunch was always a picnic and they had supper in their dressing gowns after a bath. 'Sixteen was the golden age of going downstairs,' a member of the Household recalls, 'but they preferred to be in the nursery after a day outside far more than being downstairs with the guests.'

At half-term, Edward would often spend time at Wood Farm on the Sandringham estate with only his nanny and a nursery footman for company. Mrs Hazel cleaned and cooked simple foods such as corn on the cob or the fishcakes that Edward loved, and Edward went for long walks on the beach.

At Windsor, all Edward wanted to do was ride his pony, Flame, and he would be quite happy as long as he was left alone to do so. If he was thwarted in any way his bad temper manifested itself in silence. If he was very angry he would go bright red but never shouted or screamed, unlike Andrew.

Nearly a decade and a sizeable spiritual and emotional gap separated Andrew and Edward from Charles and Anne; although they were subjected to the same kind of upbringing and accorded the same kind of privileges, the atmosphere was more relaxed and they were better equipped to deal with English public-school life, where the regimented routine was not so very different from their own. By the time they both started school, the Swinging Sixties had come and gone, Anne had married Captain Mark Phillips, and unemployment and Northern Ireland were the kingdom's main preoccupations.

While unemployment was not a problem they had to deal

with, the deteriorating situation in Northern Ireland meant an inevitable increase in royal security and when, during the Christmas holidays of 1970, Special Branch learned of an IRA plot to kidnap either Andrew or his cousin George, Earl of St Andrews, who was also at Heatherdown, the guard was increased.

These royal protection officers (though armed bodyguards would be a more accurate description) do their best to blend with the background, though some inevitably become great friends of their 'clients'. Andrew Merrylees, who was appointed a bodyguard to Edward when he was nine years old, remained with him throughout his schooldays and only left in 1991. 'Edward looked upon him as being a substitute father, as his own was often away,' a former member of the Household recalls.

Although Philip was affectionate with them when he was around, he did not agree with indulging children. They were given pocket money but only used it to buy records and tapes. They didn't have many clothes and never bought their own. Edward wore Andrew's hand-me-downs.

When it came to their senior schooling, Eton was again considered, as it had been with Charles, but again Prince Philip could not be convinced. He remained a sternly devout disciple of Kurt Hahn's guiding principle: character first, intelligence second, knowledge third. Gordonstoun in faraway Morayshire, he insisted, would be far better for them.

For Andrew, who was not intellectual, perhaps it was. He was not timid like his elder brother and soon acquired a not so enviable reputation as a joke-teller.

'He never stopped cracking them,' one of his former classmates recalled. 'Goodness knows where he got them from. But whatever the source, it showed no signs of drying up.'

Another schoolmate said that at Gordonstoun Andrew became known as the 'Sniggerer', because of his tendency to

sidle up to someone and say, 'Have you heard the one about . . .'
'The trouble is, by the time he had finished the joke he was
laughing so much you couldn't understand the punch line.'

One girl who was in the same class as Andrew at the by
now co-educational school remembered him as 'a man with a
fat bottom who laughed at his own jokes'.

Perhaps Eton would have polished Andrew's rough corners
and given him a better scholastic education. He was less adapt-
able than Charles, and judging by the comments made by his
contemporaries, it is clear that his 'I am the Prince' attitude
stood out at the determinedly egalitarian school. One fellow-
pupil called him just another poor little rich kid who, 'didn't
know whether he wanted to be a prince or one of the lads'.
His inability to resolve that dilemma proved something of a
handicap, and he did not emulate his father and elder brother
by becoming Guardian, as the Gordonstoun's head boy is
called.

Edward did. The Queen's youngest child had 'loathed' the
idea of going to Gordonstoun, and in the beginning he felt
singled out and different, if only because of the police protec-
tors who had become a permanent appendage to all royal
personages. But once he had settled in he found that he liked
the outdoor activities like sailing and rock-climbing, and
would later speak of his time there with some enthusiasm. But
he never considered schooldays 'fun'.

'A school is a school,' he said. 'I don't agree with the
statement that school days are the happiest days of your life.'

Edward was and still is a solitary person, who prefers to do
things his own way. His three A-levels got him into Cambridge
(amidst some criticism from those who said that his title had
more to do with his being granted a place than had his mid-
dling grades), and the relative freedom he enjoyed there gave
him a taste of a world not normally accorded to royal princes,
and he liked that.

Neither Edward nor Andrew has expanded to his full potential as an adult, however. They were quite loving children, but neither of them generous. They both enjoyed play-acting, but not the real life their sheltered upbringing had ill prepared them for. They were also more immature than most of their contemporaries—what other children at the age of fifteen, for instance, would still be having their supper in their dressing gowns with Nanny in the nursery? And they had little say when it first came to the vital matter of choosing their careers. It had to be the military. As Andrew pointed out, what other real choice was there for a prince?

As it turned out, Andrew thoroughly enjoyed the Navy. Edward's military career, on the other hand, was disastrously short-lived.

He joined the Royal Marines. In the crisis of late adolescence he left before his training had been completed. His parents pleaded with him to reconsider and stay after completing a year. Edward, as he always has done when faced with something unpleasant, switched off before allowing his emotions to escape in the privacy of his room, where he wept. After more discussions with his parents at Sandringham and with his Commandant, Sir Michael Watkins, the pressure was so great he agreed—for his sister's sake—to a meeting, without his parents, at Buckingham Palace.

Anne, Mark Phillips, Fergie and Andrew all drove to London on Sunday 11 January 1987 to meet him. They spent the afternoon talking to him gently, explaining to him that it made sense to stay in the Marines for another eight months, then announce he had decided not to pursue any more training. Without the presence of the Queen and Philip the situation seemed less oppressive and eventually Edward agreed.

Anne, immensely relieved that her brother had saved himself so much anguish, returned that night to Gatcombe Park with her husband. The following morning, as she was driving back to Sandringham in her Range Rover, she heard on the radio news that Edward had quit. Such was her shock that she almost drove the car off the road into the ditch.

My God!' she said. 'He's going to regret that for the rest of his life!'

Diana

ixteen days before Christmas, 1968, Viscountess Althorp started proceedings in the High Court in London to end her fourteen-year marriage to the seventh Earl Spencer's son and heir, Johnny. She was thirty-two, her husband was forty-four. Diana, their youngest daughter, was only seven.

The divorce quickly degenerated into a painful contest that pitted husband against wife, turned Lady Althorp's mother, Ruth, Lady Fermoy, against her daughter, and eventually lost Lady Althorp the custody of her four children. It left their youngest daughter with a psychological injury from which she is still struggling to recover.

Diana can remember the arguments that led up to the separation. In her memory's ear she can still hear the sound of her mother crying and the resonance of her father's harsh words which had provoked those tears. There were occasions when his temper drove him to violence. Too young to intervene, too immature to cope, she took the only course open to her and locked her feelings away inside herself.

Many children learn to come to terms with such early traumas; to confront them, to move on, eventually to accept them as a sad but unalterable chapter of their lives. As Erin Pizzey, Britain's foremost counselor of abused women and their children, explained: 'We all have to come to terms with our childhoods in order to cope with adult life.' Diana never did. The emotional lesion was allowed to fester untreated, and would later manifest itself in the eating disorder, bulimia. Its sufferers, convinced of their own worthlessness and frightened of failure, binge-eat and then make themselves sick afterwards.

'Most bulimics have a history of early emotional starvation and it must be remembered that Diana's mother left her when she was very young,' psychotherapist Patricia Peters wrote in *The Sunday Times*. 'Self-esteem is shattered when a mother leaves her child. The concept is, "My mother couldn't have loved me or she wouldn't have left me", and the depression that follows is an expression of the anger which is turned against the self.'

In fact, Diana's mother did not want to leave her daughter. She battled in the courts for four months to keep custody of Diana and her other children, Sarah, Jane, and their little brother, Charles.

It was Frances Althorp herself who initiated the action to end her marriage. Under the Marital Causes Act of 1965 a divorce could only be sought on the grounds of adultery, desertion 'without cause' for a period of three years, a clause that included insanity, or 'on the grounds that her husband has since the celebration of the marriage been guilty of rape, sodomy or bestiality . . .'

None of those applied, but there was one more category—'cruelty'. The destructive confrontations of the kind that the infant Diana had witnessed 'from her hiding place behind the drawing room door' gave Frances the grounds on which to seek to end her marriage. As one who knew the couple put it, starkly: 'Johnny Althorp could be horrid.'

But Frances Althorp was herself an adulteress who had been named as the 'other woman' in an uncontested suit brought against her lover, Peter Shand Kydd, by his wife, Elizabeth.

And in the late sixties, before the law adapted to the radical change in social attitudes that took place during that decade, that still weighed heavily against a woman. Viscount Althorp cross-petitioned and won. The divorce was granted in April 1969 by Mr Justice Wrangham on the grounds of Lady Al-thorp's adultery. The judge awarded Althorp custody of the children and ordered Diana's mother and Shand Kydd to pay the £3,000 legal costs. It was a social and maternal humiliation for Frances. It would have a dire effect on their children.

For a long time after the final split Diana's brother, Charles, would cry himself to sleep at night, calling out for a mother who was no longer there. Sarah, Diana's eldest sister, would later develop anorexia nervosa, a disease closely related to bulimia. Erin Pizzey, who in 1971 founded Chiswick Women's Aid to help battered women and their children, said: 'Diana forcibly lost her mother when she was very young and this loss—of a good, warm, loving figure—would have had a major effect on her. If you don't resolve the damage you take it with you into adulthood where it can affect your relationships with men. She would have grown up with a great deal of fear and have probably over-compensated with her own children. She would be anxious to give back what she had lost.'

There was little their father could do to reduce this long-term damage. He was a man who always did his civic duty, but he believed that it was a woman's job to look after the children and he had not the faintest idea how to tend to the needs of his own distraught brood. He also happened to be suffering from what his son would later describe as 'shell shock'. Looking back at the ruin of his marriage he asked: 'How many of those fourteen years were happy? I thought all of them, until the moment we parted. I was wrong.'

Frances and Johnny were engaged in October, 1953. She had known him, it was reported at the time, 'since she was a schoolgirl'. That was no time at all. Frances was seventeen

years old when she became betrothed. The period of their
engagement did not allow the couple an opportunity to get to
know each other any better; three weeks after their engagement was announced Johnny left Britain on the Queen's six-
month tour of the Commonwealth. He took with him a portrait of his fiancée painted in red oxide by the society artist
Nicholas Egon, which he hung in his cabin aboard the royal
tour liner, *Gothic*.

Frances was still only eighteen when she married the thirty-
year-old heir to the Spencer earldom in a lavish ceremony at
Westminster Abbey the following May—the youngest bride
to be married there in over half a century. The service was
attended by 1,500 people including the Queen, the Duke of
Edinburgh, the Queen Mother, Princess Margaret (then in
the middle of the 'Townsend affair'), the late George VI's
sister, Mary, the Princess Royal, the duchesses of Kent and
Gloucester, and the young Duke of Kent and his sister, Princess Alexandra. The service was followed by a reception for
800—all nine members of the Royal Family attended—at St
James's Palace, which the Queen had lent for the occasion.
The bride wore 'a gown of camellia-coloured faille embroidered
on the tight-fitting bodice and full skirt with hand-cut dia-
monds, sequins, and rhinestones, and a tulle veil which formed
a short train and was held in place by a diamond tiara.' It was
a splash of high life to brighten the austere, glamour-starved
Britain of the fifties and was duly named 'the wedding of the
year'.

Sarah was born the following year, Jane two years later. The
Spencers made their home at Park House in Norfolk, a ten-
room Victorian mansion on the edge of the Sandringham
estate which Frances's father, who died in 1955, had leased
from his friend, George VI. Johnny, having left the Crown's
service, studied at the Royal Agricultural College, Cirences-
ter, and started to farm the 650 nearby acres bought in part

with £20,000 of his young wife's inheritance. To all outward appearances they were a contented, well-to-do country family, rooted to the land, filling in their time with good works and civic duties. The seeds of their future troubles had already been planted, however, though Johnny, so decent, and essentially so naïve, didn't realize it.

He had served in the war with the Royal Scots Greys and been mentioned in dispatches, and then as aide-de-camp to the governor of South Australia. He had seen all he wanted of the world and now wanted to enjoy the life of a country squire before he inherited his father's title and attendant responsibilities. The same was not true of his wife. She was young and had never had the opportunity of enjoying her youth. She was married to a man twelve years older than herself and she soon became bored with what she felt was the deadening routine of her life.

In 1960 she gave birth to her third child, a son named John, who died ten hours later. Johnny felt it his duty to produce an heir: they tried again and on 1 July 1961, Frances gave birth to another child. It was not, however, the son Johnny had so set his heart on that he had only considered boys' names. It was another girl.

A week later she was named Diana Frances and her father declared her a 'perfect physical specimen'. But the need to produce a son to inherit the earldom was still a paramount consideration for Johnny. He unfairly blamed Frances for the failure (it is the man who determines the sex of the child) and she was dispatched to Harley Street for tests.

'It was a dreadful time for my parents and probably the root of their divorce because I don't think they ever got over it,' Charles, the son who did eventually arrive, would later say.

Diana formed her own poignant opinion on the subject: 'I was supposed to be a boy.' To add to her sense of inferiority, to the feeling that she was in some way a 'nuisance' to her parents, Diana came to believe that, had that first boy survived, she would not have been born at all. That might well have been true, but her parents none the less did what they could to give her a happy childhood.

Park House was the ideal setting for young children: big, rambling and very homely. There were romps with her father in the nursery, 'a wonderful room for playing bears in', as he recalled. Diana was surrounded by animals—rabbits, hamsters and gerbils, gun dogs, a springer spaniel named Jill, and a cat called Marmalade. There were woods and fields to roam in, and quiet country lanes to ride her bicycle along. There were ponies and horses, though Diana did not care for them. She had taken up riding at the age of three but when she was eight had fallen off and broken her arm. She fell off again two years later when her pony caught its foot in a rabbit hole. 'We walked the rest of the way home and the doctor checked her out and said she was fine,' Mary Clarke, her nanny at the time, recalled. Fear, however, got the better of her and it was not until she was married that she could again be persuaded to mount a horse.

Diana much preferred the outdoor heated swimming pool where she developed her excellent diving technique, and the family's summer visits to the seaside at Brancaster to bathe and build sandcastles on the beach. There were also visits to the 'big house' for tea with Prince Andrew and, later, with Prince Edward who succeeded in covering himself with honey.

'The children were socializing all the time and Diana loved parties,' recalled Janet Thompson, her nanny for two and a half years.

She saw little of her parents, it is true, as she spent most of her time in the company of her nannies and her governess, Gertrude Allen, who had once taught her mother. But that was not unusual, given the Althorps' social background, and she was certainly never left to fend for herself.

'The Althorp children never tidied their rooms or made their beds,' Nanny Thompson said. There was no need to. The Althorps employed six servants, including a full-time cook. 'We're not at all grand,' Frances would say. That depends on your definition of grand; another nanny, Mary Clarke, felt that she was 'seeing a bit of old England that was dying fast'.

Diana's brother, Charles, who was born three years after her, agreed. 'It was a privileged upbringing out of a different age.' Not that they regarded it as such. 'As children we accepted our circumstances as normal,' he said. But for all the comfort and advantages something, as Charles said, was 'certainly' lacking—'a mother figure'.

In the summer of 1966 Frances met Edinburgh University-educated wall-paper heir Peter Shand Kydd at a dinner party in London. He was everything her husband was not—witty, raffish, extrovert and blessed with an ability to make women laugh. They soon became lovers. Within a few indecent months Shand Kydd had left his wife and three children and Frances had moved out of Park House with her children and into an apartment in Cadogan Place in Chelsea to be near him.

Sometimes Johnny would come to London to visit them at weekends and holidays. But it was an unsatisfactory state of affairs and, badly wounded by his wife's defection, he made up his mind that he, not their mother, would have care and control of all the children.

Johnny Althorp doted on his youngest daughter, but it was his son, who would one day inherit his title and his lands, who was the object of his familial ambition, a point made clear by the religious ceremonies held to mark their respective births. Diana was christened at St Mary Magdalene's, the local church in Sandringham. Her godparents were John Floyd, Alexander Gilmour, Mrs Timothy Colman, Mrs William Fox, and Mrs Michael Pratt, worthy friends of her parents. Charles was christened in Westminister Abbey with the Queen as one of his godparents.

Althorp had waited ten years for his son and he had no intention of losing him.

Frances returned to Park House for the Christmas of 1967, for the sake of the children. It was the last time the family would be together. Johnny, consumed with rage, was in dark and violent mood. His self-control deserted him and his rows with Frances were extreme. Frances cried and pleaded but her husband was adamant: the children, he insisted, would stay with him.

'He refused to let them return to London,' Frances said. She, in turn, refused to stay with her husband and returned to London, leaving the two youngest children behind (Sarah and Jane were at boarding school). 'It had become apparent that the marriage had broken down completely,' she said.

Althorp was not capable of looking after the children by himself, and the following February he advertised for a nanny to take 'full charge' of his children. So began an even more unsettled period in their young lives, with nannies coming and going with distressing regularity.

'As children we accepted this as quite normal,' Charles Althorp recalled. 'But now it seems so frightening. We were very lucky in that we had three or four nannies during those years who were exceptionally nice, devoted, loving people— but there were some strange ones as well. There was one, I believe, who attacked my father with a carving knife. She didn't catch him, then disappeared shouting, "To the river, to the river!" And that was the last we saw of her!'

Diana, Nanny Clarke said, was 'seriously affected' by the breakdown of her parents' marriage. Once so lively, the little girl the staff had nicknamed 'Duchess' became introverted and nervous and acquired the lifetime's habit of always looking down. Always headstrong, she became even more wilful and on occasion downright disobedient. She resented the parade of nannies who she believed where trying to usurp her mother's place.

'Manners were very important,' Nanny Clarke remembered. In the confusion generated by her mother's departure they were frequently forgotten. She locked one nanny in the bathroom. She threw another's clothes out on to the roof. Sometimes the nannies responded in kind. One used to bang Diana and Charles's heads together. There were, Diana recalled, 'too many nannies. The whole thing was very unstable.'

Her father found it hard to cope. He did not have the required skills to be a single parent. He never spoke to them about the problems that had engulfed the family, Diana would later complain. He would sometimes join them for tea in the nursery but it was, so Nanny Clarke recalled, 'very hard going. In those early days after the divorce he wasn't very relaxed with them.'

Their mother, who had married Shand Kydd within a month of her divorce, continued to see her children, but she was not in a position to assuage their distress. Whatever the brutal background to the divorce—Johnny was not as easy to live with as his later image of a warm-hearted, tweedy, country man, might have suggested—Frances would henceforth be labelled a 'bolter', condemned to carry the stigma of a woman who had run out on her family and her responsibilities.

Diana has never publicly criticized her mother for her actions. It is none the less notable to her friends that the adult Diana does not mention her name if she can avoid it. Her sense of rejection became embedded, and all the holidays she spent with her mother and all the presents Frances lavished on her did not alleviate it. She felt unwanted, a feeling compounded when she was sent away to boarding school shortly afterwards.

Diana had been to school before—in London, when she briefly lived there with her mother, then to Silfield, a pre-prep in King's Lynn; but that had been a day school, and every afternoon she had returned to Park House. The atmosphere at Park House may not have been a happy one—filled with her own anxieties, the silence of the country night played on her terrified imagination. She had no mother on hand to comfort her and she would lie awake, listening to her brother crying in his sleep, often too frightened to get out of bed to soothe him. But it was still her home, full of familiar objects and the animals she loved. There was Charles to help dress— and a teddy bear to dress in the clothes her little brother had outgrown. 'She's always had a very loving nature,' Charles Althorp said. 'She was very good with me as a baby. She used to look after me.'

Now she was being wrenched away from the only security she had left. Her parents had decided that it would be in their troubled daughter's best interests for her to have the routine and discipline of a traditional English boarding school, and Riddlesworth Hall, some forty miles away from Sandringham, was duly selected.

Johnny Althorp drove her there and left her clutching a stuffed green hippopotamus and Peanuts, her pet guinea pig. It was, he recalled 'a terrible day'. So it was for his eight-year-old daughter as well. It was the beginning of eight years of institutional care, first at Riddlesworth, later at West Heath, the smart girls' public school which her mother and her two older sisters had all attended.

As it turned out, Diana settled in quite well. The British boarding school can be an intimidating institution, but by its insistence on rules and order it can provide a sense of security—which was exactly what Diana needed. She made friends. She was good at sport—she was an excellent diver and did well at netball because, as she said, 'it was much easier for me to get the ball in the net because I was so tall'. She excelled at dancing. And if she could be a little boisterous on occasion—she was an enthusiastic participant in the dormitory romps and midnight feasts and custard-pie fights, and if she didn't like a particular sporting activity she would smear her knees with blue eye shadow and pretend it was bruising—that was more than compensated for by her attitude towards others.

Jean Lowe, her headmistress at Silfield, recalled her 'kindness to the smaller members of the community'. At West Heath she became involved in community work in nearby Sevenoaks, paying regular visits to old people to sit and talk to them for hours. It came naturally to her: she had an intuitive sympathy for others and she enjoyed the work. She also visited the Darenth Park mental hospital near Dartford for the Voluntary Service Unit. Some found the experience harrowing. Not Diana. Always most at ease with people younger or less fortunate than herself, she derived personal satisfaction from trying to elicit a word or a smile from the physically and mentally handicapped inmates. Muriel Stevens, who helped to organize those visits, said: 'That's where she learned to go down on her hands and knees to meet people because most of the interaction was crawling with the patients.'

On the academic front, however, Diana was always in difficulties. She was, Jean Lowe recalled diplomatically, 'extremely average'. Her brother, spotting her difficulties, unkindly nicknamed her Brian, after the particularly dim-witted snail in the children's television programme 'The Magic Round-about'. She learned enough at Riddlesworth to pass the Common Entrance examination that gave her her passage to West Heath, but the rigours of study all but defeated her. She took a modest five O-levels—and failed every one.

Her middle sister, Jane, who was a senior girl when Diana arrived, had passed her O-levels and had gone on to take A-levels. Her elder sister Sarah's education was disrupted when she was expelled for drinking. ('I was bored,' she explained). Her brother, however, had sailed through Eton and gone on to Oxford University. Diana, still very unsure of herself, found the comparisons odious. She felt herself to be 'hopeless, a dropout'. Confronted with those stark academic results, Diana had no choice but to do exactly that and drop out of school, an unqualified sixteen-year-old without obvious prospects but with the not inconsiderable advantage of her family's name and wealth to fall back on.

In 1975 her irascible grandfather had died and Johnny Althorp was now the 8th Earl Spencer, owner of one of the finest houses in Britain and, despite the taxing problem of over two million pounds' death duties, a very rich man. And Diana Spencer, as the daughter of an earl, was now a Lady.

She was sent to the *Institut Alpin Videmanetée*, an expensive finishing school in Switzerland. Young for her years and desperately homesick, she only stayed there briefly before flying home again. She got a job as a teacher with Madame Vacani, the dance school so favoured by the Royal Family, but did not have the dedication to make a career out of it. 'She had rather a full social life,' Miss Vacani recalled.

So she started working as a baby-sitter—'She was a positive Pied Piper with children,' her mother remarked. She also worked as a daily cleaner for her sister Sarah's flatmate, Lucinda Craig-Harvey, who said: 'She dusted, she cleaned, she did the washing-up, she cleaned out the bathroom, she scrubbed the loo. And she was very good, well, good enough. She lasted a year and Sarah, as her older sister, would have got rid of her and got someone else if she hadn't been.'

It was not long before a hint of competition had crept into Diana's relationship with her sister. Sarah, initially the most attractive of the Spencer girls, enjoyed her status as the oldest in the family. It was Sarah who made the first move to London,

Sarah who first attracted the attentions of Prince Charles. Now her younger sister, whose looks were rapidly improving with age, was moving in on what she regarded as her territory, and she did not like it. It was yet another problem to add to Diana's pile.

Of more substantial importance was her relationship with her father. Diana had continued to see as much of her mother as circumstance allowed, visiting her at her home in West Sussex and, later, on the thousand-acre sheep farm she bought with Shand Kydd on the Isle of Sill off Scotland's west coast, and staying with her at her home in Chelsea when she first moved to London. It was Johnny, however, who was the pivot of her life.

Relations between Johnny and Frances never recovered from the bitterness of their divorce and there was inevitable and sometimes blatant rivalry between the two for the affection of their children, which meant that they showered them with more presents than was good for them. It was a contest in which, in Diana's case at least, Johnny emerged victorious. Diana adored her father, whom she perceived as a warm and kindly man who had given her the devotion she always felt herself in such urgent need of.

'A child is not only emotionally bonded to its parents but also chemically bonded,' explained Erin Pizzey. The bitterness of the divorce—and the ferocity of her father's treatment of her mother—was submerged in her youthful subconscious. 'With a violent parent the relationship is emotionally intense, and life for the child is fraught with drama,' Erin continued. 'In later life the child recreates the drama of childhood.'

'There is a thing called the Spencer temper,' Charles Althorp admitted. 'We are renowned for having a very bad temper. But, at the same time, in adversity I hope that we are fairly solid and calm.'

When Diana was fifteen years old Johnny Spencer fell in

love and found someone to take the place of his departed wife. Her name was Raine. She was the daughter of Barbara Cartland, the romantic novelist whose rose-tinted view of human relations Diana was so addicted to. She also happened to be married to the Earl of Dartmouth, an old friend of Johnny's since their days at Eton together, and for the second time in less than a decade Spencer was involved in a messy divorce case.

Diana and her sisters never took to Raine. They resented her airs and graces, and the way she took charge of their father's life. The first time she came to lunch gave a foretaste of the squabbles to come. Nanny Mary Clarke said: 'I remember feeling tense and trying to distract Diana without success. Sarah was sent from the room and Diana followed her. We did not lunch again with Lady Dartmouth.'

When Raine eventually left her husband in 1976 after twenty-eight years of marriage and moved in with Johnny, Sarah coldly remarked: 'Since my grandfather died last June and we moved from Sandringham to Althorp Park, Lady Dartmouth has been an all too frequent visitor.'

The teenaged children would sing 'Raine, Raine, go away'. She didn't. Two months after her divorce, Raine married Earl Spencer in a five-minute ceremony at London's Caxton Hall register office and became the chatelaine of Althorp. The battle lines were drawn, and when Raine started selling off many of the family treasures (to help pay off her husband's death duties, as she would explain), and redecorating the house according to her own sometimes gaudy tastes, the hostility between the two camps became almost palpable. The row would rumble on for the rest of Johnny Spencer's life.

'No step-relationships are easy,' he once observed. 'It was hard on my children and hard on Raine, moving into a family as close as we are. You couldn't expect it to work wonders at the start.' Or at the finish, as it happened.

Charles, who inherited the house and the earldom on the death of his father in 1992, felt that an important part of his birthright had been sold off.

Diana's sense of loss was more subjective. The product of a broken home, she had focused her affections on her father. Now he had married a strong-willed woman she didn't like who quickly took charge of his life. Diana, her insecurity by then firmly established, felt herself pushed into the emotional background, a gawky adolescent who felt uncomfortable, too big, and out of place.

The accompaniment to this sense of rejection had been three notably unpleasant divorce cases. Looking at the wreckage of broken homes and bitter partings, Diana would declare: 'I'll never marry unless I really love, really love, someone. If you're not really sure you love someone, then you might get divorced. I never want to be divorced!'

The Gloucesters

*P*rince Henry, Duke of Gloucester, was born in the twentieth century. He more rightly belonged in the nineteenth. Son of a king, brother of two more, he was grumpy and difficult, drank too much and had an impulsive and volatile temper.

Yet his son, Prince William, is remembered as the most glamorous, the best looking and the most stylish member of the new generation of royal men. Self-confident enough to ride out his obstreperous father, William made his own mark in his own way until his untimely death in August 1972. Two years later his father, handicapped by two strokes and unable to speak, died, aged seventy-four, and the dukedom passed to William's younger brother, Richard. The last link with Victoria had been broken, a royal chapter ended.

Born on 31 March 1900, Prince Henry lived to be the last surviving child of the six born to Queen Mary. Sandwiched between his sister, Princess Mary, later Princess Royal and Countess of Harewood, who was three years his senior, and his brother, George, later the Duke of Kent, who was almost three years his junior, he was born fifth in line to a throne on which Queen Victoria still sat—just.

His mother, the future Queen Mary, then still the Duchess of York, hoped he would be her last child.

'I think I have done my duty and may now stop,' Mary wrote to her Aunt Augusta, the Grand Duchess of Mecklenburg-Strelitz, 'as having babies is highly distasteful to me, tho' once they are there they are very nice! The children are so pleased with the baby who they think flew in at my window and had to have his wings cut off!'

Some years later this same Grand Duchess was the recipient of a sharp slap on the cheek when she was introduced to 'a small boy in a stiff white petticoat with an angry look on his face'.

Little Henry had escaped a cruel and sadistic nanny who wreaked havoc with the emotions of his elder brothers, and may even have gone so far as to sexually abuse them. But if he had been spared that nursery nightmare, he was still frightened of his parents, and often, when asked to do something, was so stricken with anxiety that he was incapable of carrying out their request. He turned in on himself—and then out in explosions of rage of the kind which left Augusta nursing her cheek.

When his mother tried to make him speak to the old lady, he had refused. When she proffered her face for a kiss, his anger and frustration had been such that he slapped her instead.

Like so many of his royal relations, it was only in the nursery that Henry felt truly secure. It was a protected world and much more relaxed than it had been. The sadistic nanny had been replaced by the gentle and more loving Mrs Bill, whom Henry and his sister Mary called 'Lalla'. Henry's fear of his parents, however, would have a lasting effect on his development and throughout his life he found human relationships difficult and never managed to overcome his distaste for physical contact.

By today's standards Henry's childhood was miserable, the treatment meted out to him cruel. He was nervous and prone to illness. Like his elder brother, Prince Albert, later George VI, he was forced to wear splints to correct his knock knees.

As a toddler his pent-up frustrations manifested themselves in temper tantrums and crying, which were later replaced by uncontrollable fits of giggling. His parents, knowing no better, regarded his behavior as pure naughtiness and instructed his teachers and nannies to punish him accordingly, which they did.

To add to his troubles, he seldom mixed with children outside his own family and his loneliness was compounded when ill-health forced him to convalesce for long periods at York Gate House in Broadstairs, the seaside home of his father's physician, in the care of his nurse, Sister Edith Ward, who had nursed his father, King George V, through one of his illnesses.

His parents took a little more interest in his education than they did in his emotional development and he was entrusted to the capable hands of his brothers' tutor, Henry Peter Hansell, a kindly man who helped him learn how to control his tantrums. He decided the routine of a classroom with other boys would help him far more than being tutored at home.

The King was opposed. 'You must learn to behave like a boy and not like a little child,' he wrote to his son. Henry was ten years old at the time. He wrote back, 'Dear Papa, Thank you very much for the nice letter you so kindly sent me.' To Hansell the King wrote: 'Keep an eye on Harry, he looks very frail, but when well must be kept up to the mark and you must be strict with him . . .'

Eventually his father gave in and at the age of ten Henry became the first son of a British monarch to go to school. The problems that faced a royal prince attending school for the first time in 1910 were the same as they are today. He had to be protected from journalists and photographers. He had to be treated much the same as the other boys and make friends amongst those same boys—who knew very well that he was different.

Henry, who wrote dutifully to his parents every week from his new school, St Peter's Court in Broadstairs, was homesick, often ill and suffered the embarrassment of still having to wear painful splints and special boots to correct the arches of his feet. When George, his more academically gifted brother, joined him at school two years later, he was made to appear even more clumsy. The brothers did get along, however, and Henry was pleased to show his sibling the ropes, as George dutifully recorded in a letter to the King dated 12 May 1912.

'I rather think that I like school,' ten-year-old George wrote to his father in his neat, distinctive hand. 'I play cricket every day, but I can not play well. I am very pleased that Harry is with me here or otherwise I would not know what to do and where to go.'

They seldom saw their parents in person. Their father had acceded to the throne in the year Henry had first been sent to school. With the Crown came Buckingham Palace, Windsor Castle and Balmoral. The court migrated between them and during their holidays the children also travelled between them, always in the care of servants, before being deposited back at boarding school. Their only real communication with their mother and father was by the rather stilted over-polite little letters that they were obliged to send each week.

On 2 June 1912, for instance, Henry wrote to his father from St Peter's Court to wish him Happy Birthday.

'Dear Papa,' he wrote to the King-Emperor who had just returned from India. 'I wish you many Happy returns of the day. I hope you will have a very nice birthday and very nice presents . . . I would like to see the animals you brought back from India very much. Thank you very much for your letter. I have planted quite a lot of flowers.' And he ended as he always did, 'Best love from your devoted son, Harry.'

Despite his slow academic start, Henry managed to pass into Eton where he was put into the care of Mr Lubbock in the same house as Prince Leopold, later King of the Belgians. His headmaster at St Peter's Court was sorry to see him go and wrote, 'He has developed so much in seriousness and thoughtfulness without losing any of his love of fun.'

His experience at prep school stood him in good stead and his Eton days were amongst his happiest. Although still dogged by ill-health, he made friends and, for the first time in his life, assumed some sense of responsibility, even visiting his retarded younger brother, John, at Frogmore to ride and play with him. John, who was born in 1905, only lived to the age of thirteen and spent most of his short life away from his parents and family, as he was an epileptic and mentally retarded.

Henry did well enough at Eton to pass into the military college at Sandhurst where he found that army life appealed to him. As a youngster he had never mastered the art of small talk and consequently found the round of social engagements at Court dull and depressing. To most of his parents' friends he appeared graceless when compared to his dashing eldest brother, David (later the Duke of Windsor), and his glamorous younger brother, George. When faced with society Henry retreated into his shell.

His escape was outdoor pursuits. He was a good shot, and as he had always preferred animals to people, became an expert horseman. When he joined the 10th Royal Hussars, he was so at home on a horse he could sit upright while sound asleep, a habit which earned him the nickname 'Uncle Pineapple' as his bearskin nodded like the top of the fruit when he dozed off during rehearsals for the Queen's Birthday Parade.

Because of his social awkwardness, Henry was inclined to seek solace in drink and often drank too much. There were other unsuitable diversions. During a visit to Kenya in 1928 he became romantically involved with a married woman—Beryl Markham, who set her sights on the unworldly half-drunk prince—who reciprocated with enthusiasm. When he sobered up, he became smitten with the daredevil Beryl, who would become the first woman to cross the Atlantic east to west on a solo flight. The ensuing scandal, which resulted in her divorce a year later, was settled by a financial arrangement which continued until Beryl's death in 1986.

In 1935, and in greater keeping with his position, Henry, who had been created Duke of Gloucester just before he went on that fateful trip to Kenya, proposed to and was accepted by the Duke of Buccleuch's third daughter, Lady Alice Christabel Montagu-Douglas-Scott. Her brother William was his best friend, and the Buccleuch family provided George with some of the affection and warmth he had never found in his own home. It should have been a glorious wedding, befitting the son of a King-Emperor, but Alice's father died shortly before the ceremony and instead of Westminster Abbey they were married in the chapel at Buckingham Palace.

Happiness, which had been so elusive in Henry's life, still evaded him, however, and it wasn't until 1941, six years after their marriage, that Alice was able to maintain a pregnancy. The news that the Duchess, who had suffered an earlier miscarriage, was pregnant so delighted Queen Mary that she admitted to nearly falling off her dressing-table stool with excitement.

Rigid decorum quickly reasserted itself, of course, and the Queen was soon writing to her daughter-in-law Alice, daughter of one of the richest and grandest noblemen in Europe, saying, 'Fortnum and Mason are so expensive I think you had better go elsewhere for the cradle.'

On 18 December 1941, Alice gave birth to their 'much longed-for' child at Lady Carnarvon's Nursing Home, conveniently near Mr Cedric Lane Roberts, 'the eminent gynaecologist, who had to perform the necessary Caesarean operation'.

'Oh the joy I felt when I heard you and Alice had got a boy!' Queen Mary wrote to her son the next day. 'And that your great wish has been fulfilled after all these years.' The baby was delivered at 5.35 p.m., and Henry was with his wife when she came round from the operation at 6.05. The baby had a shock of brown hair and very bright blue eyes, and according to his mother looked 'most absurdly like Harry— Though how it was possible in anything so small I cannot think.'

Henry was given leave from the army to be with his wife, but for much of the first years of baby William's life he was away on military duties. 'I am so envious of you having William all to yourself,' he wrote.

Although it was wartime, William's early childhood lacked little. His mother looked after him with the help of Nanny Lightbody, who later cared for Prince Charles, and the country life at Barnwell Manor, the Duke and Duchess's family home, provided a safe and comfortable home. There were dogs, horses and farm animals to play with and, in the garden, a sand pit and a swimming pool. He visited Queen Mary at Badminton, and his cousin Michael, who was six months younger, came to Barnwell with his mother, the Duchess of Kent.

William, surrounded by caring, loving people—when 'Nana' Lightbody went on holiday, his father's old nanny, Mrs Bill, would come and look after him—grew to be a confident, happy child. He was thoroughly spoilt by the elderly estate workers and never short of playmates.

On 26 August 1944, Alice gave birth to a second son.

'What joy! another boy,' Queen Mary wrote to her son. 'I hope this time you will call him Richard, which sounds so well with Gloucester.'

His father, who had never been able to pronounce his 'R's, was not keen. He had no choice but to comply, however, just as his brother Bertie had had to give in over the naming of Princess Margaret, and the baby was duly christened Richard Alexander Walter George.

William had been excited at the prospect of another playmate. It proved to be a disappointment. When he went to the nursing home with Nanny Lightbody he turned to her and said, in an accusing voice filled with disappointment, 'You told me it was a little boy for me to play with and it's only a baby.'

William didn't have much time to be upset, as just before Christmas the whole family, including Nana Lightbody, set off by boat for Australia, where the Duke was to take up the position of Governor-General.

When he saw the Royal Mail Steamer *Rimutaka* that was to transport them to the other side of the world looming through the fog of the Liverpool docks, William asked 'Is that Granny Buccleuch's house?' (referring to Drumlanrig Castle, the family seat of the Buccleuch family). He went on board hand in hand with the captain, with Alice and Nana Lightbody following behind with Richard in a basket.

'I am so fond of Alice,' Queen Mary wrote to her brother in Canada as the family sailed off. 'She is a treasure and they are very happy unlike many married people in these peculiar times. I hope they will be a success. It may give Harry a chance of showing what he is made of.'

Six frigates, two destroyers and a battleship protected the royal party as they headed for Australia. Princess Alice recalled how William crept into her bed on the second night, during a particularly fierce gale, while Nanny Lightbody announced that if the ship went down she would go down with it and never leave baby Richard.

The following morning Alice told her weary son he was three years old and it was his birthday. A tired little voice replied, 'I don't want a birthday.' He was feeling so seasick the thought of a birthday cake was most unappealing, but after the first few days he thoroughly enjoyed shipboard life, especially the lifeboat drill, when he could wear his life jacket with the electric bulb he could switch on and off.

The journey was exciting for three-year-old William. There were more storms, the heat of the tropics and, just before they left the Atlantic, an encounter with a German U-boat, which was sunk by one of the escort vessels.

Life was considerably more peaceful in Australia where the family spent the next two years. The ravages and deprivations that afflicted wartime Britain had skipped the Antipodes. William and Richard ate bananas for the first time, tasted pineapples and mangos, and spent holidays on the beaches of New South Wales. They also spent time with their father—a particular treat in a family where children were rarely seen or heard.

Henry was proud of his little boys and, anxious to compensate for the severity of his own childhood, tended to overindulge them. They had everything they wanted. When they returned to England they were allowed to bring their little Australian terriers, Piper and Jean, and were given a pony called Minnie Mouse and bikes to ride. He remained, however, an essentially gruff and retiring gentleman farmer at heart, but one forced to assume unexpected and greater duties when his eldest brother abdicated and he found himself closer to the throne.

'It was a terrible responsibility for a man who had never envisaged anything other than a military career,' Prince William later told journalist Audrey Whiting. 'He did his best, which is all any man can do in life.'

The best thing he could do for his children, the Duke decided, was to give them a decent education. A governess, Miss Rosamund Ramirez, was duly hired. Miss Ramirez had taught the late King Faisal in Iraq, and she taught both the Gloucester boys until, at the age of eight, William went to Wellesley House prep school, where Richard followed him three years later.

Recalling her first meeting with William at Marlborough House, Miss Ramirez said: 'I was struck by the beauty of his face and skin. The blue coat he wore accentuated the colour of his eyes which were, in fact, grey rather than blue.

'He was the most rewarding pupil, never at a loss for something to do or talk about—a characteristic later shared by Richard, who at this time was still too young to be a satisfactory playmate for a brother nearly three years older.'

Life for William was always an adventure. He was active from the moment he woke in the morning until he could finally be persuaded to go to bed at night. But he had a surprisingly well-developed sense of duty which in later life manifested itself when he fell in love with divorcee, Zsuzui Starkloff, whom he met in Japan. William was torn between his duty and his personal feelings, but his duty won and he told Mrs Starkloff he could never marry her.

'He's too much of a man to be happy in the prince's role and he's too much of a prince to be happy in the ordinary man's role,' Zsuzui observed.

'My younger brother and I experienced greater freedom in childhood than perhaps any other member of the Royal Family of our generation,' William later recounted. 'It says a great deal about my parents when I tell you I think the only request my father ever asked of me was that I should follow him to Eton. This I did, but if I had not been happy there he would have certainly let me change schools.'

William never managed quite to find his niche, however. After Eton and Cambridge he spent a total of five years abroad in the Diplomatic Service, was a first-class pilot, an excellent shot and an all-round skilled sportsman. He was an adventurer with a conscience, a playboy with a heart, and reconciling those two sides of his character sometimes proved difficult.

'I often think I rejected my role because of the awful problems my father faced,' he said. 'He couldn't have been very happy until he met my mother, who did so much for him. She's an incredible person. I often feel I have let her down.

But there has never been a word of criticism or reproach. It would have meant a great deal to her if I had married and had children.'

That commitment to the future was left to his younger brother Richard, whose early life followed the same pattern as William's. He was educated at Wellesley House and Eton and then followed him to Magdalene College Cambridge, where he read architecture. From there on their lives took a decidedly different turn.

In his second year at Cambridge in 1965, Richard met his wife-to-be, Birgitte van Deurs, a nineteen-year-old Danish student who was studying English at the Bell School of Languages. The daughter of a Danish lawyer from Odense, Birgitte returned to Copenhagen the following year to enrol in a three-year diploma course, before finding a job as a secretary in the Danish Embassy in London so she could be near Richard, who at that point had no expectation of inheriting the royal dukedom.

When the couple were married at Barnwell Church on 8 July 1972, the old Duke was in a sad and sorry state. The last surviving child of King George V, he was virtually paralysed by two strokes and confined to a wheelchair. 'The great thing was to give him the comfort of knowing someone was there,' his wife, Princess Alice, recalled.

Unable to communicate, but able to understand, he had wept as he watched his brother David's funeral on television a month before. He was unable to attend the wedding service of his youngest son, where Prince William was best man, but shared an awareness of the happiness of the occasion at the reception afterwards.

He also understood, all too well and all too painfully, when his elder son Prince William was killed in a flying accident six weeks later.

On the morning of 28 August 1972, William, who had a competition flying licence, was killed competing in the Goodyear International Trophy in Staffordshire. His father lingered on in a void for another two years until the evening of 9 June 1974, when the slender thread of his life finally gave way. It was the end of an era and he was buried at Frogmore near his brother, the Duke of Windsor, and his son, Prince William.

The last surviving child from the York House nursery at Sandringham was finally laid to rest.

The tragic death of his brother and father gave Richard the dukedom and propelled him and his wife into a life they neither expected nor wanted. Richard was forced to abandon his architectural practice in Camden Town and take up the management of the family's 2,500-acre estate in Northamptonshire. His duchess, a shy and self-effacing woman, found herself with a diary of royal appointments.

On 24 October 1974, four months after the old Duke's death, Birgitte gave birth to a son in the Lindo Wing of St Mary's Hospital, Paddington. He was christened Alexander Patrick Gregers Richard Windsor and would be known as the Earl of Ulster.

William once said that being royal inhibits you, and you can never be your real self. 'I simply knew that whether I liked it or not, I was automatically separated by my heritage from the rest of the world.'

But he also thought that the next generation of the 'family' would be better equipped to deal with people and be 'far less cautious, far less inhibited and much better adults'.

This is exactly what the Duke and Duchess want for their children. Their daughters, Lady Davina Windsor, born on 19 November 1977, and Lady Rose Windsor, born on 1 March 1980, and both educated at St George's boarding school in Ascot, will never have to carry out official royal engagements.

Their brother Alexander, who followed in the family tradition and was educated at Eton, will one day inherit Barnwell Manor and the Dukedom of Gloucester.

But he will not carry the prefix His Royal Highness. And his sisters will have no more of a title than Lady—royal by descent but not by name.

The Kents

n 1935 the Duke of Kent and his elegant wife, Princess Marina, were the focus of much the same sort of adulation and interest that the Prince and Princess of Wales attract today.

It was the year of George V's Silver Jubilee, and the King's subjects regarded both him and his family with a respect boarding on reverence. The Kents were the glamorous, golden couple in this royal pantheon, and the news that the Greek-born Marina was expecting her first child drew large crowds to the street outside their rented home at 3 Belgrave Square.

George, Duke of Kent, in the company of his wife's father, Prince Nicholas of Greece, and her sister, Elizabeth, spent the day of 8 October pacing the drawing room, smoking endless cigarettes and drinking cups of coffee, which were two of his safer habits. Upstairs Marina was beginning her labour in a canopied bed on the second floor.

With masculine self-confidence George had insisted the baby was going to be a boy, and had had the nursery decorated in blue and white. He even demanded that blue ribbons be woven around the white lace cradle.

Shortly after 2 a.m. on 9 October, eleven months after their wedding, George's intuition proved to be right. Just before the baby was delivered he had run upstairs to her bedside. He stayed at her side throughout, holding her hand, the first royal father to be there at the birth of his child since Prince Albert, who was with Queen Victoria at the birth of all nine of their children. Also in attendance was the Home Secretary, Sir John Simon, whose presence was obligatory under the existing law, and Marina's mother, Princess Nicholas of Greece.

The baby, later christened Edward George Nicholas Paul Patrick, was seventh in the line of succession to the throne, and during the traditional Christmas get-together at Sandringham in Norfolk that year the fast failing King was introduced to his third grandchild.

'Saw my Kent grandson in his bath,' he wrote in his diary. When they left again for London George V wrote to the Duchess of Gloucester from Sandringham to say how he regretted the departure of George and Marina and 'their sweet baby'. He would not see him again. The King died shortly before midnight on Monday 20 January 1936. At his bedside were his Queen, the Prince of Wales, the Duke of York, the Princess Royal and the Duke and Duchess of Kent, who had hurried back from London to be there.

George V had been very fond of Marina and had greatly approved when his youngest surviving son had married the woman he called 'the most beautiful Princess in Europe—and the poorest!'

But if Marina was poor, George was not. The deaths of his father and his aunt, Princess Victoria, a month earlier had left him a very rich young man. Victoria left him her country home, the Coppins, near Iver in Buckinghamshire, while from the King he inherited a fortune large enough to pursue the elegant and often louche lifestyle he so enjoyed.

He and Marina transformed Coppins into a family home filled with the sound of laughter and witty conversation. Such artistic luminaries as playwright Noel Coward, conductor Malcolm Sargent and author Somerset Maugham mixed easily with Marina's sophisticated European relations, and they all expressed due admiration for baby Eddie.

Marina, with her European background, was a more tactile mother than many of her contemporaries, but in line with the custom of the day would leave her children in the care of nannies for much of the time. Few well-born mothers saw their children for more than the customary half-hour in the evening when they were washed and scrubbed and on their best behaviour. Babies were almost entirely looked after by a nurse and such duties as changing nappies, pushing the pram or getting up in the night were dealt with entirely by her. In large households like the Kents' there would also be an assistant nanny and a nursery-maid to do the cleaning and washing and lay the table for lunch. The delicate ironing was usually done by the under-nanny, who might get up at six in the morning to complete the task of pressing the many petticoats and layers of cotton and lace.

Eddie may have seen less of his mother than modern child psychologists would recommend, but he was certainly well cared for by Nanny Ethel Smith, overseen by Marina's old nanny, Kate Fox. Foxy, as Miss Fox was inevitably called, had a considerable influence on Marina's ideas on bringing up children. An English Norland-trained nanny, she had been hired by Marina's Russian-born mother, Princess Nicholas of Greece, to look after Marina and her two sisters. She had travelled all over Europe with her charges, always insisting that only English be spoken in the nursery and always feeding them plain English food: soft-boiled eggs and bread-and-butter fingers dipped in the yolk, rice pudding and shepherd's pie were the order of the day—Foxy considered Greek food unsuitable for children and firmly declined any help from the 'foreign' kitchen staff.

By the time Eddie was born Foxy was officially retired, but she remained attached to the Kent household until her death in Iver Hospital in November 1949, a pervasive influence right to the end. Marina never forgot Foxy's early training, and even as adults her children risked her wrath if they breached the rigid code of conduct Foxy had taught her. It was her second child, her daughter, Alexandra, who was singled out for particular attention in this hard training-course in royal behaviour.

Alexandra was born on Christmas Day 1936 and weighed 6½ lbs. 'The nicest thing to have happened this year,' Queen Mary observed. It was. In January her husband had died and in December her eldest son, Edward VIII had abdicated, leaving his shy, stammering younger brother to assume the burden of kingship. The thought of putting the more dazzling youngest brother on the throne had been quickly passed over, for what George of Kent made up in glamour he more than lost in decorum.

Bisexual in his youth, he was alleged to have had what were then illegal sexual relations with an Argentinian diplomat, an Italian aristocrat and Noël Coward, who made a conversational habit of bragging about his association with the prince. In his wilder moments he had been known to wear women's clothing in nightclubs. Of equal concern was his taste, which bordered on addiction, for cocaine and morphine, which he had been introduced to in the twenties by American heiress Kiki Whitney-Preston.

'It really is a terrible and terrifying thing to happen to anyone, and far worse to one's brother,' his oldest brother, David, wrote to their father, George V. It was the Prince of Wales who helped put George through 'the cure' in 1929, the results of which went some way towards improving relations between the King and his eldest son, if only for the time being. 'Looking after him all those months must have been a great strain on you,' the King wrote to his heir.

Marriage to Marina was a further help in bringing his behaviour under a semblance of control, but the flaws remained. When everything was taken into account, his brother Bertie, however reluctant he may have been, was deemed a safer choice for the difficult job of restoring the prestige of the monarchy.

But though the Crown had passed them by, George and Marina still excited considerable attention from a public that knew nothing of his weaknesses. The birth of another royal baby symbolized hope for the British people, who had been rocked by the Abdication crisis, and for months afterwards the newspapers reported even the smallest detail, such as the not very remarkable fact that their daughter was gaining weight.

On 9 February 1937, in the old chapel at Buckingham Palace, the baby, sixth in line to the throne, was christened Alexandra Helen Elizabeth Olga Christabel. The godparents were her grandmother, Princess Nicholas of Greece; her aunt, Princess Olga of Yugoslavia; her mother's brother-in-law, the Count of Torring Jettenbach—known as Uncle Toto; her great-aunt, Queen Maud of Norway, a daughter of Edward VII; Queen Mary's brother Alexander, Earl of Athlone; and her aunt and uncle, King George VI and Queen Elizabeth.

When Alexandra was just over a month old, her parents took a six-week holiday leaving her and her brother in the care of Nanny Ethel Smith and Foxy. This was not considered in the least unusual, and no objections were raised. It was still an age when children were required to fit in with their parents rather than the other way round, an age of being seen, rarely heard, and always very polite.

To that end Marina impressed on Alexandra the importance of royal discretion, the need to walk slowly with a straight back, and to keep still when she was sitting without crossing her legs. They were lessons that would be strongly reinforced by Queen Mary. As for many children, the outbreak of war on 3 September 1939 tore Alexandra and Eddie's secure world apart. They were staying at Sandringham when they were woken by an air raid signal and hurried to the basement. Queen Mary noted in her diary that 'the Children behaved beautifully. At 3.30 we heard "All Clear" so I returned to bed but not to sleep!' Later that morning the Queen and her grandchildren plus a staff of sixty-three servants and their dependants left Sandringham for Badminton House in Gloucestershire, the home of Queen Mary's niece, the Duchess of Beaufort.

Over the next two years the children were under the powerful influence of their grandmother, whose innate sense of what was proper and what was not governed the Royal Family's public behaviour for over half a century. More indulgent with her grandchildren than she had ever been with her children, she told them bedtime stories of brave deeds and adventures of the Empire over which she had ruled as Queen Consort. They were enrolled in her 'ivy squad' in her endless battle against the plant she detested. Days were spent scouring the 50,000-acre estate searching for ivy to chop down.

There was always time for lessons in discipline, however. As well as insisting that Alexandra followed her mother's instruction to walk with a straight back, Queen Mary also taught her how to curtsey properly, while the pensive and serious Eddie was drilled in the gallant skill of bowing and hand-kissing.

Alexandra, sometimes moody and frequently disobedient, was frightened of the austere woman in black, old-fashioned dresses who called her an 'impossible child'. Years later, when she was asked how she could stay still so long without tiring, Alexandra replied: 'You must remember, I was trained to do so by my grandmother, Queen Mary.'

The presence of their parents might have provided a leavening, but because Coppins was in the direct flight-path of the German bombers, the children were rarely allowed home.

And because their father was busy with his duties as an Air Commodore in charge of the welfare of the Royal Air Force units, and their mother with her work as a nurse, Eddie and Alexandra were left to deal with their grandmother as best they could.

Alexandra did not fully understand the forced separations from her mother. When Michael was born at Coppins at 7.35 on the evening of 4 July 1942, and she found that her position as the baby of the family was about to be usurped, she became even more difficult and moody and would kick and scream if she did not get her own way. It certainly did not escape her young notice that her father was besotted with the new arrival.

George of Kent was not the sort of man to spend hours cooing over a baby. Clutching a cocktail, he might stroll into the nursery to say goodnight to his children before wandering out again to resume his busy social life. He was utterly enchanted by his youngest child, however.

Baroness Agnes de Stoeckl, one of Marina's oldest friends, who lived in a cottage on Coppins' estate at the time, recorded the Duke's infatuation with the tiny infant in her diary. 'Every evening, instead of sitting up late as usual, he leaves the table shortly after ten o'clock and carries his youngest son to the nursery and lays him in his cot and stands watching and watching,' she wrote. 'Nanny told me that each night she discreetly leaves the room, but she can hear the Duke talking softly to him.'

Because their son was born on 4 July, the Duke and Duchess of Kent decided to ask the wartime President of the United States, Franklin D. Roosevelt, to be one of the godparents, and two days after the birth George extended him a formal invitation: 'My wife and I would be so delighted if you would be godfather to our son. We would be especially pleased, as he was born on Independence Day.'

Roosevelt responded by cable, which read: 'I am much

thrilled and very proud to be Godfather to the youngster and I send him my affectionate greetings. Tell the Duchess that I count on seeing him as soon as the going is good.'

It was an unlikely friendship: an American President who harboured a deep distaste for British imperialism and did much to hasten the dismantling of the Empire, and the son and brother of a King-Emperor. On a personal level, however, they got along well. They met when George and Marina were on their honeymoon in the West Indies and were invited to lunch by the Roosevelts, who happened to be cruising off Nassau. George, the first member of the Royal Family to fly the Atlantic, then stayed with President and Mrs Roosevelt in the White House.

When war broke out the President frequently sent boxes of oranges and bananas (both unobtainable in Britain throughout the war) to Badminton for the Kents' children. Sending himself over for the christening at Windsor Castle proved impossible, however, and George himself stood proxy for America's war leader.

The service, held in the private chapel, was voted by 75-year-old Queen Mary a most 'successful day'. The occasion was combined with Queen Elizabeth's forty-second birthday celebrations, and her grandmother recalled in her diaries that she saw 'lots of old friends, servants etc.' as well as many of her royal relations who had been driven from their own countries.

King George of Greece, one of the godparents, was not so happy and complained he did not seem to know anybody. This was probably true, as many of the guests were from Coppins and Household staff from Buckingham Palace transferred to Windsor Castle. The tea that followed in the Oak Dining Room went some way to restoring his good humour.

Because of rationing the only food available was home-grown produce, but the tea was still considerable, given the austerity of the time. Queen Mary meticulously measured out her favourite Indian tea at the correct ratio of one spoon for each person and one for the pot before sitting back for the footmen to pour it and hand round the sandwiches and cakes. Windsor Castle was then a wartime fortress, manned by soldiers whose duty it was to guard sixteen-year-old Princess Elizabeth and twelve year-old Margaret Rose against kidnap attempts. The princesses joined their cousins, Eddie and Alexandra, for the ceremony. It was a welcome break from their routine—and a not unwelcome change from the constrictions of Badminton.

When their little brother was born, Marina was anxious that Edward and Alexandra should not feel left out. They had been living with Queen Mary at Badminton since the outbreak of war in September 1939 and had seen their mother only once a week and their father less. When they returned to Coppins periodically, there were the inevitable tensions. Alexandra was moody and disobedient, and her brother Eddie was withdrawn. They were both confused. The war had deprived them of the steady family life they both clearly needed.

Marina discussed her problems with Dr Jacob Snowman when he arrived to circumcize the baby shortly after the christening, and she stressed how important it was that, in her view, a mother should prepare a young child for the advent of an infant brother or sister.

'It was a very cordial conversation,' Dr Snowman recalled in his diaries, 'and all the association of that visit remains the more impressed on my memory by the tragedy that occurred a few days afterwards.'

Nine days after the christening, Queen Mary drove to Coppins for lunch. She enjoyed herself so much she stayed for tea and afterwards walked in the garden chatting with her youngest son. Thirty-nine-year-old George loved his garden, and over the seven years since he had inherited the house, gardening had developed into something of a passion.

'The baby is sweet,' Queen Mary wrote in her diary; 'had lunch and tea there—walked in the garden—Georgie showed me some of his interesting things. He looked so happy with his lovely wife and dear baby.'

It was the last time she was to see her son. Twelve days later, on 25 August, a day of continuous, heavy rain, the Dowager Queen received a telephone call shortly after dinner. It was from the King and Queen at Balmoral to tell her George had been killed.

George had left Coppins the previous afternoon and driven himself to London to catch the overnight train for Inverness to take a Sunderland flying-boat to Iceland for an RAF welfare tour of inspection. After kissing Alexandra and Eddie goodbye, he had taken his seven-week-old son in his arms and held him tightly. Marina watched him drive away until the car was out of sight. She expected him to be gone for only ten days.

The following evening Marina had just gone upstairs to her bedroom intending to have an early night when the telephone rang. Nanny Kate Fox answered it. When she heard the news the elderly lady was numbed with shock. She slowly climbed the stairs to the bedroom and Marina, hearing her heavy footfall, immediately sensed disaster. The moment Foxy opened the door, she whispered, 'It's George, isn't it?'

At 1.10 that afternoon George had taken off from the Cromarty Firth for the 900-mile flight to Reykjavik. The papers relating to the crash were closed to the public for the next half century, but that did not dampen the rumour that the Duke was drunk after an all too convivial luncheon, that he insisted on piloting the plane himself, that he misjudged the high ground and crashed into the hillside near Berridale in Scotland.

Fourteen of the fifteen men aboard were killed. The local doctor identified the 39-year-old Duke by his watch, which had stopped at 32 minutes after takeoff, and his identity bracelet, which read: 'His Royal Highness The Duke of Kent, Coppins, Iver, Buckinghamshire.'

'I felt so stunned by the shock I could not believe it,' Queen Mary wrote. Her immediate concern was for Marina and the children. The following day she drove to Coppins, where she found her daughter-in-law weeping uncontrollably. As Marina grasped the deadly finality of the situation, her weeping gave way to profound shock and she sat motionless, staring at the wall. The man she loved was dead. Her seven-week-old baby Prince Michael would never know his father. Prince Eddie, almost seven, was now the second Duke of Kent, and Princess Alexandra, at five and a half, could not be expected to understand the trauma.

The funeral of Prince George, Duke of Kent, took place in St George's Chapel on the morning of Saturday 29 August. Heavily veiled, Marina was supported by the Queen and Queen Mary.

'I have attended many family funerals in the Chapel,' wrote King George VI, 'but none which have moved me in the same way. Everybody there I knew well, but I did not dare look at any of them for fear of breaking down.'

For Marina, still in an emotional hormonal upheaval after childbirth, the only solace was retreat from a world which had temporarily ended. No amount of cajoling could coax her out of her depression, and the sight and sound of baby Michael only served to remind her of George. Foxy was too old and too distressed herself to cope, so it was left to Nanny Smith and her assistant, Nanny Neald, to take charge.

In desperation it was decided that Marina's sister, Princess Olga, would have to be brought back from her exile in Kenya. Olga and her husband, Prince Paul of Yugoslavia, had exiled after Germany's pact with the Yugoslavians, and getting Olga out of East Africa presented both political and logistical problems, but on 17 September Olga arrived at Coppins to be reunited with her grieving sister.

For Marina it was an emotional reunion and the first step on her road to recovery. One of the first things she did was to send the last photograph taken by Cecil Beaton of George and baby Michael to President Roosevelt. 'I want to send you this photograph of your God son that was taken when he was six weeks old,' Marina wrote on the black-edged writing paper. 'I hope I will have the pleasure of introducing him to you in the not too distant future.'

The exiled Queen Wilhelmina of the Netherlands, another godparent, sent Roosevelt her own impressions of 'little Michael', whom she saw for the first time when he was four months old: 'He is such a darling,' she wrote, 'and he was in a very good temper and has such a radiant laugh and fine big, blue eyes and much golden hair, that even stands up in a crest. I think he will later on much resemble his father.'

In adulthood Prince Michael looks more like his mother. But his colouring—light green eyes and an olive skin—and his love of anything mechanical came from the father he never knew.

'I inherited my love for fast cars from my father,' Prince Michael said. He remembers how he 'bored everybody rigid' as a child by forever begging to be allowed to drive the cars of visitors who called to see his mother 'Every hapless guest that came to lunch was asked, 'Please can I drive your car?' Our drive wasn't more than three hundred yards long and I think my request usually served to ruin their lunch. But by the age of eleven, I had driven over a hundred different cars down our drive!'

Michael's elder brother Eddie had shown a similar interest in cars and used to spend hours in the garage listening while his father explained how they worked. At four he could take a toy car apart and then reassemble it. To the young prince his father was the fount of all knowledge, and his untimely death was a painful loss to the hypersensitive little boy, who was prone to sudden outbursts of violent temper, a family trait amongst the male members of the family since the time of Edward VII.

The months immediately after George's death were extremely difficult, and Eddie fell victim to severe attacks of asthma. With the help of Aunt Olga and the support of their grandmother, Queen Mary, the routine of their daily life was gradually restored. Marina resumed her public duties and left Nanny Neald to look after baby Michael. Coppins was now officially owned by Eddie, but held in trust until he came of age, and at the end of the war when the children's enforced sojourn at Badminton House ended, Marina determined to make it a home once again. Marina, the sophisticated, elegant woman who had shared her late husband's love of the bright lights, was forced by fate to devote herself to her children. The Royal Family, always so united in the public's perception, left her to fend for herself. She rose to the challenge.

'My mother brought us up,' Michael recalled. 'All three of us. There was nobody in the family who came forward, who became a father figure. It was very strange. I never had an older man, a father figure in my life.'

He did, however, have a 'splendid nanny'—Nanny Neald. She was the traditional starchy type who wore a uniform and reigned supreme in the nursery.

'She was much loved and very strict,' the prince recalled. 'She was a splendid figure, very wise and very sound. I owe her a lot.'

If the Duke had lived he would probably have been the most modern parent of his generation. He put Eddie's name down for Eton when he was four months old. Michael was registered for the college at birth. This would not be unusual now, but in the thirties, when royal boys were always taught at home before being sent to naval college, it was considered revolutionary.

As a single parent it was now Marina's concern to organize the education of her children. She never felt particularly close to her in-laws and was reluctant to turn to them for advice. Unlike many other royal mothers who are seemingly incapable of establishing a loving relationship with their offspring, Marina was determined to provide them with the right mixture of discipline and affection. She admonished them in her deep voice if they did anything wrong, but always made a point of praising them when they did well. To help her look after Alexandra and Michael, while Eddie was at Ludgate, a preparatory school near Wokingham in Surrey, she decided to engage a governess.

The governess was named Catherine Peebles. She would later have charge of the early education of Prince Charles and Princess Anne. She was a small, neat Scotswoman with no formal training, but according to her previous employers, Henry and Alice, Duke and Duchess of Gloucester, she was a perfect mixture of kindness and compassion. 'A dear lady and terribly strict,' is how Prince Michael remembers her.

She left a lasting impression on him; years later he would recall with horror a Highland holiday he spent with his cousins, the Gloucesters, when Miss Peebles came too.

Every morning, at 9.30, she took the young prince into the schoolroom for his first lessons of the day—usually mathematics, which he hated. 'I was terribly bad at mathematics—anything that didn't divide or multiply immediately threw me into a panic,' he says. One morning Miss Peebles asked him to solve a particularly difficult problem and as usual he panicked and was unable to answer it.

'Do you know what she did?' he said, reliving the awful

moment. 'She made me stand outside like a dunce in the passage. The house was full of servants, and as they passed me they started laughing and pointing. It was the most humiliating thing. I have never forgotten it!'

Michael may have been a dunce at mathematics, but he was gifted at languages and this was nurtured, not in Miss Peebles' strict schoolroom, but in the home of some Iver neighbours who had a French governess called Madame.

'As a small fellow of about five, I remember being shown pictures of people and underneath, written in French, was their profession,' he recalled. 'The very first thing I learned was *Le Facteur*, the postman.

'Princess Marina, my mother, used to talk French, not with us children, but with her sisters and others, so we already had the sound of the French language in our ears, without necessarily knowing what the words meant. I remember hearing this wonderful long word in French and I wanted to show it off, so I called my model lorry *quelquechose*.'

At the age of eight Michael was sent to Sunningdale prep school near Ascot. For the first time in his young life he was in a male-dominated environment, run by headmaster Mr Fox, a man he liked and respected. The only problem was the food, or rather the lack of it.

'It was ghastly beyond words,' he said. 'It was so awful I never used to eat it.' To supplement his diet the prince tried eating leaves, which he collected while watching cricket, followed by a dessert of toothpaste.

'I discovered at an early age that oak leaves were quite good, but laurel leaves made you sick! I used to eat toothpaste. Preferably Macleans.' Apart from the food, Michael loved Sunningdale and had no hesitation sending his own son there forty-five years later.

Michael was noticeably less complicated than his elder brother, Eddie, and boisterous sister, Alexandra. When Alexandra was growing up she showed little of her mother's glamour and looked plump and awkward in her cast-off clothing. She had inherited her father's quick temper as well as his infectious laugh, and her quick-witted responses could be cutting. With two brothers as companions it was not surprising that Alexandra grew into a tomboy, climbing trees, dashing about on her pony and playing at soldiers. They all had pet rabbits and the local farmer allowed them to look after some of his calves. So determined was the princess that hers should look the best that she groomed the little creature several times a day and once put brilliantine on its fur so that it would look shinier.

Marina tried to instil in her children a sense of the value of money sometimes with amusing results. Visiting a chemist's shop in Iver one day. Eddie and Alexandra bought a bar of soap with their sixpenny allowance of pocket money. Eddie considered it a waste of money because they already had soap at home, but Alexandra liked the idea of smuggling a different sort of soap into the house and secretly using it. Alexandra finally got her own way and the chemist remembered them handing over the six pennies and running off home with the soap.

Marina could handle Alexandra's stubborn and disobedient ways, and the frequent battles between mother and daughter always ended with forgiveness. Eddie's withdrawn moods continued to worry her, however, and as no one in the family came forward with any support, she decided to engage a tutor for her son, to give him the male attention she felt he lacked. Her choice was Giles St Aubyn, a history master from Eton, who came to Coppins during the holidays to teach Eddie and help him develop new interests. St Aubyn, the son of Lord St Leven, owner of picturesque St Michael's Mount in Cornwall, helped provide the stimulus Eddie needed.

For all her efforts, the young Duke's intellectual progress was not as quick as his mother would have wished. But like his younger brother, Michael, he did have an aptitude for languages, particularly French, and he had inherited his parents' love for the arts. He did not have their flair, however. He was more of a plodder.

He also found it difficult to cope with the problems and pressures of boarding school, and his stay at Eton was noticeably short. Still unsettled by the death of his father, he was very unhappy. That only aggravated his asthma, and shortly after the death in 1952 of his uncle, George VI, his mother decided that he should finish his education in the clear mountain air of Switzerland at Le Rosey, alma mater to such international luminaries as the Aga Khan and the late Shah of Iran, where the regime was less restricted than it was at Eton.

With his mixture of Russian and Hanoverian blood—he looked, Chips Channon noted, like 'all the four Georges rolled into one'—he fitted well into Le Rosey's cosmopolitan society.

Prince Michael's Eton schooldays were far more successful. 'When I went to Eton I never made a conscious effort to study French harder than any other language,' he recalled. 'It was just easier for me. There was a dear man, called Bud Hill, who was one of the Eton housemasters, and at the end of my first half [term] he took the trouble to write to me saying that in all his twenty-five years as a teacher at Eton, no boy had ever got higher marks in his French trials at the end of his first half.

'My mother was very pleased, but I, like a fool, lost the letter. If there was ever a case to frame something, that was it. I was terribly touched and I am delighted my son seems to have inherited the gift.'

Alexandra, too, reaped the benefits of her mother's cosmopolitan background and was also fluent in French. Her uncle, George VI, stirring himself out of the indifference that had marked his attitude towards his two fatherless nephews, had remarked on her talent and her temperament and advised Marina to send her away to school. The sturdy pony-mad ten-year-old, who had once dreamed of being a bareback rider in a circus, duly went to Heathfield in September 1947—the first royal girl ever to be sent to boarding school.

Unlike her own daughter, who would rebel against tradition and her royal status, Alexandra took everything in her characteristically down-to-earth stride. Unlike her cousin, Princess Elizabeth, who found it difficult to mix with strangers, Alexandra opted for sharing a dormitory with five other girls.

Unsophisticated though she was, she was never at a loss when it came to making conversation, nor intimidated by people in authority, and she was immediately popular. There were no problems about her mixing with the other girls, her former headmistress Kathleen Dodds remembered. She was anxious to get to know them and mixed in well.

It was the matrons who had the problems, Kathleen Dodds said, for though she was capable of making friends, she had no idea of how to behave in a school environment.

The headmistress recalled: 'When a matron said: "Alexandra, you forgot to clear your shelves," she was apt to fling her arms around the astonished woman's neck and cry: "Oh, darling Matron! I am so sorry!"

'Similarly, when something nice happened, she would rush down a school corridor and ecstatically embrace the first mistress she collided with. She was a hefty child, who'd nearly knock people off their feet.

'She also had a clear, carrying voice. It wasn't even muted for her bedtime prayers. God must have found Alexandra's supplications very revealing—not least because of the nicknames she had for her royal relatives.

'In the dormitory she was pure hell. One night I was working late in my study when thumps, thuds and bangs from overhead made the great bronze chandelier start to swing. Next day I sent for the head of the dormitory—Alexandra. In answer to my accusation that she had nearly brought the chandelier down on my head she looked up at the ceiling then said: "Oh, it's only a small chandelier. I thought it was like the huge ones they have at Windsor."

'Despite her royal connections, Alexandra was not rich. "We can't afford expensive things," the Duchess had told me. Some girls had their school coats and skirts hand-tailored. Not Alexandra. Her under-clothes were mended, her uniform off the peg. Her everyday clothes were hand-me-downs from her royal cousins. Princess Margaret's clothes were an especial trial. "I'm so huge and she's so small. I'll never get into them," Alex would lament.

'She made great efforts to polish herself up for her mother's birthday, but with a great shout of, "Mama! Your present!" Alexandra hurled herself at her mother and dropped everything she was holding.'

On 21 December 1951 Princess Marina and her three children travelled as usual to Sandringham House to spend Christmas with the King and Queen. Eleven months before, the King had been diagnosed as having lung cancer and had had a lung and some of the nerves in his larynx removed, leaving him in a weakened state and hardly able to speak. But the traditional family Christmas was a time of forced cheer and the children were told nothing more than that Uncle Bertie 'wasn't very well'. After Christmas, Alexandra returned to school, Eddie returned to Switzerland, and Marina flew to Germany to visit her sister. Only Prince Michael, almost ten years old, remained at Sandringham with his cousins Charles and Anne.

On the morning of Tuesday 5 February the children watched King George set out on a rabbit shoot after breakfast, and return home in time for tea in cheerful mood. He retired to bed early having said goodnight to his grandchildren. Later that night his body was discovered by his valet. He had died peacefully in his sleep. Cousin Lilibet, far away in Nairobi, was now Queen.

That term Alexandra was described in her end-of-term report as a girl 'with all the lovable qualities of quick sympathy, affection, generosity, laughter and total honesty.' The traits that were there in the child flowered in the woman, and when Alexandra left school just before her sixteenth birthday she had just the attributes the young Queen needed to support her in her role as monarch. Alexandra was asked to enter public life earlier than any other member of the Royal Family before.

'However the monarchy changes—and change it must—' the late Lord Mountbatten said, 'the Queen and Prince Charles will need the support of people like Alexandra and Eddie. They don't grow on trees, you know. To be a monarch and have cousins like the Kents is of untold value—they are both relatives, friends and, at the same time, bloody hard-working people.'

Events would not always be kind to the children of Prince George of Kent. The war had deprived them of their father. Alexandra would suffer enormous problems with her daughter, Eddie with his sons, and Michael with money. All three, however, would perform their duties with admirable, old-fashioned dedication.

As Prince Michael explained: 'If you have privilege, which in my case came from birth, you have no option but to accept some kind of obligation. You can't have all the perks without pulling your own weight.'

George, Helen and Nicholas

hen the Earl of St Andrews was asked what his father did for a living he replied, 'He changes in and out of uniform.'

The question was addressed to George, the Duke of Kent's son, on the stage of a theatre in London's West End when he was three years old. He had been taken to see Harry Corbett's annual 'Sooty's Christmas Show'. The puppeteer had asked children in the audience to come up on stage and George St Andrews had gone forward. A confident little boy, he sang 'Away in a Manger' in a shrill voice and won the prize of a Sooty glove puppet.

Georgie, as his parents called him, was born on 26 June 1962, at Coppins, the Kents' family home in Buckinghamshire. He weighed 6lb 4oz and was the first male child in the direct line of succession not to have the title 'Prince', casualty of his great-grandfather George V's ruling that the royal title should extend only as far as the grandchildren of the sovereign.

Without a royal handle, it was easier for his mother, Katharine, to play down her son's royal connections. He would never be involved in royal duties and she was determined to stave off the day when her firstborn realized he was 'different'. Her good intentions were thwarted almost immediately, however, when she gave in to pressure from both her husband and her mother-in-law, Princess Marina, and agreed to have the infant christened in the Music Room of Buckingham Palace with the panoply of royalty, and to name him George, after his paternal grandfather who had died during the Second World War, Philip after his godfather, Prince Philip, and Nicholas after his great-grandfather, Prince Nicholas of Greece.

A devoted mother, Katharine shared the duties of looking after her son with a Scottish nanny, Mary McPherson, who had once been a nursemaid to the Factor of Balmoral. In the mode of all the royal nannies, she soon established an unswerving routine for the baby's nursery life at Coppins.

The tranquility of the Coppins nursery did not last for long, however, for when George was six months old he was uprooted to a small army flat when his father, a uniform-wearing (and changing) officer in the Royal Scots Greys, was posted to Hong Kong as second-in-command of C Squadron. There were no special facilities for the Duchess on board the army 'women and children' flight to the colony, and Katharine and Nanny shared the journey's duties of nappy-changing, feeding and mopping up the overtired infant. The flight, with brief stop-overs, took two days and George, according to his mother, behaved surprisingly well. Always a happy baby, he didn't seem to mind being carted around and quickly settled into his new home. The Duchess enjoyed being an army wife—and being spared the regular round of royal duties. She now had the time to enjoy motherhood. With Nanny McPherson and the help of an *amah*, or nursery maid, who did all the washing and ironing, Kate could concentrate on her son. The Chinese staff were very taken by the blonde, blue-eyed infant, who, once he started crawling, was so quick they called him 'the little one with the winged knees'.

It was a happy interlude in the Kents' life. The Duchess was able to push the pram in a nearby park without a police escort, or take the baby to see his father play polo. Eddie and Katharine both enjoyed the sights and sounds of Hong Kong and made friends with the other army officers and their wives. It was a decidedly unroyal existence—when guests came to stay, nanny and George moved into the spare room of their neighbour, Captain Cox, who lived in the flat below.

Noël Coward, who had been so close to the Duke's father, stayed with them on one of his trips to the Far East. The playwright wrote in his diary: 'A really enchanting evening with Prince Eddie and Kathy, who live in an ordinary officer's issue flatlet in the New Territories . . . merry as grigs and having a lovely time untrammelled by royal pomposity. They really are a sweet couple and it is a pleasure to see two people so entirely happy with each other. I also saw George who is thirteen months and blond and pink and smiling.'

Katharine was very attached to her baby. It was only after much discussion that she agreed to leave him behind with Nanny McPherson when she and Eddie returned to England for Princess Alexandra's wedding to Angus Ogilvy in April 1963. In the absence of a father, Eddie gave his sister away. The Duchess, determined not to be parted from George any longer than necessary, hurriedly took a flight back only two days after the wedding.

The Hong Kong tour lasted only a year and in 1963 Katharine and Eddie returned to England with Nanny and George for the traditional Christmas at Sandringham. It was to be a special occasion. Katharine had just learnt that she was pregnant again. So had the Queen and Princess Margaret. And Princess Alexandra was expecting her first child. There had not been such an example of royal fecundity since George III's four daughters-in-law were all pregnant at the same time, and when the four modern royal mothers-to-be gathered in the mock-Jacobean mansion, the conversation, much to Prince Philip's hearty amusement, revolved around babies and prenatal care.

The company of so many pregnant royal relations was something of a comfort to Katharine. She was used to being part of a large family group and missed the friendliness of her Yorkshire childhood. She found the protocol that enveloped her husband's family difficult to deal with, and fond as she was of them individually, she still found them slightly intimidating *en masse*.

On 29 April 1964, in the familiar surroundings of Coppins, Katharine gave birth to a 7lb 8oz baby girl. The Duke, who was in Fallingbostel, Germany, with his regiment, arrived only just in time for the birth.

'We are delighted with my first granddaughter,' Princess Marina wrote to her sister, Princess Olga, 'especially as Katharine longed for a girl.'

Helen Marina Lucy, named after her beautiful Romanov great-grandmother, the Grand Duchess Helen Vladimirovna of Russia, later Princess Nicholas of Greece, was christened in the private chapel at Windsor. Her godparents included Princess Margaret, who had only just recovered from the birth of her daughter, and Angus Ogilvy. The Queen used the occasion of Helen's christening to celebrate this plethora of royal births and held a family lunch party at Windsor Castle.

While the adults quaffed champagne in the Oak Room the nannies were being kept busy in the nursery. Prince Edward, aged three months, and Prince Andrew, a cheeky four and a half, were looked after by Nanny Mabel Anderson. Lady Helen Windsor, aged five weeks, and George, now two, were looked after by Nanny McPherson. Thirteen-week-old James Ogilvy was with his Nanny Rattle. And Lady Sarah Armstrong-Jones, aged five weeks, and Viscount Linley, two and a half, were under the care of Nanny Sumner. It was a fraught occasion—

nannies Sumner and Anderson did not like each other, and everyone considered Nanny McPherson to be rather difficult. Only Nanny Rattle was above the nursery fray.

Such moments of below-stairs confrontation were unusual. The early childhood years of George and Helen revolved around their father's army life. Home was not a palace but an army base in Hanover where they were allowed to mix in normally with the other children.

In the summer of 1966 the Kents moved back to England and reopened Coppins. George, then aged four, was enrolled in the village school, while Helen, by then a two-year-old toddler, played in the upper-floor nursery as her father had done before her. Some pre-war toys were discovered in the attic, including an old swing made by their grandfather, which Kate dusted off and put in the garden. It was the happiest of times for the Duchess. Her husband, who could sometimes be cold and reserved, was attentive and pleased to have his family under the familiar familial roof.

When the Duke was away at staff college, Katharine's mother, Joyce Worsley, came to stay to see her grandchildren. George, she noted, was far more Worsley than Windsor and was already a bright little boy, who enjoyed tinkling on the piano and riding on his pony. Those sunny days gave no hint of the troubles to come.

The first shock came when Eddie's adored mother Marina was admitted to hospital with pains in her arm and leg. Tests revealed she had a brain tumour and six months at most to live. Eddie was distraught, and when he told his brother and sister they agreed to spare their mother the news, so that she could see out her life in peace. The end came quickly. Just over a month later, on 27 August 1968, two days after the anniversary of her husband's death, Marina died.

The death of her mother-in-law propelled Katharine into a round of royal duties which kept her away from her children more than she would have wished. Because of Eddie's nomadic army existence, the children were used to his absences, but they had always had their mother around. They relied on her—and she on them—and however late and tired she might be she was always home in time for their bath and to read them a story. Music was her great love, and she sang to them and taught them a few simple notes on the piano. She enjoyed motherhood and was keen to extend her family.

Having a baby at the age of thirty-seven carried considerably more risks then than it would in later years. Screening tests were not so thorough and the medical equipment available was less sophisticated. Although Kate was in good health, her gynaecologist, John Peel, preferred to oversee the birth in hospital rather than at home, where every instrument had to be thought of and brought in beforehand. Another reason why Coppins was a less than suitable place to deliver a baby was that it had been burgled several times over recent months.

So it was that on 25 July 1970 Katharine gave birth to a son, not in the familiar surroundings of the family home, but at Kings College Hospital in London. This time Eddie, who was stationed in Cyprus, was unable to be at his wife's side, but minutes after the birth she telephoned him herself, to give him the news that a son had been born and that mother and baby were doing well.

The baby was christened Nicholas Charles Edward Jonathan Windsor, and Prince Charles agreed to be one of the godparents.

Katharine's hopes of enlarging her family after the birth of Nicholas were to be thwarted. Try as she might in following years, she could not keep a pregnancy intact, and perhaps because she was so tense and wanted more children so much, it made it all the worse.

Three years after Nicholas was born, Katharine's father died and she took it badly.

'I loved him very deeply,' she said sadly.

It was the beginning of a downward slope for Katharine. It was difficult for Eddie too. He had no one to turn to—and like other members of his family, leant on Lord Mountbatten for advice. Uncle Dickie's advice was that he should leave the army, get a civilian job, make himself financially secure, and spend more time with his increasingly troubled wife. The Queen offered them a London base, York House in St James's Palace, and encouraged her cousin to find a civilian job, which he did, as Vice-Chairman of the British Overseas Trade Board.

Far from allowing him more time with his family, however, the job frequently took Eddie away from home. They decided to sell Coppins and take up the Queen's offer of a lease on Anmer Hall on the Sandringham estate. For Helen, who had spent all her childhood in the leafy lanes of Buckinghamshire—she went to a local nursery before going to Eton End at Datchet—it was more of a wrench than for George, who was at Heatherdown prep school with his cousin, Prince Andrew. A bright but serious child, George appeared to have inherited the style and artistic temperament of his grandfather, Prince George, and, from his mother's side, the Worsley academic mind. But unlike his sister Helen, who could wrap the Duke around her little finger, George was nervous of his temperamental father.

'The Duke was hardest of all on George, being a firstborn,' a family friend recalled. 'He couldn't get away with a thing as a child and if he took one step from the straight and narrow he was knocked into the middle of next week.'

Despite his own unhappy spell there, the Duke decided to follow the newly founded family tradition and send his son to Eton.

In May 1975, when he was twelve, George competed with seventy-six other candidates for fifteen Eton scholarships. A month before his thirteenth birthday, the Eton authorities announced that he had come overall top in French and well above average in his general papers. He came eighth in the success list and thus was the first member of his family to win a King's scholarship since they were granted by Henry VI in the fifteenth century.

Eddie and Katharine were well pleased. Their shy young son, who felt so out of place with his rowdy royal relations, had proved himself to be the first truly intellectual member of the family. Both George's father and his uncle, Prince Michael, had excelled at languages. Princess Marina was an excellent painter and had exhibited in the Royal Academy, and Prince George could sit at the piano and 'strum Debussy'. But none of the family had enjoyed this kind of academic success at such an early age.

George enjoyed his time at Eton. The ancient grandeur of the school allowed him the anonymity he wished for. There were no photographers lying in wait as there were during the family gatherings at Sandringham or Windsor Castle, and he blended comfortably into the background.

There was one nagging problem, however—his mother's health. Throughout his Eton schooldays Katharine was constantly being admitted to hospital with one ailment or another. Being the eldest, George felt responsible for his increasingly fragile mother, and when she discovered she was pregnant again in 1977, aged forty-four, George was one of the first people she told. Sadly the pregnancy wasn't to last. Katharine was admitted to the King Edward VII Hospital with complications. Her psychological problems made it very difficult for her to deal with the trauma of the situation, and when doctors failed to save the baby after a thirty-six-hour battle, Katharine sank into a deep depression.

Neither the support of her husband, who had returned from a business trip in Iran to be by her side, nor the appealing letters from her teenage son, nor the youthful exuberance of seven-year-old Lord Nicholas and thirteen-year-old Lady Helen could pull her round. For the next seven years the Duchess spun on an emotional roller-coaster. Her depression was sometimes so overwhelming that she was admitted to hospital. At other times she would sit at home, looking blank, not talking.

The death of her mother, Lady Worsley, who had been such a support to her, contributed to her suffering, and although Eddie did everything he could, he was all but helpless. The situation had its inevitable effect on her children and George, who had started out at school with such promise, failed two out of three of his A-level exams.

Helen, whose education had taken her from Eton End to St Paul's Junior School for Girls in London, which was renowned for its academic record and teaching of music and drama, talked to her mother's doctors about depression and learnt how to understand the problems it presented. But she was now at boarding school, St Mary's, Wantage, and was far enough removed to be spared the worst. Nicholas was more directly involved. His presence was a great comfort to Katharine, who guiltily spoilt him. 'Nicholas was always very much a mummy's boy,' a friend said. 'He was forever being cuddled by his mother, who's an amazingly affectionate lady.'

Nicholas was wary of his father and did his best not to upset him. If he did and the Duke lost his temper, Nick would go running to his mother. They used to sit in the kitchen and listen to music until the Duke calmed down.

Music was a great therapy to the Duchess, and much to her delight Nicholas was given a walk-on part in Mozart's *The Magic Flute*, thus becoming the first member of the Royal Family to perform in a Covent Garden opera.

Two years later, at the age of thirteen, instead of following his brother to Eton, Nicholas started his public-school life as a day boy at Westminster School, in Dean's Yard, Westminster. One of the most high-powered academic schools in the country, its reputation thrives on the arts rather than sport—Andrew Lloyd Webber is a former pupil—and what is done outside school hours is supposedly under parents' jurisdiction.

After school, instead of hanging out with his friends, Nicholas would loyally return home to his mother in York House. Unlike many other royal homes, York House, the former residence of both the Duke of Windsor and Nicholas's grandfather, Prince George, had a 'homely' atmosphere. On the evenings when his father was out, Nicholas would sit in the kitchen doing his homework while his mother cooked supper, lavishing her attention on her youngest son whom she called by the pet name 'Snoopy'.

Helen, meanwhile, having completed a sixth-form year at Gordonstoun, had extracted herself from the family nest and was sharing a flat with a girlfriend. Together with her cousin Lady Sarah Armstrong-Jones, she was making the most of the youthful freedom that had been so noticeably denied other royal children. Men swarmed around her, attracted by her beautiful blonde looks. So did the media, drawn by her royal pedigree. After she had been discovered sunbathing topless during a family holiday on the island of Corfu she became a regular item in the London gossip columns, which irreverently labelled her Melons.

'A lot of things were quite shocking for her, and at heart she was younger than her years,' her former boyfriend, Nigel Oakes, remembered. 'She came from a very protective background and was charmingly naïve. It was quite obvious she was a very innocent person who was doing her best to go out and be a wild child.

'The nice thing was that she wasn't very good at it. She's better at what she is doing now, with a respectable job and leading a quieter life.'

Of the three Kent children, Helen was the one who appeared to cope best with life outside the Royal Family. Her two brothers, both of whom had shown so much intellectual promise, did not fulfil their parents' early expectations.

In 1988 Nicholas took A-levels at Harrow and gained a place at Manchester College, Oxford, where he studied philosophy. He was caught smoking cannabis with a friend in St James's Park the same year. His highly-strung mother was mortified and ordered her son home to Anmer Hall, where he spent a miserable Christmas walking around the grounds with his dog. Restless and unfulfilled, he seemed unable to commit himself to anything more than wandering around the Third World on the fringes of charity projects. But that was his choice and he had the freedom to make it.

When it came to matters of the heart, the Kents' children were also able to exercise their independence. In 1992 Helen married contemporary art dealer Tim Taylor, who has made her extremely happy. Three years earlier George St Andrews had given up his right of succession to marry Roman Catholic divorcée Sylvana Tomaselli. As she was head of the Church of England, it was impossible for the Queen to attend the register office ceremony. The links with the main branch of the Royal Family, never close, were becoming ever more tenuous. That did not concern the shy, self-effacing Earl.

'I am never going to carry out engagements,' he had said as a teenager. 'I have managed to remain anonymous so far in life and I want to stay that way.'

He joined the Diplomatic Service and was posted as Third Secretary to the British Embassy in Budapest in Hungary. For all his undoubted intellectual ability, however, he could not pass his Foreign Office exams and was forced to leave the service. He did not seem unduly upset by that downturn in his career, and spent the next four years of his unemployment learning languages, during which time he achieved a passable knowledge of Arabic, Hebrew, Persian and Polish to add to the French, Italian, German, Russian, Hungarian and Sanskrit.

'It gives me something to do,' he explained.

While he studied, his wife worked, writing books and tutoring Cambridge undergraduates. The couple did not employ a nanny and the Earl became a 'house husband', shouldering much of the early responsibility for bringing up their son, who was born in 1988, christened Edward, and bore the courtesy title Lord Downpatrick.

George St Andrews appeared happy with his domesticated lot. Like his sister, he had married, not for dynastic advantage, but for love alone.

The golden-haired boy who won first prize at the Christmas pantomime, the little girl playing with her father's old toys in the nursery at Coppins and the nervous schoolboy walking on to the stage at Covent Garden Opera House—all have played their part on the stage of royal life. But unlike their cousins in Buckingham Palace, they were able to write their own scripts. If their marriages are as successful as they appear to be, then the Kents will have proved themselves, against all odds, to have been successful parents.

James and Marina

As children move towards adulthood and start flexing the developing muscles of their impending independence, relationships between offspring and parents are frequently strained to breaking point.

They were in the case of the Ogilvys—to a catastrophic extent. It was as if all the faults in the royal method of raising children had been visited on one family, and there would be no recovery from the bitterness and acrimony generated.

In 1989 Princess Alexandra's 23-year-old daughter, Marina, complained, 'Who cares about family background these days?' It was the prelude to a public, emotional family row in which a daughter rejected every value that was dear to her mother and father, including her lineage, saying she felt persecuted because her royal genes prevented her from being anonymous.

The sense of duty, instilled in Princess Alexandra by her grandmother, Queen Mary, was one of the things Marina was complaining about. Duty, she said, took her mother and father away from her and prevented them from being there when she needed them. When she asked her father what came first, Queen and country or his daughter, he replied: 'Queen and country.'

Her grandmother, Princess Marina, would have echoed those sentiments. Within months of her husband's death she

189

put royal duty before private grief and went back to royal work. She expected the same devotion from her children. As they matured she tried to persuade Alexandra, Eddie and Michael that it would be a good idea if they eventually married into one of Europe's royal families.

Arranged marriages, she said, were no bad thing, especially if they involved a royal blood line. Who else was going to understand what life as a member of the family was like but someone from a similar background? When her son Eddie Kent met and fell in love with commoner Katharine Worsley, two years his senior, Marina was so displeased she made them wait five years before she would even consider allowing them to marry.

When they eventually did, in June 1961, Marina had to give up Coppins, her home of twenty-two years. Her apparently lonely plight produced such a deep sense of guilt in Alexandra that she felt it was her duty to stay with her in their Kensington Palace apartment. She drew the line at her mother's suggestion that she should marry the King of Norway's son, Crown Prince Harald, a second son. Even so, it was another year and a half before Alexandra finally had the courage to commit herself to Angus Ogilvy, who had been courting her for eight years.

Angus, a chain-smoking businessman with craggy good looks, was nine years her senior and noticeably masculine compared to the kind of fey men whose company her mother preferred. He was the second son of the 12th Earl of Airlie, a former lord-in-waiting to King George V and Lord Chamberlain to Queen Elizabeth, and his background of Eton and Oxford followed by a spell in the Scots Guards was impeccable. Even Marina, with her high standards, found it difficult to fault him. She did, however, leave her distinctive thumb print on their marriage by insisting the engagement be announced on 29 November 1962, the anniversary of her own wedding.

Marriage altered Alexandra's perception of life. For the first time she was out from under the watchful eye of her mother, with a home of her own—Thatched House Lodge in Richmond Park, a magnificent Georgian lodge with four acres of land and an outdoor swimming pool. And for the first time she had responsibilities other than her royal duties—to her husband and her unborn child.

In July 1963, as was still the custom for royal ladies at the time, she withdrew from public life for the first time since she was sixteen. On Saturday 29 February 1964 she gave birth to a 9lb 6oz baby boy. As she toasted the baby's health she laughed about the wretched luck of her being born on Christmas Day and her son being born on 29 February in a Leap Year. But she was a calm and devoted mother; her earlier experience as a nurse at the children's hospital, Great Ormond Street, stood her in good stead.

It was not long after the birth, however, that duty again called and within ten weeks Alexandra resumed her royal duties. James Robert Bruce was christened in Buckingham Palace on 11 May with the Queen, who had a two-month-old baby of her own, and the Duchess of Kent, who had given birth a month before, acting as godmothers. Prince Michael and Sir Robert Menzies, Prime Minister of Australia, who was a longtime acquaintance of Alexandra's, were the godfathers.

When his mother went off to work James was left in the care of Miss Olive Rattle, a traditional English nanny who soon had the newly-decorated nursery organized and running according to a well-ordered routine. Nanny had made only one demand—for a rocking chair, which she said she needed for rocking the baby to sleep. In their desire to keep nanny happy, Angus had driven into Richmond the next day and bought her one.

Overseas tours, always of several days and sometimes of several weeks, were to be the pattern of the Ogilvys' lives over the next few years. Although he had made it a rule not to be involved with his wife's royal duties, Angus agreed to accompany her when she travelled abroad—at his own expense. When they travelled, little James would remain at home in the care of Nanny Rattle, who would often take him to visit his godmother the Queen, whose youngest child, Prince Edward, had been born ten days after James. Two other cousins, Lady Sarah Armstrong-Jones and Lady Helen Windsor, were all born within a few months, so providing three companions of the same age within the family circle.

Of these four great-grandchildren of George V, James was the only one without a title, his father having refused the Queen's offer of an earldom. Alexandra knew cousin Lilibet was anxious for them to accept a title, but bowed to her husband's determination.

'I don't see why I should get a peerage just because I've married a princess,' he explained.

On Sunday 31 July 1966, with her husband at her side, Alexandra gave birth to her second child, a 7lb 8oz baby girl, who was later christened in the Chapel Royal of St James's Palace. Amongst the godparents were Princess Margaret, the Duke of Kent and eighteen-year-old Prince Charles. The infant was given the names Marina Victoria Alexandra—Marina after her grandmother, Victoria after her great-great-great-grandmother, and Alexandra after her mother. It would have been hard to foresee what anguish the angelic little baby lying in her cot was to cause not only her parents but all her mother's family.

Princess Alexandra and Angus Ogilvy tried to play down the royal connections of their children, but it was difficult. The Queen wished that James might join her son Prince Edward and her niece Lady Sarah Armstrong-Jones in the Buckingham Palace schoolroom. Initially Alexandra was not totally in favour of the idea, but went along with it partly to please

Lilibet and partly because it presented an answer to the immediate problem of what to do about her son's early education. And besides, James could be driven to school each morning by his father on his way to the City. The governess who had replaced Miss Peebles was a young woman called Lavinia Keppel, whose forebear was Alice Keppel, for many years the mistress of the children's great-great-grandfather, Edward VII. Lavinia's patience and imaginative teaching inspired the lively group of five-year-olds to do well, and both Princess Alexandra and Princess Margaret took a great deal of interest in their progress.

Margaret would often pop into the schoolroom to offer encouragement to Miss Keppel. All the facilities were certainly there to ensure they got a good head-start. There were few groups of five-year-olds who could boast their own private swimming pool, music room and tennis court, as well as the nursery cuisine organized with such care by Prince Edward's devoted nanny, Mabel Anderson, and served by a nursery footman.

Unlike his uncle, Prince Michael, who had been so hopeless at maths that his governess, Miss Peebles, had made him stand in disgrace outside the schoolroom, James did well at arithmetic. He was also good at music and learnt to play on the large grand piano at Thatched House Lodge.

While James was in the schoolroom, baby Marina was cared for by Nanny Rattle. She adored her little charge and would stand by her when the troubles started—so much so that, at eighty-two, she was the only family link at the reception when Marina married photographer Paul Mowatt in 1990.

'My nanny is a wonderful person,' Marina said shortly after the birth of her baby. 'She's one of the best. James and I were her last children, so I was her last baby. She came to our wedding and she thinks Zenouska is a little darling.'

As 'Jo' and 'Mo', as James and Marina were nicknamed,

grew up they saw less and less of their parents. Alexandra was involved with her royal duties, Angus with his business commitments. James was sent to Gibbs, a smart London prep school in Kensington where he was later joined by Prince Edward, while from the age of five Marina travelled to Chelsea where she was taught by a governess with a small group of other children.

The small amount of time they were able to devote to their children worried Alexandra and Angus. They were determined to bring up their son and daughter as much like other children as possible, but the royal connection was always there. How many of their friends' parents had a staff of eight, a chauffeur and police protection twenty-four hours a day? And how many children spent their summer holidays on the Queen's Norfolk estate or their Christmas holidays at Windsor Castle?

It was a dilemma which both the Duke of Kent and Princess Alexandra had to deal with, and which Angus Ogilvy summed up in an interview with Audrey Whiting. 'It is very difficult for the children when they go back to school at the end of a holiday,' he said. 'They are inevitably asked where they went and they can only reply truthfully "Balmoral" or "Windsor Castle". You can imagine what happens then. They are bombarded with questions such as "What is the Queen really like?", "Do you eat with the Queen?", "Is Princess Alexandra as nice as she seems?"

'We are trying to bring up two children with their feet firmly on the ground. When they grow up they will each have to earn their own livings. Being related to the Queen will not help them and nor will the fact that they spend holidays in magnificent royal castles assist them to get on in life. My wife and I have done our best to make our children recognize that the royal way of life they experience now and then is something to enjoy and appreciate, but that it will never be a permanent part of their future lives.'

Marina Ogilvy would later say that the dilemma of being partly royal and never having her parents around when she needed them affected her far more than her brother. As small children they had enjoyed a pleasant existence, playing in the grounds of Thatched House Lodge, riding through Richmond Park on their ponies, spending holidays on one of the Queen's estates with their cousins. 'I was two years younger than "the foursome",' Marina says, 'but I followed Sarah Armstrong-Jones to Frances Holland when I was seven and joined Helen Windsor at St Mary's when I was about thirteen.'

Marina was a confident, happy child, always laughing and joking, but she was sensitive about her royal position.

'Obviously I was very aware of our situation,' she said. 'We had a bodyguard, called Mr Street. I would die of embarrassment at being driven to school. I used to beg the driver to take his cap off.

'It was odd, but it wasn't a truly royal upbringing. I was half in, half out. My mother had the title, but not my father. I wasn't a Lady-something at school. I was plain Miss Marina, but obviously I was very aware of our situation.'

James was less complicated than his sister. He was not academic, but he found school work easy and had no trouble passing exams. At the age of seven he was sent to Heatherdown in Ascot together with his older cousins, George St Andrews and Prince Andrew, and his contemporary, Prince Edward.

Like his father and uncles, James went on to Eton where he joined his cousin George St Andrews, who was two years his senior. His charm and enthusiasm, which were set off by a combination of his parents' good looks, made him popular, and he did quite well academically. He left with thirteen O-levels and three A-levels and got a place at St Andrew's University in Scotland, where he met banker's daughter Julia Rawlinson whom he married in 1988. They moved to Scotland last year and she gave up her prestigious job as PR representative to Garrard, the Crown jewellers, to work in Hamilton and Inckes, Edinburgh's premier jewellers. They both commute into the city, where he works in a shipping company, from a country house in Fife.

Sadly, the close bond that once existed between Marina and James was broken when James refused to accept Paul Mowatt. 'He decided not to acknowledge Paul and wouldn't shake his hand at the wedding,' Marina said. 'James and I got on very well as children and throughout our teens. It is very sad.'

It was when Marina was at Frances Holland that her position as a member of the Royal Family began to dawn on her. 'During one of the lessons the teacher pointed out a picture of Princess Marina of Kent in a book and said to me, "This is your grandmother",' Marina remembered. 'It was the first time I had really thought about it.'

'It was odd,' she said, 'being taught your own place in Constitutional history.' (She is twenty-seventh in the line of succession.)

'All through my life I have been used to people trading on my name, trying to use me to get to my family. People invited me to attend things, not because of who I was, but because of the family I came from.'

By the time she joined her cousin Lady Helen Windsor at St Mary's, Wantage, a fashionable girls' boarding school, Marina was better equipped to deal with the situation. 'I got on well because I was popular and did well at music and drama. I was anti-elitism, but not all the girls were like that.'

The conflicts which had begun to threaten Marina's happiness came to their first crisis point when, at the age of fifteen, she developed anorexia nervosa. Figures suggest that as many as one or two in every hundred girls suffer from the slimmers' disease during some part of their adolescence, and Marina was one of them. Anorexia, according to Penelope Leach, 'is about dependence. It makes her [in this case Marina] the subject of much care and concern and puts off inner or outer pressure on her to become more independent of her parents. It gives her a rich and endless source of conflict, which effectively replaces the more usual and age-appropriate fight for freedom from parental control.'

Despite her anorexia, which continued for several years until she went into the Priory Clinic for treatment, Marina left school with seven O-levels and two A-levels, determined to make her own way.

'When I left school it seemed incredible to some that I actually worked for a living,' she said. 'An illusion exists that princesses' daughters never lift a finger, that they sit in some ivory tower willing the hours away until introduced to some suitable young man with a double-barrelled name. I tried to live the life of a young royal: I went to all those awful parties where people are so superficial. I did the things that were expected of me—but, from an early age, deep inside, I knew this life wasn't for me.'

At this stage relations with her parents were all right, according to Marina. But not right enough.

'I wanted to do things like develop my music, while they wanted me to do cooking and a typing course. I felt pressure to do that rather than go into the world of music. I felt I was being pushed into place, and I wanted to lead my own life and earn my own living.'

Though her parents were loving, they remained distant, and she spent long periods on her own, depressed and confused. She reached an 'all-time low' before she went on her Operation Raleigh expedition, but the challenge of going on one of their exacting, tough expeditions gave her confidence.

Prince Charles, who was one of her godparents, had long been a keen supporter of Operation Raleigh, and was pleased when Marina told him she had passed the selection test.

'She wrote to me and said she was keen to do it,' Charles remembers, 'which I was very impressed with because she'd worked it out entirely on her own—her parents hadn't said anything, nobody else had—I hadn't. I encouraged her and thought it would be marvellous. She did extremely well and passed the selection test, which is hideous. They have to plunge their hands into tins of maggots and wrestle with pythons and measure the chest size of gorillas, or something! And she did that marvellously and was selected and so I was thrilled.'

So were her parents, although Marina admits to having had some qualms about telling them she had been accepted. Such was the distance building up between them that she thought they would dismiss the idea as being too tough for her. But they were anxious to help their daughter out of the depressions she had suffered from the onset of her teenage years—depressions that both Angus and Alexandra were instinctively aware of.

Marina's main love, however, was her music, and between various jobs and running in the London marathon she won a coveted place at the Guildhall School of Music. Six years later she had to her credit scores for television, films and a theatrical production, and in 1993 produced her first solo album which she financed herself.

Unlike her brother and royal cousins, who celebrated their twenty-first birthdays with a large joint party at Windsor Castle, Marina didn't care about a smart social life. She was happy to spend her twenty-first birthday eating porridge with a group of deprived children on a special course operated by the Drake Centre in Scotland. Everyone liked her down-to-earth approach to life, and she was described by the deputy director as 'a lady of personality, understanding, a considerable presence and a terrific sense of humour'.

Some years before Marina's problems had taken hold, Angus Ogilvy had voiced his worries about the long-term effects of absentee parents to journalist Audrey Whiting. 'I think the time is coming very shortly,' he said, 'when if we don't see more of our children, we're going to pay the price at the other end, when they're older. But it's very difficult. You decide to spend an evening with the children, but then someone rings up and says, "Will you please come to a film première? If you come it will help us raise another £1,500 and this could help three hundred spastics." Well, who are more important, three hundred spastics or your own children?'

The Ogilvys made their choice and paid a terrible price for their misjudgement. In October 1990 Marina announced she was expecting a child by her photographer boyfriend, Paul Mowatt, whom she had met at a dinner party in 1987. Naive and unworldly for her twenty-three years, Marina half expected her mother, if not her father, to be pleased that they were to be grandparents. 'They knew we were very much in love and our whole future was going to be together,' Marina said. 'But the first thing my father did was say, "What shall we tell the Queen!" It felt like we were performers on television and I was watching. I couldn't believe it was really happening.'

Instead of seeing her daughter as a confused and emotional woman, Princess Alexandra saw her as a naughty little girl and with Queen Mary's strict admonishments still ringing in her ears, according to Marina, she 'turned her mouth into a kind of snarl' and ordered her to get married immediately or have an abortion.

'Dad said that if I had the baby without getting married it would change history and bring disgrace on the monarchy,' Marina explained. 'He said there hadn't been an illegitimate birth in the Royal Family for a hundred and fifty years. My father loves being married to a Royal. He has always gloried in it.'

To the misfortune of all involved, Marina felt too confused and distraught by her parents' attitude to act rationally. She felt the weight of the Family bearing down on her. Instead of talking it over with her relations, she told all to a national newspaper.

'My intention was just to get my side of the story across,' she explained. 'I wasn't doing it out of revenge.'

Angus and Alexandra's world fell apart when they read their daughter's allegations in the newspaper over the next few days. Marina left no stone unturned when she described how they had never been there for her, how her father drank too much, how all they cared about was their devotion to 'Crown and country'.

Sir Angus countered by admitting that they had let Marina down, that they had failed her. 'When a child grows up and behaves in a certain manner you can only look to that child's parents if blame is being apportioned. And we must take the lot.'

The damage had been done, however. 'We thought about my parents and how it would affect them and we discussed it endlessly, but I just wanted the baby,' Marina remembers. 'I was very upset they never accepted Paul—the atmosphere [at home] was unbearable.'

Relations between Marina and her parents were not properly mended. They appeared for the wedding, but not for the reception. The only person from Marina's childhood who was there was eighty-two-year-old Nanny Rattle. 'Where Marina goes, I go,' she said defiantly. Angus and Alexandra did not see their first grandchild, Zenouska, who was born on 26 May 1990, until the baby was fifteen days old, and her brother, with whom she was once so close, hasn't spoken to her since the wedding. Other members of the Royal Family have ignored

Marina, even her favourite godfather Prince Charles, who supported her over her Operation Raleigh mission. He sent her a bitter-sweet present that Christmas. It was a copy of his own book, *A Vision of Britain*, inscribed with a message that told Marina off for causing trouble.

The trap of royalty had opened, and Marina had been dropped through. A member of 'The Family' remarked when I asked if Marina had been invited to Lady Helen Windsor's wedding: 'Marina who?'

But they had reckoned without Marina's determination to create a secure and happy family life for herself, her husband and Zenouska. By self-righting irony, Marina chose to bring up her daughter in a conventional manner and send her to private school. Like most parents she and Paul wanted the best for their child, and although it was some way from their semi in Teddington, Middlesex, they started her at the same Montessori school near Windsor that her cousin Princess Eugenie attended. They did not, however, give in to the convention of having a nanny. 'Paul's changed nappies since day one,' Marina said. But when it was announced that she was expecting her second child in the middle of June 1993, she admitted they would need some help.

The news of the second pregnancy provoked Marina into talking about a reconciliation with her parents, who hadn't seen Zenouska since she was a fortnight old. 'I don't want anything material from them,' Marina said. 'I just want us to be friends and them to support us as a family. I'd like there to be some harmony. I don't understand how my mother can go to church each Sunday and yet not find it in her heart to forgive.'

Freddie and Ella

P rince and Princess Michael of Kent were dining at home. Their 'guests', in the panelled dining room of their seventeenth-century manor house in Gloucestershire, had not changed for dinner. They were in their dressing-gowns.

The conversation that particular evening in the summer of 1992 was about football, a subject about which one of them, a fair-skinned, large-eyed young man, was very knowledgeable. The other, a young golden-haired girl, was obviously tired. Turning to their elegant hostess she asked if she could be excused, explaining that she had to get up early the following morning to go riding.

The 'guests' were Lord Frederick and Lady Gabriella Windsor, the then thirteen-year-old son and eleven-year-old daughter of Prince Michael and his wife, the former Baroness Marie Christine von Reibnitz. And those evenings around the dining table are what the Princess calls an 'important' part of their education. During the school holidays, and if their parents are not hosting a more formal dinner party, they are allowed to stay up for supper to learn 'the art of conversation'. And if Gabriella failed the test that evening, there would be many other occasions for her to polish up on it. For although they will not have to fulfil a round of royal duties when they grow

202

up, their royal pedigree ensures they will never have the privilege of anonymity.

Both Freddie and Ella are titled according to a provision made by George V, who decided in 1917 that the change from prince to commoner would be too sudden if there were not the cushion of a minor honorific to help those lesser branches of the Royal Family on their way. Both children were brought up to understand that although they are not Royal Highnesses, they are still the children of a Prince of the Blood and will have many of the privileges associated with being a member of the reigning house.

'We say to them, "Never forget people look to you to set an example",' Prince Michael explained. 'Sometimes it works, sometimes it doesn't. But the children are conscious that high standards are expected of them.'

Lord Frederick was born on 6 April 1979 in the Lindo Wing of St Mary's Hospital in Paddington nine months and one week after his parents' wedding in Vienna. The Queen's gynaecologist, George Pinker, delivered the baby. He was baptized Frederick Michael George David Louis in the Chapel Royal of St James's Palace. Prince Michael's sister, Princess Alexandra, and his nephew, the Earl of St Andrew's, Marie Christine's cousin, Prince Karl zu Schwarzenberg, and her Austrian friend, Mrs Jacqueline Geddes, were the godparents.

The service was an Anglican one. When Prince Michael married the Roman Catholic Marie Christine he automatically lost his right to the succession as a consequence of the Act of Settlement 1702. By law, their children would have to be brought up in the Church of England and would also thereby retain their right of succession. 'It was not "our decision" as is often written,' said Marie Christine. 'We were not in a position to *make* a decision.'

Home for Freddie, as he was called, was the attic nursery suite of his parents' grace and favour apartment in Kensington

Palace designed by Sir Christopher Wren. Its windows looked out over a courtyard. He was cared for by 'a really remarkable' Norland-trained nanny called Jean Rowcliffe, who had once been employed in the nursery at Buckingham Palace, but had then enrolled in the famous Berkshire school in order to improve her career prospects.

Norland College had contacted the Princess when she was three months pregnant and informed her that they had an outstanding pupil who would be qualified by the time her first baby was born.

'I was so overwhelmed by being pregnant I had not yet thought of getting a nanny,' Marie Christine recalled, 'so I said "Yes please". When Jean arrived for an interview, I immediately liked her.'

Jean, a 27-year-old Canadian from a large family, arrived at Kensington Palace in April 1979 and stayed for six years. Among the royal neighbours she was known as 'that wonderful nanny'. Prince and Princess Michael showed her their confidence by allowing her to run the nursery in her own remarkable way.

'We were older parents,' Princess Michael explains, 'so we didn't do too much experimenting. But Jean was fresh out of Norland and their prize pupil, so we let her get on with it. I do not recall changing a nappy once and I don't think I ever pushed the pram!'

On 23 April 1981, almost exactly two years after Freddie was born, Marie Christine gave birth to her second child, again in the Lindo Wing of St Mary's Hospital. One of the first people to see the newborn girl was her brother, by then an enquiring, precocious two-year-old. Both Marie Christine and Michael were anxious that their son should not be jealous of the new arrival, and had made an effort to try and prepare him for the discovery that he would no longer be the centre of attention by assuring him that the bulge in his mother's tummy was a new playmate.

'He came to the hospital the next day,' Princess Michael remembered, 'and looked at the worm swaddled in its plastic cot. He just looked at it and said with the greatest disappointment in his shrill childish voice, "I can't play with that!" But when he reached into the cot and discovered the baby had given him a little present, a little model car he had long been wanting, he declared she might not be such a bad thing after all!'

Lady Gabriella Marina Alexandra Ophelia Windsor was christened as her brother had been in the Chapel Royal of St James's Palace. Her godparents were King Constantine of Greece; Lady Elizabeth Anson, sister of the photographer, the Earl of Lichfield and a cousin of the Queen; Prince Hugo Windisch-Graetz, a cousin of Marie Christine's; and Princess Alexandra's daughter Marina Ogilvy (a choice which, according to Princess Michael, 'her mother wanted very much').

Ella's birth coincided with the engagement of Lady Diana Spencer to the Prince of Wales. The world was gripped by Di-mania and everything from her hairstyle to her sapphire engagement ring was being copied. Members of the Royal Family were in great demand and the glamorous Kents were no exception. As soon as she had recovered from the birth, Princess Michael resumed her round of royal engagements.

She loved her children, but she did not want to be with them all the time. Like many women, Princess Anne amongst them, she found them more interesting as they matured and preferred to leave the everyday baby care in the hands of her nanny, with Ruth Wallace, who later worked for the Princess of Wales, standing in for Jean on her days off.

'I couldn't even cope for two days a week,' Marie Christine admitted. 'I'm very impatient and think it's important that a child doesn't see you being irritable. You have to be a patient person to deal with a young child's mentality and I am not.'

Prince Michael had recently exchanged his military career for full-time employment in the City, and although the apartment in Kensington Palace was grace and favour and cost them little to run, Nether Lypiatt Manor, which they bought in 1980 for £300,000, cost almost as much again to refurbish. As a second son, Prince Michael is not eligible to receive any monies from the Civil List, and the expenses of doing official royal duties have always been met out of their own pockets.

'Of course it is a burden,' the Princess told me, 'but we manage. Our hefty expenses are staff, cars, stationery, postage and the telephone. The telephone never stops ringing.'

As children, neither Prince nor Princess Michael knew their fathers—Princess Michael's had parted from her mother when she was a baby. They were none the less determined not to overcompensate for that by spoiling their own children.

Prince Michael was certainly no New Age husband, but he did enjoy nursery teas and romping around on the floor. And he liked reading to his children and, when they were older, playing word games like Scrabble with them. Each day the Prince and Princess had what they called 'quality time' with their children pencilled into their daily programme.

'It was usually teatime,' the Princess recalls. 'They would come downstairs after their nap looking clean, tidy and scrubbed. They'd be all bright and bushy tailed so in a sense they'd give us quality time too.'

Once the children started school (at the Norland Nursery in Notting Hill Gate, followed by Queen's Gate for Ella and Wetherby for Freddie), 'quality time' fell in the late afternoon. Homework was left to the supervision of Nanny, who according to Marie Christine had Freddie reading *The Times* newspaper at three and spelling 'almost every word in the English language' by the time he was five.

'I'm not eager to force them to do things at a younger age than they should,' Princess Michael said, 'but if they are keen, I let them. Freddie is hungry for knowledge, while Ella is more laid back, which I think is the right way round—intellectual girls can be an awful pain at times.'

One aspect of their childhood that their parents considered most important was that the two children should be good friends. Marie Christine was close to her own brother, and Prince Michael to his elder sister, Alexandra. Ella and Freddie were encouraged to be protective of each other and to show genuine concern for other people, something Marie Christine credits entirely to Nanny Jean. When they went for walks with their nanny around their 'little world' of Kensington Palace, they were taught politely to greet the policeman on duty, the milkman, the gardener and all the other members of staff they encountered.

' "Show concern", Jean used to say in her charming Canadian lilt; "Freddie Windsor, show concern",' their mother recalled.

Nanny's teachings left their mark and even the Prince of Wales once remarked on Freddie's good manners, muttering to himself that he wished William and Harry were the same. When Ella broke her leg in a skiing accident in 1992, however, the two young princes were her first visitors. Marie Christine recalls: 'William and Harry came for five minutes clutching a bunch of daffodils for Ella. They just popped in, gave her a hug and a kiss and went out again. So kind.' Her first delivered flower arrangement came from Prince Charles.

Ella enjoyed being pampered after her accident, and was very brave about staying in bed for four months flat on her back. Unable to ride, play tennis with her friends or even run, she missed her schoolfriends despite the attention at home. 'A Taurean, she's determined, but has the sweetest nature,' her mother observed, adding: 'Ella's sort of "somewhere else" much of the time. Deliciously vague, and the funniest thing unless you are the one trying to get her to the airport on time!'

On the matter of how best to deal with her children's royal background, Marie Christine said: 'I've not been tougher on them because of who they are and I've not been more lenient either. I'm rather indulgent, but at the same time there are rules and those rules have to be kept. I just think over-indulged, spoilt children are insufferable and I won't have mine behaving like that. They eat what's put in front of them, and they say "Yes please" and "no thank-you" and get up when someone comes into the room. Good manners are for everybody, and I would have brought them up in exactly the same way, no matter whom I married.'

Being married to a prince of the royal blood did create certain uncomfortable pressures, however. In 1985 it was disclosed that Marie Christine's father, like all enlisted German men, had once been a member of the Nazi party. In the ensuing furore Marie Christine and her husband found themselves under intense media scrutiny. Freddie was only six, but was bright enough to understand that something awful was going on. It was an early lesson in the pitfalls of royal life, and ever since then they have made a point of explaining things to their children in order to protect them.

'Knowledge is power,' says Marie Christine, 'and knowledge of self invaluable. They have quite a healthy suspicion of the media, because in their experience the media tells lies.'

When the children went to boarding school—Freddie attended his father's old preparatory school, Sunningdale; Ella was at Godstowe, an all-girls junior school in High Wycombe—they were allowed 'a certain number of newspapers, so they read not only about us, but also about other members of the family, and it can be quite hurtful.'

Prince Michael said: 'We try not to show them anything, but at school little children talk. Sometimes they come home rather tight-lipped, and when I ask what is wrong, it all comes tumbling out. You discover they have been got at or teased about something and that upsets them. But life isn't fair, you have to accept it.'

'I tell them that they also have to be better behaved, because they can't get away with the things that other children might just get away with,' Princess Michael added.

The subject of what exactly is fair and what isn't sometimes bothers their young minds. 'Children have this great obsession with what is fair,' Princess Michael said. 'I say to them, "Is it fair that you have this lovely house to live in and another in the country? Is it fair that you're healthy? Is it fair that you go abroad on holidays to ski or whatever, and other children don't?" I mean that's "not fair" either. If you're one of the lucky ones who "have", then you have an obligation to help those who "have not". I think they are getting the message.'

Both Freddie and Ella were slightly in awe of their forceful mother, and once they discovered their life was easier if they did what she wanted, they usually did it. 'I'm a non-stop nag,' she said. 'And I think at times they become numb hearing me too.'

Both Prince and Princess Michael feel strongly that apart from unlimited unconditional love, a good education, self-discipline and good manners are the three greatest gifts you can give a child. These advantages, they hope, will one day allow Freddie and Ella to move from the Buckingham Palace balcony into the crowds below with easy dignity. The object of parenthood, they argue, is to develop in the child the faith and inner strength necessary to deal with whatever life might throw at them.

Freddie, who spent a year at school in France perfecting his French grammar and conversation, had certain hereditary advantages apart from his royal pedigree. He was bright enough to gain a scholarship to Eton. His parents are very proud of that achievement, as Eton, under the head-mastership of Dr Eric Anderson, ceased to be a bastion of the old-boy network and reverted to being a school noted for its high academic standards which only offered places to those intelligent enough to pass the entrance exam, regardless of their parentage.

Prince Michael said: 'His housemaster is a rugger-playing classical scholar—a splendid combination! Freddie loves football and is very knowledgeable about the game. He's very single-minded and a linguist, but he does have an academic bent and might become something of a historian. I want both children to have done lots of things at school and had the experience of different things in life.'

On a formal level, he is keen for Freddie to go to university and, later, to acquire a knowledge of business. Ella, meanwhile, is encouraged in whatever area she shows talent—at this stage, mostly artistic.

'They have wonderful conversations with their father,' Marie Christine said. 'He's very patient with them, while I'm rather twitchy and impatient.'

Matters of discipline their father leaves to his wife. She believes in immediate retribution and punishment by deprivation. When he was young, if he misbehaved Freddie would not be allowed to watch a football match on television, or would have the plug pulled out of his computer game. Princess Michael's theory is that all children have some favourite game or toy, and if that is the very thing they are deprived of when they are badly behaved, they seem to respond very quickly.

Horses and riding consumed much of Ella's youthful enthusiasm. She first sat on a pony at the age of three, screamed with delight and soon became a keen rider with a pony of her own. During the school holidays she was happiest in the stable yard, cleaning tack or grooming her pony, and the highlight of her summer holidays was going to Pony Club camp.

Freddie didn't much care for horses. He preferred motorized

horse power. Michael, a former rally driver, did not believe that his son had inherited his love of speed, but Frederick was none the less taught to drive at the age of eleven and both he and Ella enjoy driving his father's old Mini round the private roads of the Queen's Windsor estate.

That is one advantage of being a part of the Royal Family. But Freddie and Ella do not have access to one of the greatest advantages of all—the royal fortune. They, like their Kent and Gloucester cousins, will have to make their own way— armed with the good manners and the conversational adept-ness their parents have made such efforts to instil in them.

David and Sarah

O f all the royal children, Lady Sarah Armstrong-Jones and her brother David, Viscount Linley had most reason to feel emotionally confused.

When Antony Armstrong-Jones, a photographer from *Queen* magazine, married the Queen's sister and became the Earl of Snowdon, society was convinced the union would never last. It didn't, but the two children from Princess Margaret's eighteen-year marriage survived their upbringing and emerged comparatively unscathed.

'I don't know what it means to have the Queen as an aunt,' David Linley said. 'I just consider them as family.' There were certain advantages thrown in, of course.

David Albert Charles Armstrong-Jones, Viscount Linley of Nymans, was born into the family on 3 November 1961 at Clarence House. The small Kensington Palace apartment his parents occupied immediately after their marriage was considered unsuitable for a Caesarean birth. The Queen Mother was at her daughter's side. The infant, weighing 6 lb 4 oz, took the title Viscount Linley, after his paternal great-grandfather, Linley Sambourne, and was christened in the Music Room of Buckingham Palace on 19 December, with the Queen, Lady Elizabeth Cavendish, Lord Plunket—then Master of the Queen's Household—Lord Rupert Nevill and the Reverend Simon Phipps, later the Bishop of Lincoln, for godparents.

Before their marriage, Margaret and Tony had discussed the possibility of having children and decided they didn't want any. Margaret liked children, but the responsibility of motherhood didn't appeal to her. 'After we got married Tony changed his mind,' she said. 'So I gave him two children.'

In the early sixties, London was a 'swinging' city and Margaret and Tony were in the cultural vanguard. They dined in trendy Italian restaurants frequented by the new working-class elite, like actors Michael Caine and Peter Sellers. They went to parties with pop stars, amongst them the Beatles, whom Margaret greatly admired 'because they were poets as well as musicians'. John Lennon irreverently called her Priceless Margerine, and Lord Snowdon Bony Armstrove. The rest of their set simply called them 'the Snowbums'.

Sometimes their avant garde life appeared to interfere with their parental duties. Only seven weeks after their son was born they were to be found revelling in Antigua in the West Indies. One newspaper report went so far as to label the princess 'callous' for leaving her baby behind in the care of a nanny. She was simply following royal tradition. And despite the press criticism, Margaret was a far more affectionate mother than her background would have led people to believe.

On one issue, however, she was immovable—the nannies—and her children were entrusted to Nanny Sumner, a nanny of the old school who provided them with their stability in a somewhat rocky household.

When Nanny went to stay in the Queen's homes she was disliked by some of the other staff because she was extremely fussy and very demanding. She did not get on with Mabel Anderson—the feeling was mutual—and they fought their genteel battles in the nurseries of Balmoral, Sandringham and Windsor.

'There was a lot of tension between them,' a former member of staff remembers. 'They were very formal with each other but had their breakfast separately even though the nursery quarters at Balmoral are quite small. It was like two rival camps.'

Every summer Tony and Margaret partied in Europe with their sophisticated friends while Nanny stayed with the children at Balmoral in Scotland. The Queen liked having them there, and when Margaret gave birth to a second child, a daughter, on 1 May 1964, it was not long before the infant was seconded into the Highland nursery, while her parents were transported to Porto Cervo on the Costa Smeralda in the Aga Khan's private jet.

The infant, Sarah Frances Elizabeth Armstrong-Jones, was christened on 13 July, in the Private Chapel at Buckingham Palace. Her godparents were Lady Penn, sister of *Queen* magazine's former proprietor Jocelyn Stevens; Jocelyn's now ex-wife Jane, who became one of Margaret's ladies-in-waiting; Miss Marigold Bridgeman, the elder sister of artist Gerald; the Earl of Westmorland; and Antony Barton, a friend of Tony's from his Cambridge University days. It was a jovial group that wet the baby's head with champagne in the Queen's Gallery after the ceremony. Behind the smiles, however, doubts about the future of her marriage were already building in the princess's mind.

Despite those strains and the seemingly endless round of parties, Margaret proved herself to be a good mother. Once her pregnancies were over—both births were by Caesarean—and she had lost some of the excess weight she gained, she settled down well to the routine of motherhood.

On her doctor's advice she breastfed her babies for the first few weeks of their lives and formed the fashionable 'bonding'. If they started crying in the night she would be the first up—

if she had gone to bed—and much to Tony's annoyance took Nanny's side on everything.

The continual presence of Nanny Sumner irritated Snowdon. He had little respect for the formality of nursery routine and insisted on seeing his children when he wanted to. Once, much to Nanny Sumner's fury, he woke David at ten o'clock in the evening just to tell him off for some misdemeanour committed during the day.

On another occasion when he was 'having a go' at Sarah, he could see she desperately wanted to go the lavatory. She kept crossing and uncrossing her legs as she listened to her father's ticking-off. He wouldn't let her leave the room until he was finished and by that time the poor child was in tears of embarrassment—again to Nanny's intense annoyance.

He disapproved of the long-term retention of a nanny for the two children, who he felt should be allowed to stand on their own feet. Margaret disagreed and argued the children must keep the one stable thing in their life. Without ever having read them, she subscribed to the theory of child psychologists Mussen, Conger and Kagan, who said that by the age of two the love that a little child has for its nanny can be one of the most important emotions in its life. By then, they argued, 'a child's feelings acquire the strength and variety of adult love'.

Not unnaturally, Nanny Sumner could not stand Snowdon and they never spoke, passing each other in the corridor as if they didn't exist. Not that Snowdon's Bohemian theories about bringing up children were unkind. It was just that they were very different from Nanny's. He did not believe that children would develop to their limits if there was always a nanny on hand to pander to them.

He believed, for instance, that toys had always to be constructive. That stemmed in part from his own experiences at

Eton where boys were banned from having radios or gramophones in their rooms unless they had made them themselves, which he did. He applied that principle to his own children, and as both his children testified, the early encouragement he gave them stood them in good stead.

As a very young child David would watch his father in his workroom at Kensington Palace. 'I used to stand beside him and then started making things myself at school, putting together small Christmas presents for the family,' David recalled.

Notwithstanding Margaret's famous remark, 'My children are not royal, they merely happen to have the Queen for an aunt,' that meant a lot of presents. For the two Snowdon children were an integral part of the Royal Family.

At the age of five, David started lessons with Prince Andrew in the large Buckingham Palace schoolroom. The cousins, twenty months apart, tolerated each other, but did not really get on well together until they were adults.

Sarah, on the other hand, was always very close to Prince Edward, with whom she shared lessons with governess Lavinia Keppel.

The Queen was very fond of her sister's children and took them under her wing as the quarrels between Margaret and Tony intensified. It was the Queen who taught Sarah to ride—on a silver Palomino pony presented to them by Peter Sellers—and it was the Queen who helped give them the semblance of a secure background.

In 1973 the Snowdons went to Italy on a family holiday. It was to be their last. Almost as soon as they arrived, Snowdon lapsed into one of his silent moods. He was either late for meals or didn't bother to turn up at all, and was rude to Margaret in front of the children.

'Papa, Mummy is talking to you,' one of them would say.

'I know,' was the only answer.

At the end of the first week Snowdon packed his bags and

returned to London, leaving Margaret and the children to continue the holiday alone. The effect of this squabbling had a predictably detrimental effect on twelve-year-old David and nine-year-old Sarah, both of whom were protective of their mother and very attached to their father.

According to psychologist Penelope Leach, younger children, who are unable to fathom much of the reality of an adult relationship, tend to assume that they were the cause of the problem. It is difficult for a child who is the centre of his or her own life and thinking to believe that they are not similarly the centre of their parents'. 'Furthermore,' Leach says, 'much of the friction which they have seen has often involved their own behaviour—their noise or their discipline, their mother's spoiling or their father's neglect—so they easily see these accumulated small issues as the cause of the crash.'

David's school work suffered and it became apparent that his poor grades at Ashdown House, his pre-preparatory school, would not get him through Common Entrance, let alone into Eton, his father's old school. It was decided to send him to Millbrook House near Abingdon, which specialized in tutoring boys to pass their Common Entrance. The idea of Eton was abandoned and instead he was entered for Bedales, a co-educational school in Hampshire, best known for its arts and design centre.

It was a happy choice for David and his sister, who joined him after completing four years at Frances Holland near the Sloane Square end of Chelsea's King's Road. They both flourished in the relaxed informal atmosphere of the school where freedom and responsibility were both given and the progressively-raised pupils ran their own committees. Careers were discussed as part of the general curriculum and no one seemed to take any undue notice of Princess Margaret's two children.

It was at Bedales that David and Sarah came to accept that

their parents could not be happy together, would henceforth lead their own lives and would eventually divorce (a step that had caused the children much initial concern). In March 1976 a formal statement to that effect was issued by Buckingham Palace.

Under the terms of the separation, Lord Linley and Lady Sarah, then aged fourteen and eleven respectively, were to remain at Kensington Palace with their mother, while Lord Snowdon, on whom the princess had agreed to settle a six-figure sum, was to be granted free access to them.

It was the prelude to one of the worst periods of Margaret's life, dogged by bad health and bad publicity, particularly over her friendship with Roddy Llewellyn, a young gardener sixteen years her junior. She was subject to severe bouts of migraine, and flu prevented her from attending her daughter's confirmation on 5 April 1978. For Margaret, a deeply religious woman, who had sought solace in her faith after her romance with Peter Townsend ended, to miss so important an occasion was very upsetting and she issued a statement explaining her absence. It stated: 'Against her personal wishes, but on the strict advice of her doctors, the princess was prevented from attending the service.'

Tony was there, however, with David, who had been confirmed three years earlier in St George's Chapel at the same time as Prince Andrew. Her royal cousins, Prince Edward, Lady Helen Windsor, and James Ogilvy joined Sarah and were confirmed before the Archbishop of Canterbury, Dr Donald Coggan.

At the lunch party afterwards at Windsor Castle, where all the children's numerous godparents were present, Margaret was allowed to look in for a short time. Guests noticed how drawn and thin she appeared. A few days later it was discovered the princess had hepatitis.

If it was a difficult time for Margaret, it was also hard on her children. As well as the health problem, there was also the procession of men who were not their father to contend with. Sarah's attitude towards Roddy Llewellyn, according to Margaret's authorized biographer, Christopher Warwick, 'was ambivalent. She accepted Roddy because of her mother'.

She was always polite, though, just as Nanny Sumner had taught her to be. Nanny's influence was felt by David too, although he had been somewhat more rebellious. Once out of his adolescence, when he had been rather imperious—he once demanded of a footman at Balmoral that he immediately mend the puncture in his bicycle and return it to him within the hour—he proved he knew how to behave.

'I believe in old-fashioned courtesy and manners,' he said. 'It makes me laugh when people wonder whether they should open a door for a feminist. I would.'

Professional to the last, Nanny Sumner had not allowed her dislike of Snowdon to manifest itself in front of 'my children', as she referred to them, and they both grew up adoring their father. He in turn was proud of them both, especially when Sarah's artistic talent began to reveal itself.

'It became obvious when she was at Bedales school that she was quite good at painting, art and design.' Snowdon said. 'Sarah is a very creative person.'

When Snowdon first took his daughter to Venice, he told her the only way to see the 'best city in the world' was without any people, 'so we got up at four o'clock in the morning and roamed around Venice together enjoying the buildings. St Mark's Square was breath-taking in the early light.'

Sarah was very much her father's girl. He taught her to ski and took her on boating holidays along the vast networks of English canals, and when the divorce came through in 1978 and he married Lucy Lindsay Hogg, he included her in his new life by later making her a godmother to their daughter Frances.

She was still the Queen's niece, however, and while being not quite royal did get her work attention that might otherwise have been denied so early in her career, it also had its drawbacks. She never liked the round of glitzy parties enjoyed by her friend and cousin Lady Helen, and used to complain, 'No one wants to date me because of who I am.'

That was not true, but after the very public break-up of her parents' marriage, it would be remarkable if she had not been left with some insecurities. According to George Hatton, however, who first taught Sarah art when she was at Bedales, she was 'the most normal, down-to-earth character you could meet. She made nothing of her royal background. We never pried. Yet you knew that she'd been up painting and sketching at Balmoral and Sandringham during the holidays.'

Inheriting his mother's acerbic wit and strong character and his father's small stature and artistic temperament, David developed quickly. His early obsession with distancing himself from the Royal Family and making his own way in the world earned him praise, but left him confused. He admits he was always trying to please his parents, especially his father, and felt guilty that he was neither an academic nor keen to go into the army as his mother wanted. He had no interest in the Services and was not of a temperament that would have enjoyed an evening's bawdy banter in the ship's wardroom, as did his cousin the Duke of York.

'I suppose I have inherited bits of both my mother and father,' Linley said. 'They are both artistic. My mother has great taste. Both of them taught me an invaluable lesson—always look at things, always be inquisitive. Some people go through their whole lives without looking at things properly.'

The events of their childhood opened both David's and Sarah's eyes wide. But if it made for a painful upbringing, it also provided them with the foundation on which to build their own careers—he as a carpenter, she as a painter.

David and Sarah

Princess Anne once remarked that she knew of parents who did 'everything right', only for their offspring to turn out 'wrong'. And she knew of others who did 'everything wrong' but whose children turned out 'right'. She could well have been referring to the Snowdons.

Peter and Zara

Motherhood was an inconvenience to Princess Anne. She resented being pregnant because it curtailed her riding activities. She heartily disliked the fuss. And by her own admission, she 'wasn't particularly keen on children'.

'Being pregnant is a very boring nine months,' she said. 'I am not particularly maternal,' she continued, adding, in her typically matter-of-fact way, 'It's an occupational hazard of being a wife.'

When, on 15 November 1977, one day after her fourth wedding anniversary, she gave birth to a 7lb 9oz son in the Lindo Wing of St Mary's Hospital, she didn't feel an overwhelming rush of 'mother love'. Her lack of enthusiasm over the baby was compensated for by her husband, Captain Phillips, who was with her throughout her labour—and by the Queen.

When the Queen heard of the birth of her first grandchild, she was about to conduct an investiture of people who had been granted titles and medals. The baby was born at 10.46 and the investiture scheduled to start at 11, but she was so overjoyed she delayed the ceremony for an unprecedented ten minutes while she recovered her composure. Prince Philip, who was in Germany, was equally pleased. He admired his forthright daughter and had always been very close to her. He was convinced motherhood would soften her edges and give her another dimension to her life.

Peter Mark Andrew Phillips, as the baby was to be known, was fifth in line to the throne and the first royal baby to be born to a commoner for five hundred years.

Anne, who firmly believes she is a princess only by accident of birth, was adamant she would not accept titles for her children. It was for that reason that Mark refused the Queen's offer of an earldom. Anne has always rejected the idea of ennoblement for reasons other than notable achievement and disapproved of Antony Armstrong-Jones's elevation to the Earldom of Snowdon following his marriage to Princess Margaret in 1960. Everything about Anne and Mark's domestic life was calculated to distance them from the 'royal' aspect of their lives and in spite of the Queen's pleadings, Anne stood firm. She nourished the ambition that her children should be able to take up whatever career they wanted, without always being dogged by their royal heritage.

Commoner or not, Peter had a special place in his grandmother's heart. Normally undemonstrative, the Queen was always picking him up, much to the amusement of her Household, who had never seen her touching anything other than her dogs with such outward affection.

Anne and Mark's no-nonsense approach to their firstborn reflected itself in their choice of godparents for his christening on 22 December in the Music Room at Buckingham Palace. His godparents, apart from his uncle, Prince Charles, were close friends: Captain Hamish Lochare and the Right Reverend Geoffrey Tiarks on Mark's side, and Lady Cecil Cameron and former equestrian, Jane Bullen, now Mrs Timothy Holderness-Roddam, on Anne's.

Back at Gatcombe Park, the Gloucestershire home the Queen gave them as a wedding gift, the warren of attic rooms had been transformed into a nursery suite with its own bedrooms, bathrooms, sitting room and kitchen. The furniture, mostly from the old nursery wing at Sandringham, was comfortable and cosy.

Royal nanny Mabel Anderson arrived shortly after the New Year. Mabel, whose duties at Buckingham Palace were virtually over, had been asked by the Queen if she would like to help look after baby Peter and establish a proper nursery for Anne. Her appearance, along with the sound of her Roberts radio tuned to Terry Wogan on Radio 2, completed the familiar picture. She soon established her routine and, apart from having to lay the nursery table for meals instead of having her own footman do it, seemed to adapt to country life. It was a young, happy household where even the butler wore jeans and the wellington boots stood in silent formation in the stone-flagged hall alongside the pram.

Anne's less than notable fervour for motherhood did not mean she was not a good mother; quite the reverse. She was. She just approached motherhood differently from someone such as the Princess of Wales.

'The assumption that everyone wants a child and will love it from the moment it is born is responsible for a great deal of unhappiness,' child psychologist Penelope Leach has observed.

Anne agreed. 'You don't actually have to like children very much to be interested in giving them the best possible start in life,' she said. And one way to achieve that was by having nanny Mabel there. If Anne didn't have the patience or the will to play the devoted mother, she was intelligent and shrewd enough to allow someone else to do the job for her.

During the next four years Anne experienced all the usual and some of the more unusual difficulties associated with working mothers. Her seemingly limitless energy enabled her to juggle her time between her child, her husband and her increasing number of royal engagements with some dexterity.

'Whether I'm getting the balance right or not I'm not sure,' she said. 'It's too early to say. I've been a princess all my life, but I've become a wife and mother comparatively recently.'

When the occasion demanded, Anne put being a wife and mother first. At harvest time, for instance, she put aside her royal duties and stayed at home. Everyone, including the household staff, helped in the fields, while little Peter trotted about on the fat pony he had been given. Prince Edward and sometimes Prince Andrew would come along to spend the days in the fields and the evenings around Mabel's nursery fire, which Mabel insisted be kept burning even if it was eighty degrees outside. It was as if nothing had ever changed.

'It was very informal,' a former member of the household remembered. 'It was a smart farmhouse which just happened to have a princess that lived in it.'

When Peter was four years old, Anne found she was expecting another baby. Mark was relieved; during their seven-year marriage they had stayed together by staying apart and he hoped the baby would bring them closer. So did the Queen when they told her at a belated fiftieth birthday party held for Princess Margaret at the Ritz Hotel in London. News of royal babies travels fast and the following morning Buckingham Palace was inundated with calls. There was only one problem. Mark Phillips's parents didn't know.

Anne was close to her mother-in-law and anxious for her to hear the news before she read about it. The difficulty was that Anne Phillips and her husband, Peter, were on holiday in a remote Cornish cottage without a telephone. Eventually Anne contacted the local police to ask if they would send someone round with a message to telephone her 'urgently'.

The communication got through, and shortly afterwards a worried Mrs Phillips was on the line from a local callbox.

'What is it?' she asked.

'Thank goodness I reached you,' Anne replied. 'I'm pregnant!'

On 15 May 1981, in the Lindo Wing of St Mary's Hospital, Paddington, she gave birth to a baby girl. She weighed 8lbs 1oz and was delivered by the Queen's gynaecologist, George Pinker, at 8.15 a.m. That evening, in the unglamorous surroundings of the fourth-floor Lindo Wing, the Queen took her first granddaughter from her perspex cot beside Anne's bed and held her gently. Like her brother, the baby had no title, but she was eighth in the line of succession.

In contrast to her feelings after the birth of her first child, Anne was besotted with her daughter. Guests were dragged off to see the baby in her cot or Anne would wheel the pram around the garden whilst chatting to them. Because of what Anne describes as 'her somewhat positive arrival', they named the baby Zara, meaning 'bright as the dawn'. According to Anne it was Prince Charles who thought of the name, when he visited her in hospital and she told him about the infant's early and noisy entrance into the world. Her other names were Anne, after Mark's mother, and Elizabeth after the Queen.

The godparents were again selected from amongst their closest friends, and apart from Prince Andrew included no royal relations. Colonel Andrew Parker Bowles, who lived nearby with his wife Camilla, and equestrian Hugh Thomas, who had been in the 1976 Olympic team with Anne, were the other godfathers; the Countess of Lichfield and former world champion racing driver, Jackie Stewart's wife, Helen, the godmothers.

Two months before Zara was born, nanny Mabel Anderson had decided it was time for her retirement. She had fulfilled her promise and brought up Peter Phillips—and coped with the informality of Gatcombe, to which she had never totally adapted. The absence of a nursery footman, a nursery maid and her own chauffeur had not deterred her unduly, but she felt a second baby would be too much. Mabel's life had revolved around the royal children for thirty-three years. It was time to fold away her stiffly starched uniform. South Africa beckoned and Mabel handed over the nursery reins to a northerner, Pat Moss, who was brought in, not to take over, but to share the duties with her royal employer, who started taking a decidedly unroyal practical interest in her children.

If anyone had told her she would actually enjoy changing nappies and prefer to be bathing a baby than out riding, Anne would probably have told them to 'naff off', but Zara had stirred her maternal instincts. It did not mean she loved Peter any less; it was simply that she felt more protective about Zara.

As the children got older and their childish pranks naughtier, it was Anne who dished out the discipline. She was stricter than Mark, though not obsessively so. If the children were noisy when they should have been quiet she would shout and tell them to shut up, but she did not mind their childish mess—or when Peter clambered on top of the piano in his wellingtons. If they did irritate her, however, she had no qualms about slapping them—even in public—and packing them off to bed.

The Queen, who loved having the duo to stay, was equally firm. She might have been a doting granny, but she was a strict one too. 'She was always chastising them,' a rating on board *Britannia* remembered. 'I've even seen her shake Zara when she's been naughty.'

That happened when Zara was caught running up and down the stairs. 'Don't do that,' said the Queen. When Zara carried on the Queen grabbed hold of her and shook her.

On Nanny's day off, Anne would look after the children herself. She would go upstairs in the morning to wake them, then dress them and prepare them a cooked breakfast. If it was a weekday either their policeman or Mark would then take them to school, while Anne made the beds and tidied up the nursery. If it was a weekend they would all go riding together, staying up in the stable yard until lunchtime. Mark would take over when they came home, playing hide-and-seek or rolling about with them on the floor. He had no qualms about playing childish games or teaching them to ride. Nor did Anne.

From the start Anne refused to be influenced by public opinion in the way she brought up her children. 'If you start down that road there's no end to it,' she said. 'You must do what you think is best for your child.' For a farmer's wife that meant country pursuits and country schools. And so it was that the Queen's first grandchild, the great-great-grandson of George V, began his education, not with a governess in the peaceful atmosphere of the Buckingham Palace schoolroom, but at a local nursery school in Minchinhampton.

Zara followed him there and fitted in so well that for some time other mothers with children there did not realize who she was. Staff were at pains not to single Zara out as someone special. 'I treat Zara just like all the others,' the headmistress said. 'She is a lovely little girl—and just like any other child of her age she can be a rascal. She has made lots of friends and is very popular and she really enjoys learning.'

Like most four-year-old girls her favourite lessons were music and movement, and the only hint that there was something different about her was the presence of one of the ubiquitous royal detectives. Zara followed Peter to Blueboys school in the same town. She stayed there until its closure in 1989, when Anne moved her to the more upmarket Beaudesert prep school. By this time Pat Moss had left and been replaced by a less traditional nanny, Sarah Minty, who helped around the house and on the farm when the children were at school.

'I think the Queen found this rather alarming,' says a former member of the Household, 'but Anne wanted to deal with the children herself.'

'You've got to be completely objective as far as children are concerned,' Anne explained. 'Consider the personality of your child and try to work out what's going to be the right thing for him or for her at the end of the day.'

The right thing for Peter and Zara, she decided, was a co-educational prep school, Port Regis, near Shaftesbury in Dorset. Both she and Mark felt the school suited the strong personalities of their children. Peter started there as a boarder aged seven, and Zara four years later when she was eight. The Phillipses liked the headmaster, David Pritchard, whose ideas on bringing up children were similar to their own.

Despite her royal duties—Anne carried out eighty-four royal engagements the year Zara was born and 168 the year after, plus her Save the Children trek—Anne still found the time to be with her children. Her extraordinary physical energy allowed her to work all day, get home, change into jeans, cook supper for the children, and then help them with their homework without turning a hair (not that that ever worried the fashion-unconscious princess).

While Mark snoozed in front of the television, Anne struggled to help Peter and Zara with their prep. 'To try to help my children to read was actually very difficult,' she confessed. 'I was concerned that I was doing them a disfavour, because my logic worked differently from theirs.'

Whatever skills they lacked in the schoolroom, Peter and Zara made up for outside. They both learnt to ride as soon as they could walk and by the age of four were quite capable of managing without a leading rein. Their life revolved around country pursuits and at weekends, instead of being left behind with Nanny, they went with their parents wherever they were going.

Sometimes they misbehaved and sometimes their mischief

made headlines, as when Peter, much to his mother's silent amusement, turned on the pursuing photographers and yelled at them.

'Shove off, you spastics,' he is reported to have said to one photographer, but no one could confirm if it really was Master Phillips in full cry or one of his friends.

When the children joined the Gatcombe Park shooting parties, their presence caused criticism amongst anti-blood sport groups. One year Peter, then aged seven, carrying a toy pistol of his own, swung a dead pheasant round and tossed it into the air. Five years later Zara, dressed in a miniature Barbour jacket and wellies, was helping to pick up dead birds when she discovered an injured one. Unable to kill it, she stamped on its head unsuccessfully—and once again the League Against Cruel Sports spoke out. The headlines ran: ANNE'S GIRL STOMPS ON PHEASANT'S HEAD! Anne took no notice. The Royal Family, like most country people, take a fatalistic view of the balance between man and nature. Dealing with guns and dying birds was regarded simply as part of their training. And while Zara was not all sweetness—she could be a 'bossy little madam' as one of the staff recalled—she was not cruel. She was just being brought up as her parents wanted— as a country girl.

Living in the rural retreat of Gloucestershire did not stop Zara from enjoying dressing up, and when the Queen gave her granddaughter special permission to attend the Royal Ascot meeting in July 1989, the eight-year-old proudly wore, 'a blue spotted dress with a straw hat', carried a tiny handbag and looked immensely pleased with her grown-up self.

In the days before Zara and Peter formed firm friendships of their own, they saw a lot of their cousins William and Harry. Gatcombe Park is not far from the Waleses' country home, Highgrove, and Diana would ensure the children had tea together every few weeks—especially if Anne was away.

When the Waleses' entourage was due to arrive at Gat-combe everyone was apprehensive. The little princes would arrive flanked by a back-up car and two detectives, looking, as one guest observed, 'as if they were going to a party in Belgravia,' with carefully pressed shorts and shiny leather shoes. Anne's offer of a trip to the stables was greeted with enthusiasm by the boys, 'less so by their mother, who never managed to bring their wellingtons.' For all Diana's efforts, however, William and Harry would always return to High-grove as dishevelled and muddy as boys like to be.

When the Prince and Princess of Wales both came over, which they occasionally did for a shooting weekend or birthday party, the house was thrown into turmoil. Three back-up cars with armed police would race up the drive and when they arrived no one was sure what to do. Charles was very particular and everything in his bedroom had to be just right or he made a fuss. He had no time for Mark and he was rather awkward with his godson, Peter.

'He was rather bemused by children,' a member of the Household remembers. 'He was not a natural like Mark Phillips. Instead he would try and be funny in that Goonish sort of way which children don't respond to. He would affect strange voices which would tend to frighten them rather than encourage them to play.'

A few years ago, one of Anne and Mark's guests was unable to join the shoot and they were racking their brains to think of a local substitute who they knew well enough to ask at the last minute.

'What about Wales?' someone helpfully suggested.

'Oh no!' Anne said, 'he's far too grand.'

'Too grand?' the perplexed guest piped up. 'But you had the Queen and the Duke of Edinburgh last weekend!'

'The trouble is,' Anne said, 'the Queen and Prince Philip aren't grand and Charles is.'

In spite of their differences, however, brother and sister get on well and they have been supportive of each other during their respective marital problems. But like her father, Anne has little time for the minutiae of protocol. She also has the self-confidence of her father and, knowing how important it is, has tried her best to develop it in her children.

Her no-nonsense approach to motherhood meant she always treated them as mini-adults. She taught them to enjoy the things she enjoyed like riding, sailing and shooting. She also impressed upon them the importance of good manners, though, like their mother, they did not always reach the exacting standards set for them.

And she always tried to work out what was best for them.

'The child must come first,' she said.

She believes that a child's home life has a greater influence on it than school and, like Prince Charles, believes in the importance of parental example. Even during the height of their marital discord, Anne and Mark tried to adhere to that creed. They never rowed about their children and they never rowed in front of their children. They tried to be the ideal parents, but they weren't the ideal couple.

When Anne first discussed the possibility of a separation with the Queen, her mother's first concern was her grandchildren. She couldn't understand why Anne couldn't stick it out, as she had done herself for so many years. The Queen liked Mark—she admired his horsemanship—and Prince Philip saw him as an achiever. Until Prince Charles married in 1981, Mark's parents were always invited to Windsor for the Christmas celebrations. Anne Phillips and the Queen had more in common than just their grandchildren, and the two women would meet at Chelsea Flower Show and dine at Buckingham Palace afterwards.

Princess Anne was not to be swayed, however, and the couple were finally divorced in 1992. They still made every effort, none the less, to remain on amicable terms for the sake of their children, and continued to put on a show of togetherness when the occasion demanded. In September 1991, for instance, when Peter started at what is now the Royal Family's alma mater, Gordonstoun, his parents drove him there and spent almost three hours at the school—before leaving in separate cars. Peter, who had already displayed his prowess at sport, settled in well—certainly better than his uncle Charles.

The divorce did not cause any noticeable disruption in Zara and Peter's life. They had been brought up with a father who was frequently abroad on business and a mother whose royal duties and work for the Save the Children Fund took her away from home for long periods. And when they were all together, Anne and Mark always made an effort to shield their children from their own problems.

When Anne married Commander Timothy Laurence in December 1992 they appeared to adapt very well to this change in their domestic circumstances. The only real difference now was that their father, instead of living in the big house with them, was based nearby at Aston Farm, two miles away, but still part of the 730-acre Gatcombe estate. Peter and Zara continued to see as much of their father as they had before. He had unlimited access to them and they joined him for as many holidays as his work schedule permitted.

Anne's efforts to keep her children out of the limelight, while letting them know the limelight is there, seem to have paid dividends. She conceded that it is perhaps too early to judge, but there was enough evidence to suggest that you don't have to be someone who has always yearned for children in order to be a good mother—and that a rigid and lonely regime is not the only way for a princess to raise her children.

William and Harry

〜

iana is a tactile mother. She is forever embracing and cuddling her sons. She holds their hands and vows they will never suffer the kind of childhood she did. She was a product of what is now known as a dysfunctional family, the survivor of emotional abuse, which according to today's psychologists is a very real form of child abuse. She is determined that William and Harry will never lie in their beds frightened, lonely and confused, as she did. 'A child's stability arises mainly from the affection received from their parents, and there is no substitute for affection,' she said. Whatever happens in her rapidly changing world, they come first.

In that she is like millions of other young mothers with two lively and occasionally naughty boys to contend with. She misses them 'like mad' when they are away at school, writes to them at least twice a week, and longs for their misspelled Sunday letters in return, with their schoolboy lack of detail. And she has resolutely stuck to her avowed intention—to bring up her children in as 'ordinary' a way as possible. Unlike her mother-in-law, who also had the same intention but whose definition of the word was always circumscribed by her royal position, 'ordinary' means precisely that.

Diana was not raised in a royal palace surrounded by courtiers. Her childhood was certainly privileged, but it was not constrained by that suffocating commitment to appearances and *form* that marked royal as opposed to aristocratic upbringings. She had been allowed to make friends and get dirty; to show emotion, to cry (indeed, there were times when it had been hard to stem the tears); to pursue her interests to the best of her abilities.

For all Philip's innovations, the ghost of old Queen Mary still seemed to be stalking the corridors of Buckingham Palace, watching over her royal descendants. Diana was only three and a half weeks past her twentieth birthday when she married Prince Charles in St Paul's Cathedral that summer's morning in July 1981. She belonged to another world, and would find it difficult to come to terms with life as a member of the Royal Family. Her relations with her husband would cause her enormous and very public problems. On matters pertaining to her children, however, Diana was insistent on having her own way, right from the start.

By tradition royal babies were born at home, usually a royal one. Diana, like Anne, broke with that convention. William was born in the private Lindo Wing of St Mary's National Health hospital in Paddington. His mother had her own room, but it was neither large nor luxurious. The bed was standard hospital issue. The walls were covered with dull floral-patterned paper. And though she had windows on two sides of her room, the view, out over the rooftops and down on to a dirty back street, could not be called scenic. The bathroom was across the hallway.

That was the way Diana wanted it. Her doctor, George Pinker, surgeon-gynaecologist to the Queen, did not subscribe to home births. And Betty Parsons, who helped thousands of women in childbirth with her relaxation techniques and assisted the Queen at the birth of Prince Edward, held that if complications were to arise a hospital was the best place to deal with them. That was a good enough argument for Diana, and on 21 June 1982 she was duly delivered of a son weighing 7 lbs, 1½ oz. 'He has a wisp of fair hair, sort of blondish, and blue eyes,' Charles proudly told the crowd waiting outside.

Diana was back there two years later to give birth to Prince Harry.

They were not easy confinements. Diana, like many first-time mothers, believed in 'natural' childbirth. William's arrival changed her view; after several hours in labour she had to be given an epidural injection to relieve the pain. Harry's birth, his father remarked, was 'much quicker'. Even so, it still took nine hours, which prompted Diana to say, 'If men had babies, they would only have one each.'

The results were worth the effort, though, and Diana, still a child herself in many ways, took pride and maternal comfort in her sons. Seeking compensation for the lack of stability and affection in her own childhood, she was intent on building a secure and loving home for her children. Charles respected this. Raised in a matriarchal family, always closer to his mother than his father, Charles had decidedly old-fashioned views on a wife's duty. 'Although the whole attitude has changed towards what women are expected to do, I still feel, all the same, at the risk of sticking my neck out, that one of the most important roles any woman could ever perform is to be a mother,' he said. 'And nobody should denigrate that role. How children grow up, what attitudes they have, are absolutely vital both from the social point of view and for the future. And all this stems so much from the role the mother performs. I know it's awfully difficult nowadays because women want to work and have to do so, to earn enough. But the role of the mother is so terribly important.'

From the beginning, Diana was determined to exert her authority in the upbringing of William and Harry. If she did not do so, she knew she would lose them to a system she neither liked nor understood, but she was still very much a newcomer to royalty and had to tread warily. The choice of godparents for William was very much Charles's—Princess Alexandra; the Queen's lady-in-waiting, Lady Susan Hussey; ex-King Constantine of Greece; Lord Romsey, grandson of Earl Mountbatten; the South African mystic Sir Laurens van der Post, in whose philosophy and story-telling ability Charles placed such great store; and the Duke of Westminster's wife, Tally, the only one of the six who was anywhere near Diana's age.

When it came to Harry, however, Diana insisted on having the final say, and his godparents were Carolyn Bartholomew; Princess Margaret's daughter, Lady Sarah Armstrong-Jones; Cece, Lord Vestey's second wife; Prince Andrew; old Etonian farmer Gerald Ward; and artist Bryan Organ, who had painted Diana in 1981.

Charles was an enthusiastic father at the beginning. A child, he mused, in the manner of Laurens van der Post, 'is the culmination of who knows how many thousands of years and the genetic make-up of your ancestors.' He read copiously on the subject of how best to bring up children, including Betty Parsons' amusing guide, *The Expectant Father*, which advised him how to help and encourage his wife. Always on the look-out for some guiding truth, he developed his theories on how best to bring up children.

'I would like to try and bring up our children to be well-mannered, to think of other people, to put themselves in other people's positions, to do unto others as they would have done to them,' he said. 'That way, even if they turn out to be not very bright or very qualified, at least if they have reasonable manners they will get so much further in life than if they did not have any at all.'

Charles seemed to be implying by that remark that intelligence and qualifications were of secondary importance, and in a sense they are. The Royal Family is judged on the way it conducts itself on public and state occasions, not by its academic prowess. To be able to stand still for hours on end, to make small talk with complete strangers, to appear dignified in even the most undignified of situations is more important, as old Queen Mary astutely pointed out, than an ability to pass a bookkeeping exam. To acquire those requisite royal manners—'simple, old-fashioned values for survival', as Charles called them—takes training of a disciplined, old-fashioned sort associated with a traditional British nanny.

'There are some experts who were very certain about how you should bring up children.' Charles said. 'But then, after twenty years, they turned round and said they'd been wrong. Think of all the poor people who had followed their suggestions.'

One of those experts was Diana's distant relation, Dr Benjamin Spock, the most influential advocate of the new permissive attitude towards child care. He would later recant many of his theories. By then, however, his *Common Sense Book of Baby and Child Care*, first published in 1946, had become the authoritative home reference work, its call for a closer, more compliant relationship between parent and child the accepted orthodoxy even amongst people who had never read it. And Diana was one of those 'poor people' who had every intention of doing exactly what Spock had advised.

The arguments between husband and wife started almost as soon as William was born. Charles wanted to name his son Arthur Albert. Diana objected and the child was christened William Arthur Philip Louis instead. On the subject of nannies she was also adamant. Her own experience with them had left her with unhappy memories. 'A mother's arms are so much more comforting than anyone else's,' she said.

Charles had wanted to employ his old nanny, Mabel Anderson, who, along with Helen Lightbody, had played such a significant role in his young life. Diana vetoed the suggestion. Mabel, she argued, was too old and too traditional. If she had to have someone—and it was pointed out to her that because of her public duties she needed someone to help her look after the children—it would be someone of *her* choice, someone who agreed with her ideas.

Charles, keen to do what his valet called with exaggeration 'anything for a quiet life', gave way, and Barbara Barnes was duly hired. She was the first royal nanny not to have at least two footmen and two housemaids to help her.

'I'm here to help the Princess, not to take over,' Barbara tactfully announced.

The daughter of a forestry worker, Barbara came to the Waleses on the recommendation of her previous employer, Lord Glenconner, whose wife, Anne, was a lady-in-waiting to Princess Margaret. Calm and capable, she had an easy manner which children responded to, and she got on extremely well with her young charges. Possibly too well, for one of Diana's less laudable characteristics is her jealousy. Always possessive, she even secretly came to envy the early rapport Charles established with his sons.

Charles had revived the ritual of bath-times and, unlike his mother, who used to sit majestically on her chair to view the proceedings from a splash-free distance, Charles made a point of joining William for his evening bath to encourage him to get used to it. One night when they were both due to go out for an engagement, Diana couldn't find Charles anywhere. She eventually discovered him in the bath with William.

'They were having a great time,' she said. 'There was soap and water everywhere.'

Diana approved, but only for a time. As the difficulties in her marriage developed into a chasm, she came to regard him as a poor father and those moments of tenderness as nothing more than paternal window-dressing. 'Charles knows so much about babies, he can have the next one,' she once irritably remarked.

That was unfair. He does not find it easy to communicate with young children who respond to the person, not the position, and his Goonish jokes and funny faces frightened as often as they amused. With his own kin, however, he established an intimacy he had never enjoyed in any relationship and he derived immense pleasure from it. It was Diana he had the problem with.

At the same time her relationship with Nanny Barnes started to fray. Not in any obvious way, but the atmosphere at the Waleses' London home in Kensington Palace changed. Diana wanted her sons to herself and came to see Barbara as a potential rival for their affections. A feeling of tension crept in.

The final parting came shortly after Barbara had flown to the West Indies just before Christmas 1986 for the sixtieth birthday party her former employer, Lord Glenconner, gave for himself on his private island, Mustique. She was photographed enjoying herself in the company of such fellow revelers as Princess Margaret, Jerry Hall and Raquel Welch.

Charles, as a defensive mechanism designed to safeguard his own sense of dignity, had become something of a stickler for the finer observances of royal protocol. One royal servant observed, 'He will not sit down at a table unless it is correctly laid. If there is a speck of dust on the cream, for instance, he will ring the bell and have it taken away. He is waited on hand and foot in a way that is almost obscene.' In this cloistered world nannies had their place—and it was not being photographed on a beach in the West Indies. He also became irked at the way people would compliment his nanny, as if he had nothing to do with his sons' manners and generally personable behaviour.

In the end it was Nanny herself who decided that it would be better for all concerned if she left. On 15 January 1987 it was announced that Barbara Barnes would be leaving the royal employ. The statement was timed to coincide with William's first day at his new school. 'I thought no one would notice,' Diana later said, 'but I was wrong, wasn't I?' She was. The British press, sensing a story, put the news of Barbara's departure on page one, and relegated William's arrival at pre-preparatory school to the inside. In fact the parting, all speculation to the contrary notwithstanding, was amicable. Barbara was consulted about her replacement and was given a grace and favour home in Kennington. She continued to exchange Christmas and birthday cards with the Waleses and their sons. She left simply because her term of employment had run its natural course and William's arrival at Wetherby in West London had seemed the ideal moment to make the break.

The young prince had already had a taste of life on the other side of the Palace walls and in that Diana had again taken the lead. When she had visited the Young England kindergarten in Pimlico where she had taught before her marriage, William had been dispatched to play with the other children. They were playing 'Galloping Horses', but he did not know how to join in that game of putting one foot in front of the other and clip-clopping around the room. Incidents like that convinced Diana, as sensitive as her son to any feeling of being 'different', that William would greatly benefit from mixing with others of his own age.

Young England was too far away and Mrs Mynors' nursery school in nearby Notting Hill was selected. 'His classmates hardly know who he is,' Mrs Mynors commented. That was not strictly true. He was soon informing his classmates, 'My daddy's a real prince.' In a fit of temper, he once threatened an adversary with all the Queen's horses and men—his grandmother's.

For William and, later, Harry to have been kept in ignorance of their position was simply an impossibility. The escort of detectives and the palaces and the subservient attitude of those who came into contact with their parents inevitably made an impression on their young minds. As one member of staff pointed out, 'There is nothing normal about those children—there is nothing normal about having two back-up cars wherever they go.'

Nor was that awareness to be entirely discouraged. However 'ordinary' their parents might wish their sons' childhoods to be, they *were* royal, and the best way to learn how to deal with that was from the earliest possible age. As their mother's adjustment problems testified.

But if their future was unquestioned, the manner of their education was not. There was consultation. In the end, though, it was Diana who had the deciding voice. 'She is very good at getting her own way,' her father observed.

William and Harry were not first taught at home by a governess, but instead started their schooling at a nursery school. They then went to Wetherby and then on to Ludgrove, a preparatory boarding school in Berkshire where Henry Hansell, who was tutor to George V's children, was once a master. They did not attend Cheam, Charles's old school, and Diana argued vehemently against Gordonstoun.

It was a clear break with royal tradition—and her husband. In the British upper classes it is almost invariably the father who makes the final decision in the choice of schools for a son. In this family the father was overruled. As one of her royal relations remarked: 'She's the strong one in the marriage—especially when it comes to the children.'

There was another sign of Diana's resolve to break free from the constraints of royal convention and that was in the all-important area of clothes. The Royal Family, with the loud-checked exception of the Duke of Windsor (and he was hardly an example to follow), have always been careful to eschew high fashion. Their clothes, down to the length of the women's hemlines and the cut of the men's suits, have been determinedly conservative, as befitting a family which sees itself as the guardian of conservative values.

Diana changed that. She turned herself into a fashion plate—much to the chagrin of the Palace old guard who believed that by dressing like a soap star she was devaluing the currency of majesty. But high glamour none the less became Diana's style and she dressed her sons to reflect it. Abandoning the velvet-collared coats and short trousers of her husband's youth, she had them wearing striped T-shirts by Jean Bourget, sweatshirts and corduroy trousers from Benetton and Osh Kosh dungarees. For one photo session at Sandringham in the winter of 1988 she turned out William and Harry in matching pale blue coats trimmed with white and fastened with mother-of-pearl buttons. She had the design copied for her by Catherine Walker, but this was one occasion when her fashion sense deserted her; when she and William later appeared in their his-and-her outfits, she was exposed to exactly the kind of ridicule she always went to such pains to avoid.

She was on safer ground when she insisted on taking William with her to Australia when he was only a few months old. The Queen and the Queen Mother had both left their young progeny behind when they had visited the Antipodes and this separation of mother and child had become the established custom. Diana was a strong believer in 'bonding'. She refused to leave her newborn in the care of nannies as her in-laws had, and it was a wet, wailing and jet-lagged infant prince who accompanied his parents to Woomargama in the Australian outback with a supply of food supplements, fluoride drops and multi-vitamins.

Diana's possessiveness sometimes bemused Charles, who was conditioned to put duty before family. He could share her feeling of loss when Harry followed William to Mrs Mynors'. 'It made me feel very sad—I had a big lump in my throat when we left Harry,' he said. He understood why Diana, as she put it, 'dived into the Kleenex box' when William left home to go to Ludgrove. ('It's quite something putting one's eldest into school,' she wrote to a friend, 'but William seemed quite confident about everything.') These were emotional set-pieces which echoed his own childhood experiences. But on general issues—how much time they should spend with their children, where to take their holidays—they were moving ever further apart. It was a sour overspill from their marital problems, and sometimes a focus for them.

Michael Shea, the Queen's former press secretary, said: 'The only arguments they had were over the children.'

William and Harry were two decidedly different characters who reacted to these strains in their own way. William, a bothersome baby much given to tears, a troublesome infant who took delight in throwing shoes into lavatories, was always portrayed as being adventurous and forceful; his brother as sweet and rather shy. In the beginning that was true. William had always seemed the more anxious of the two to get out into life, to make friends, to make the explorations expected of a little boy, while Harry had a tendency to hang back. At Mrs Mynors' Harry had hidden in the playground and refused to join the other children in their playground games, and had been too embarrassed to hold up his hand in class to be 'excused' to go to the lavatory.

That changed as they grew older. Harry fought his way past the troubles in his parents' marriage to become a confident and rather mischievous boy, better at riding and skiing than his brother. 'Harry's the naughty one, just like me,' his mother said.

The younger prince had a particular fondness for the flora and fauna of the countryside and took pleasure in his menag-

erie of pets, as both his mother and father did when they were
young. When one of the pet ducklings he kept at Kensington
Palace went missing, the worry was that it had wandered next
door and been devoured by Princess Michael of Kent's cat.
One of the policemen was sent on a search and rescue mission.
It was found unharmed in the care of Princess Michael's secretary.

'Harry loves animals and plants,' his father observed.
Charles tried to pass on his New Age philosophy to his son.
'I tell him all about them and say they have feelings too and
mustn't be hurt.'

That does not extend to the field sports so beloved by the
Royal Family. Charles rides to hounds, stalks stag on the
Balmoral estate, and shoots pheasant at Sandringham. It is
not an interest he shares with his wife. She is not an enthusi-
ast. She allowed William and Harry to join the large weekend
shoots at Sandringham because they are such an established
royal tradition, but when Anne once suggested taking the boys
out shooting herself, she firmly said no.

It was not a decision William would have questioned. For
all his initial boisterousness, he was a sensitive youngster who
intuitively picked up the tensions. He was very close to his
mother. 'William is a very self-possessed, intelligent and ma-
ture boy and quite shy,' said his uncle, Charles, now the 9th
Earl Spencer. 'He is quite formal and stiff.' It was William
who always tried to take care of his mother in her moments
of crisis, and Diana's friends remarked how she spoke to her
eldest son almost as if he was an adult; how mother and son
held hands and cuddled each other frequently.

'I want to bring them security,' she said, explaining her
approach to motherhood. 'I hug my children to death and get
into bed with them at night. I always feed them love and
affection—it's so important.'

Especially to William and Harry, who could not help but

be aware of their parents' unhappy relationship. William, being pre-adolescent, became alternately attention-seeking then introverted, consumed with the idea that his mother's unhappiness might be his own fault. When she locked herself in the bathroom to cry uncontrollably, he tried to help by pushing tissues under the bathroom door. When he was away at school where telephone calls are not allowed, he never missed an opportunity to speak to 'Mummy'. Once during the summer of 1992, when the scandal surrounding the Princess was at its height, he begged to be allowed to use a friend's parents' mobile car phone, 'just to call Mummy'.

William tried to become what is known in psychological terms as 'a controller'—a little child, burdened with his family's distress, trying manfully to carry all the problems on his own shoulders.

The granddaughter of children's author Roald Dahl, Sophie, whose own young life was scarred by similar scenes of familial conflict, says: 'To start with the publicity made me feel important because Mummy was in the newspapers. But then I started to think, "How could they do this to Mummy—and why didn't Daddy protect her?".'

For William it was the hardest, cruellest training for the job he was born one day to inherit. For whatever feelings he may have had, he still had to behave in the way his position demanded. Sometimes the strain became too much. 'I don't want to be a king,' he told a schoolfriend that miserable summer. 'I want to be a policeman.'

Both boys, however, had the good manners their father wanted, politely shaking hands, writing thank-you notes, coming down in their dressing-gowns to say goodnight to whatever guests their parents might be entertaining at Kensington Palace or Highgrove, their country house in Gloucestershire.

There had been a few early difficulties. When Bob Geldof

called at Kensington Palace to discuss the famine problem in Africa with Charles, William took one look at the perennially dishevelled Irishman and declared, 'He's all dirty. He's got scruffy hair and wet shoes.'

The iconoclastic Geldof retorted, 'Shut up, you horrible little boy. Your hair's scruffy, too.'

. 'No, it's not,' William replied, taken aback by the visitor's outspokenness. 'My mother brushed it.'

It was the kind of exchange William was discouraged from repeating. His nannies would not allow it. Diana's early reluctance to entrust her children to the care of someone else had been modified by necessity and after Barbara Barnes left she 'poached' Ruth Wallace from Prince and Princess Michael of Kent. Next was Jessie Webb, who had worked for the Duchess of York's interior decorator, Nina Campbell, for fifteen years. Giving consistency to these domestic arrangements was Olga Powell, who had started as under-nanny at the same time as Barbara Barnes. All were 'old-fashioned' nannies, in the sense that they subscribed to the notions of routine and order and, of course, to the 'Ps and Qs' and the general politeness expected of any 'well brought-up' child.

As Dr Charles Lewis of Lancaster University explained: 'However fraught the parents' relationship might be, and however often they are absent from home, a loving nanny can stabilize the situation for the children and fulfil the parents' role quite happily.'

There was inconsistency in Diana's approach to discipline, however. A couple of years ago, when William was in the Royal Mews at Buckingham Palace, he was about to get into one of the carriages when he delivered a sharp kick to the leg of the footman helping him in. Diana was very angry and immediately slapped him on the bottom. Yelling with hurt pride, William clambered inside the carriage and sat next to his mother, sobbing. His tears made her feel so guilty, she immediately picked him up and cuddled him, so negating the punishment she had just administered.

Her wish not to spoil her sons was equally fraught with contradiction. Diana tried not to spoil them as she and her brother had been by two parents who had tried to buy their affection. At Christmas they were given a Hamley's toy shop catalogue and asked to tick the presents they wanted. 'It makes you very materialistic,' Charles Spencer remembers. But executing the good intention not to spoil her children proved very difficult for Diana. She asked her friends to give them books instead of toys, but the gifts still showered their way. Barry Manilow the singer gave Harry a valuable five-inch antique baby piano, and Jaguar presented William with a miniature motor car which he crashed into the garage wall. And when it came to things like parties, Diana, for all her good intentions, could be equally indulgent.

One year William had a tea party in the inset house of London Zoo. Smarty Arty, the entertainer much favoured by the well-to-do of London society, was usually hired to provide the entertainment. In 1992 ex-King Constantine gave him a cowboys and Indians birthday party at his home in North London. Diana wore a cowgirl outfit; Charles, who is an honorary Indian chief and has the full regalia, including the feather bonnet, confined himself to a stetson, while both William and Harry wore cowboy outfits. It was at the height of the speculation about the royal marriage, but Charles and Diana presented a united front in the presence of the children. 'You wouldn't have thought anything was the matter,' said Smarty Arty, who was there to organize the games, dressed as the big fat cowboy. 'They both joined in all the games like running with a plate of water and appeared to be thoroughly enjoying themselves. At another fancy-dress party, this time at Christmas, William dressed as Michael Jackson while Harry went as a Ninja Turtle, complete with shell.

Although Charles and Diana attended these family celebrations together, the problems in their marriage were never far from the surface. She tried to arrange her schedule to fit in with her children; he would not cancel an engagement or alter an arrangement and sometimes chose to stay away from home for weeks on end. And as they grew ever further apart, an element of what looked like malice crept into their relationship. She would go out of her way to upstage him. He in turn took cold delight in upsetting her.

When Sergeant Barry Mannakee, her former bodyguard, whom she had grown particularly fond of, was killed in a motor accident, Charles did not tell her straight away. He waited until the car that was taking them to an official engagement came to a halt. Then, just as she was opening the door, he said, 'Mannakee's dead!' and pushed her out.

Such incidents only heightened their conflict, which came to a public head when William was rushed to hospital in 1991.

A group of boys, accompanied by a master, were walking along, swinging their golf clubs, when the lad in front of William swung his club over his shoulder, catching William full on the temple. Without having time to press the emergency bleeper on his wrist, William fell to the ground with blood pouring from his head. No one knew how badly he was hurt and Graham, his detective, put the emergency plans into action, alerting the Royal Berkshire Hospital with one call and the Princess of Wales with another. Within minutes William was in an ambulance on his way to the Royal Berkshire Hospital in nearby Reading. Transferred to the Great Ormond Street Hospital for Sick Children in London, he was operated on under a general anaesthetic for a depressed fracture of the skull.

Charles and Diana had hurried to his bedside—she from a luncheon at the San Lorenzo restaurant in Knightsbridge, he from Highgrove.

Diana insisted on staying at the hospital during the operation. Charles left to attend a performance of Puccini's opera, *Tosca*, at Covent Garden where he entertained a party of European Community officials. It was, he insisted, his duty—and in the Royal Family duty always comes before any personal consideration. Diana was appalled by what she saw as his callous indifference to the plight of their son. He accused her of overstating the severity of the injury—of playing the role, not of princess, but of drama queen. The British public appeared to take Diana's side. The *Sun*, in one blazing headline, summed up the argument that raged in the newspapers for several days afterwards: 'What kind of dad are you?' it asked. Not a very good one, it concluded.

Once he was better, William enjoyed the attention showered on him. He accompanied his mother to Wimbledon—both he and Harry have had tennis lessons from former champion Steffi Graf—and was allowed to invite whoever he liked out from school. Unlike his father, who was very much a loner, William has always been popular and able to deal with the inevitable teasing that comes his way. The other boys are protective of him, especially his few special friends. When he wrote to one of them after the accident, he asked them to be sure to lock the letters away so they didn't fall into 'enemy hands'. If they are questioned by their parents, William's pals dismiss him with a shrug of their shoulders. He's good at games, loves football and plays in the under-11s team, they say—and nothing more.

William is bright. His exam results are pinned in the corridor at Ludgrove along with the other boys', and he is usually in the top half of his year. Since Harry's arrival at school, William has been accused of flexing his muscles and was said to have held a fellow student's head down the loo and flushed it. This punishment, William reckoned, was fair enough for someone telling tales, but despite his royal status William was hauled before the headmaster and warned not to repeat the feat.

Harry is popular too, but only with his contemporaries. The older boys find him just a bit too self-assured and cheeky. But the school has a reputation for smoothing the rough edges of its pupils and no doubt they will encourage Harry to assume a sense of humility.

Even with the hounds of speculation baying at their heels, Charles and Diana have always tried to put on a united front when they are all together. They have done what they can to shield their sons from the unpalatable and all-too-public enquiry into their marriage, and in that they have been helped by the schools.

The headmaster of Ludgrove, Gerald Barber, and his wife Jane take great care of their young pupils—whoever they are. They are allowed to take a favourite teddy or cuddly toy back to school, but radios are forbidden. There are no newspapers available at the school, and last year the boys were more interested in the current craze for brightly coloured key-holders and how many different items they could hang from them than reading about the problems of William and Harry's parents.

As Prince Michael of Kent would observe, however, bad news has a way of filtering through. If the children didn't gossip, their parents certainly did, and Diana found herself wary of almost everyone. She would laugh to observe how some of the parents fawned around her, bowing and curtseying when she came into the dormitory—she called them affectionately the 'nods and the bobs'—but she didn't trust them.

It was the constant backdrop of William and Harry's childhood. It would leave an indelible impression on both of them. But from her own experiences Diana knew that however poor the relationship between the parents is, most children would prefer them to stay together. It was not to be. In December 1992 it was announced by the Prime Minister to the House of Commons that the Prince and Princess of Wales were to separate officially.

William and Harry were at school. Charles and Diana went to see them to break the news. They went separately. It was the first taste of their future.

Their Christmas holiday that year was divided between their parents—with the royal side of their family taking precedence. They spent Christmas Day at Sandringham with their father who, anxious to reassert his parental position, had re-employed his old nanny, Mabel Anderson.

'It's just like old times,' said the Queen.

When they rejoined their mother she went one better than the dull flatlands of Norfolk and whisked them off to the Caribbean. The difference in the holidays was symbolic of the different interests and contrasting priorities of their parents. But Diana insists she will not be pushed into the background.

She is their mother and is determined to have her say in her sons' upbringing. If there is one inheritance she can give her children, Diana has constantly reminded her friends, it will be to allow them to grow up in an emotionally healthier and less deceptive environment than she did herself.

Beatrice and Eugenie

he Duchess of York once confided to me that she hated pregnancy, that she didn't want to breastfeed, that she just wasn't the 'mumsy' type.

As with many women, the arrival of her children changed her attitude. She became deeply attached to her daughters. And the end of her marriage to the Queen's favourite son drew her even closer to them.

'They are the only thing in my life that I know is one hundred percent safe, loving and wonderful. They are my world,' she said, as she contemplated life without a husband.

In a real sense, Sarah was always a single parent. As a serving officer in the Royal Navy, Prince Andrew was away from home for months at a time and in 1990 only managed to spend forty-two days with his family. When their first child was born, Andrew's ship was in the Far East. He flew back from Singapore the day before the birth. Two weeks later he was back with his ship. For the birth of their second child just over a year later, he made it just in time, though Sarah wasn't sure if he would make it at all until he actually arrived.

'I don't like it,' Andrew said, 'but you just have to take it otherwise the Navy wouldn't exist.'

When their marriage broke up, Sarah said, with feeling, 'Never marry a sailor.'

She might have added, 'Never marry a member of the Royal Family.' Adapting to the disciplines and restrictions of royal life proved to be beyond her. Being married to someone whose own royal upbringing made him insensitive to those problems eventually proved intolerable.

On the early crest, however, of what had been a genuine love affair, and despite Sarah's initial reservations about motherhood, the Duke and his Duchess approached parenthood with youthful enthusiasm. They declared they wanted lots of children and when a 6lb 12 oz baby girl was born on the numerically symmetrical date of 8.8.88, their marriage appeared to be settled on bedrock.

So it was, for a time. They had a large home. They employed a first-rate nanny named Alison Wardley, who had been the star pupil from the elite Princess Christian College in Manchester. They had a large staff to ensure their lives ran smoothly.

In this marriage appearances proved to be deceptive, however.

On a visit to California Sarah endeared herself to the Americans with her cheery style ('I'll see you later,' she called back to a man in the crowd, who shouted, 'I love you'), but attracted a barrage of prissy-lipped criticism in Britain from people who said that she wasn't behaving in the correct 'royal' way. Then the death of the Queen's former equerry, Major Hugh Lindsay, in an avalanche at Klosters in March 1987 had greatly upset the pregnant Duchess, who was part of that ski-ing party but had stayed behind in the chalet that fatal afternoon. Next her 'darling Dads', who had been her paternal anchor since her mother had left home when she was thirteen, was discovered patronizing a West End massage parlour. And as if that were not enough, she had to contend with a continuous barrage of criticism while her husband was away at sea.

The birth of Beatrice brought some respite. Two hundred

cameramen waited for five days outside London's Portland Hospital for the first picture of the child, who was delivered by Mr Anthony Kenney. When the Duchess and her princess finally made their appearance, it was estimated that 600 pictures were taken in the first second. The public, as it does, applauded the newest member of the Royal Family. The praise would quickly die away again.

The Yorks went straight from the hospital to Balmoral where Sarah introduced the Queen to 'Baby Yorklet' who, more formally, was fifth in line to the throne. Within a few days, however, Andrew was back at sea. He was reluctant to leave, and Sarah was reluctant to see him go, clinging to him up to the last moment and complaining that she felt like a single mother.

'He was never there for me when I needed him,' she confided later. 'And I didn't think I'd need him so much.'

Six weeks later the Duchess flew to Sydney to join him for a naval review celebrating Australia's bicentennial. Beatrice was left behind in the care of her nanny. 'When would we see her?' Andrew said, defending their decision to leave her behind. 'Beatrice is much better off at home where things are stable, there is a routine and no constant upping and changing or haring around the countryside.'

It has been the fate of all royal children to be parted from their parents for long periods of time. George VI had left the Queen and the Queen had left Prince Charles at an early age. But there was an undercurrent of public hostility towards Sarah. It was her turn to become what Princess Michael of Kent called 'bad royal', and her decision to leave her child cast her in the role.

That Beatrice was in the attentive care of a team of nannies, headed by Alison Wardley and helped by Mabel Anderson, who came out of retirement to care for her favourite baby's baby, was noted—and ignored. What had been acceptable in previous generations was not acceptable now and the decision to leave Beatrice behind provoked severe and enduring criticism.

'I thought it was more important to be with my husband,' Sarah said. 'It was his turn and I think that was the right thing to have done. I'm very old-fashioned, but he comes first.'

Andrew's only advice to his wife was to ignore the criticism. It was a sad portent for the future.

Beatrice was named after Queen Victoria's ninth and final child, who is commemorated by a cairn on the Balmoral hillside which Sarah had often walked past. She was christened four days before Christmas. By tradition, royal christenings are held in the unconsecrated Music Room of Buckingham Palace, but Sarah and Andrew insisted on holding the ceremony at St James's Palace, in the Chapel Royal built by Henry VIII.

The Fergusons, including Sarah's grandmothers, Doreen Wright and Lady Elmhirst, along with most of the immediate Royal Family, crammed into the chapel which was decorated with gold and white flowers to celebrate the baptism of the Queen's fifth grandchild, Princess Beatrice Elizabeth Mary of York. Eighteen-week-old Beatrice was kept amused by her father, who clutched an assortment of toys, a bottle and a rattle. The service at the silver-gilt lily font was performed by the Archbishop of York, Dr John Habgood. The godparents were Jane, Duchess of Roxburghe, Viscount Linley, Peter (now Lord) Palumbo and two of Sarah's oldest girlfriends, Carolyn Cotterell and Gabrielle Greenhall.

As soon as the ceremony was over, the day reverted to the usual pattern. The Queen led the guests back to Buckingham Palace for the tea, neatly laid on long trestle tables in the Bow Room where little eclairs, meringues, tiny doughnuts and sandwiches were served to guests by liveried footmen. There were four sets of royal children in attendance, all with their nannies. Princess Anne took it upon herself to preside over this regal crèche.

While the guests drank tea or champagne, Andrew and his photographic mentor, Gene Nocon, hustled various godparents and children in and out of the adjoining room for the official photographs. A photograph was taken with all the various children, including Sarah's half-sisters and half-brother, Eliza, Alice and Andrew.

'Eliza being the youngest sat next to Prince Harry and in order to make her smile they pretended Harry had a big spider and was going to put it up her leg. She didn't think it was funny at all!' recalled Sarah's stepmother, Sue Ferguson.

Fatherhood appeared to give an added dimension to Andrew's hitherto regulated life. He took pleasure in bathing his baby daughter, a task he performed with military efficiency. As Sarah's sister Jane Makim recalled, 'He rolled up his sleeves, took off his watch and washed her thoroughly before he would let me play with her in the bath.' The day-to-day responsibilities of bringing her up were left to his wife and the nanny, however, Sarah had a clear idea of how she wanted things done and she did not hesitate to tell Alison what she wanted. Alison, who had been taught never to monopolize a baby and always to allow the mother time alone with it, fell in with her employer's wishes.

'I was blessed with a super nanny who taught Beatrice everything, including how to swim almost as soon as she could walk,' Sarah acknowledged.

Because of Andrew's naval duties, special occasions like christenings and birthdays had to be fitted around his schedule. Beatrice's first birthday party, for instance, was brought forward by a month and was held on 8 July 1989 on the lawns of Castlewood House. The theme that year was ragamuffin costumes for the children, dragons for the nannies. There was a jelly pit and an inflatable bouncy castle, and catering-size bottles of mustard and tomato ketchup for the children to spill over their hamburgers.

'And how many children are coming?!' the Queen enquired of her daughter-in-law as she inspected the preparations. Sue Ferguson was about to tell her that over a hundred had been invited when Sarah got her warning kick in first and replied, 'Just a few friends, ma'ama' (a blend of the formal 'ma'am' and the informal 'mama' she called the Queen by).

As it happened, the Queen enjoyed the hearty, boisterous fun, and stayed for over an hour to watch the policemen organizing races and eventually to present the prize for the best-dressed ragamuffin. Policeman's son Geoff Padgham won a prize. From the other end of the social scale, so did one of Sarah's godchildren, Arabella Llewellyn, great-niece of the Duke of Norfolk.

At the end of the lawn were outsize cardboard figures of Terry the butler in striped trousers and Alison the nanny in her Princess Christian uniform. Holes had been cut in their faces and everyone was invited to put their heads through and have crazy foam pies thrown at them (the idea was Andrew's).

'Ronald and I volunteered to do it first to get everyone going,' Sue Ferguson recalled. 'Prince Harry and Prince William thought it was wonderful being able to throw pies at us. All the adults had to take their turn, including Prince Charles, who was a good sport!'

Unknown to the guests Sarah was pregnant again. 'It was my secret and I was determined to keep it,' she said later. It was unplanned and not exactly unwanted. But she had not enjoyed her first confinement, and having just regained her figure—and her husband—was not over-enthusiastic about the idea of starting again so soon.

The struggle with what she called 'the system'—of being

continually told what she couldn't say or do—was starting to take its destructive toll and her marriage was suffering.

'The weekends were the worst,' she said. 'Andrew was tired and had the responsibilities of being a prince, not just a serving officer or husband. He had three jobs to do and I don't think anyone realized what a strain it was.'

On Friday 23 March 1990, Sarah entered the Portland Hospital. She was hoping to have the baby induced the following day, but the baby was found to be in the breech position: its feet were facing down and its head had not engaged, and Kenney was unable to turn it as he had hoped. An emergency Caesarean operation was necessary. Andrew only just arrived in time, having driven up the motorway from Plymouth where his ship, the frigate HMS *Cambletown*, was docked.

The baby, a girl, weighing 7lbs 1½ oz, was born at 7.58 p.m. After the initial shock of the operation, Sarah, wrapped in the euphoria of the new baby, welcomed a string of visitors headed by the Queen, the Princess of Wales, and her sister, Jane Makim, who had flown over from Australia.

A week later her husband drove her home—and straight into another problem. Without telling her Andrew had arranged for Gene Nocon to take official photographs of the family group. Gene had his lights already set up, and was waiting for them when she walked through the door with the baby.

Andrew wanted Gene to have the pictures for exclusive use in one magazine, but Sarah refused and insisted they go on general release. It was not their first disagreement. It would not be their last. The photos attracted another batch of criticism. It was further evidence, to Sarah at least, that her husband failed to comprehend the problems she faced. Again he left to return to his naval duties. Again she was left to deal with them on her own. But now she also had to cope with two young children, Beatrice and her sister, Eugenie.

The name Beatrice had been inspired by a heap of stones at Balmoral. Princess Eugenie Victoria Helena was named after a painting that hung in the passage at Windsor Castle.

'I liked the name at the bottom of the picture, Empress Eugenie,' Sarah explained: There is another Eugenie picture at Windsor. It is of Queen Victoria's granddaughter, Princess Victoria Eugenie of Battenberg, who became Queen of Spain. Sarah said: 'When I told the Queen I was going to call the baby Eugenie she said she remembered Aunt Ena, as she called her, who had strawberry blonde hair tied up in a bun.' The Queen was referring to the second picture.

Eugenie, pronounced, according to Sarah, U-jean-ee, or, according to her sister, Jane, 'Me Tarzan, you Janie', was christened on Sunday 23 December 1990 in the little church of St Mary Magdalene at Sandringham. The baptism was performed during the regular Sunday service, with villagers and estate workers singing Christmas carols alongside the Royal Family.

'We all sang our hearts out,' Diana said afterwards.

The godparents were Andrew's cousin James Ogilvy, Royal Navy Captain Alistair Ross, who was away on duty, Sarah's stepmother, Susan Ferguson, and two of Sarah's 'three best friends', Lulu Blacker and Jules Dodd-Noble.

Sue Ferguson recalled the day. They drove up to Norfolk with Sarah's maternity nurse Esme Tudor 'and arrived so early we had to sit in a lay-by. We had been told to go to the vicar of Sandringham's house, where we were met by Ronald's cousin, Sir Robert Fellowes [the Queen's Private Secretary], who was wearing an old tweed suit.'

After a cup of coffee with the rector and Peter Nott, the Bishop of Norwich, they were taken in by the back entrance of the church. The godparents sat in the front pew, leaving the choir stalls free for the Queen and her family. The church was a riot of festive colour, with the choir stalls decked with chrysanthemums and holly. The altar was flanked by two Christmas trees.

The congregation rose as the Queen and fourteen members of her family, including ten of the first eleven in line to the throne, filed in (Prince Charles was in the Persian Gulf visiting the Desert Rats). Andrew and Sarah came in last carrying Princess Eugenie, sixth in line to the throne, with Beatrice running along in front.

'When she saw Eliza she ran to her pew and insisted on sitting next to her,' Sue said. 'Eugenie looked unwell. She had a high flush and Sarah told me she had a temperature and an ear infection. She was very grizzly.'

Forced into a tight, itchy christening robe designed for a baby younger than Eugenie's robust nine months, she was hot and tired and uncomfortable. She squirmed and wriggled throughout the long service and when the Bishop of Norwich finally took her from her mother and sprinkled holy water on her tiny fevered brow she started screaming.

Back at Sandringham House glasses of chilled champagne greeted the churchgoers, who had been warned by Fellowes that a television crew, filming part of the celebrations, would also be present.

'The children loved it.' Sue recalled. 'They were interviewed and asked what they wanted for Christmas. When they asked Prince Andrew he said he would like a golf bag!'

Upstairs, cockney photographer Terry O'Neill was trying to organize the christening group for the official photographs. As usual, Prince Philip was tetchy and impatient.

'Haven't you taken enough?' he kept saying. 'I can't believe anyone can take so long just to take a few boring photographs.' The Queen smiled. O'Neill, the ultimate professional, ignored Philip's rudeness and kept snapping. The real problem was Eugenie's red blotchy face, made worse by her tears.

Downstairs round tables of eight had been arranged to accommodate the luncheon party. Each member of the family hosted a table. Prince Philip entertained the godparents; the Princess of Wales entertained the children. Sarah had asked the Queen if it was possible for the nannies and Terry O'Neill to join the royal gathering. The Queen found it difficult to refuse her lively daughter-in-law and an extra table had been hastily set up. And so it was that a relief nanny, who had only arrived from Australia the previous day, found herself sitting down to lunch with the Queen of England.

After lunch, Diana took all the children into another room to watch a video. Everyone else retired to the drawing room for coffee, where the Queen and Philip discussed the merits of the menu. When the party eventually broke up some of the guests paused to stand on the scales in the front hall. It is a Sandringham tradition for the guests to weigh themselves when they arrive and again when they leave, to see how much they have notched up. Beside the scales are neatly-stacked piles of dog towels. They also form part of the Sandringham ritual.

'When we left,' Sue Ferguson recalled, 'Sarah and Andrew stood at the door and waved the dog towels. It was rather strange, but obviously a Sandringham tradition.'

Such events provide the set-pieces of royal life. Contrary to impressions, however, the Royal Family does not live in an up-market commune, one on top of the other, in everyday contact with each other. Sarah had her own home to run where she was free to bring up her children in her own way. She respected the old-fashioned virtues of manners and discipline, but also embraced the more modern approach of keeping her children around her and allowing them to be part of her life.

'I was frightfully strict about manners,' Sarah's mother, Susie Barrantes recalled. 'My own mother was brought up very strictly and correctly and I think it rubs off on you.'

When the girls asked for pet rabbits they were given them, but when they failed to look after them the bunnies were unceremoniously taken away again. And each evening, after they had had their tea, they were taught to press their hands together in prayer to thank God for their food.

Sarah, without the steadying influence of a husband to call on, was not always as strict as she might have intended to be, however, and she particularly dreaded taking them aboard *Britannia* where they had a tendency to 'run riot', Eugenie especially. Beatrice was more placid, and had shown no signs of jealousy when her sister was born, regarding her not as competition, but as 'her own dolly'.

Beatrice was the more feminine of the two. She was 'passionate' about anything pink, loved having her hair tied with ribbons and was very attached to the Disney cartoon character, the Little Mermaid. She had a Little Mermaid swimsuit, lots of pink pyjamas and nighties, and her bedroom at the rented home in Wentworth her mother moved into after she parted from Andrew was decorated with pink Nina Campbell wallpaper.

Eugenie, on the other hand, was always very independent and adventurous, though in matters athletic each was as good as the other. They learned to ride on a pony called Smokey who had also been used by Peter and Zara Phillips and the Princes William and Harry. When it was Eugenie's turn to sit in the saddle, aged two, she did so with a determined disregard for personal safety. 'Boojie', as her parents call Eugenie, set her jaw and kicked away with her little heels. Sarah jokingly called her 'my monster'.

Andrew, away so much of the time, had little direct influence on the early development of his two daughters, although he did make the effort to read to them at bedtime if he happened to be at home. His interest in his children was only patchy, however, and it was Sarah's ideas that prevailed.

'I don't believe in sending them to school too early,' she said. 'I'm against boarding school, but obviously I'll be under a bit of pressure about that, but I think home life is very important. I've got two lovely girls and what's the point of sending them to school for months on end? I don't believe its right. I think it's important to see them and teach them about life through your eyes as well.

'I like to take them away with me to see new cultures and learn. The more they travel the more they can grow and learn about people in new parts of the world. It stimulates the imagination.

'I won't let them get spoiled. Beatrice might be a little precocious, but that's the fun of children that age. She's got her own character and I'm not going to squash it. She goes everywhere with me when it is possible to take her and I speak to her on a one-to-one basis. I don't talk down to her. She's my friend and we talk about everything.'

Her stepmother observed: 'She's very sensible and consistent with the children. She doesn't get hysterical and she doesn't pamper them.'

When Beatrice crashed her tricycle into a table in the hall-way and spilt the wax of a burning candle over herself, Sarah calmly took her in her arms and said, 'It doesn't hurt, it doesn't hurt. Be brave, it's all over and there is no need to cry any more,' while Andrew wiped the grease off with a towel.

'It was the right way of dealing with it,' said Sue Ferguson, who witnessed the incident. 'Sarah has the right attitude when dramas happen.'

When Sarah and Andrew separated in 1992, Sarah explained to Beatrice, who was then three and a half, that they would no longer be living with 'Papa', but they would see him just as much—and maybe more.

'Who is looking after Papa?' Beatrice enquired. 'Doesn't he miss us?'

Sarah did her best to protect her daughters from the trauma of the parting. She was helped in that by their young age, and she assured Beatrice that Papa was all right. It was not always easy, though. 'For young children in particular, exclusion from the warmth and safety of a home and family seems a horrendous exile and children worry about the absent parent,' said child psychologist Penelope Leach.

Beatrice sometimes called out 'I want my Papa'. She said just that, to her mother's considerable embarrassment, on the day Sarah left Balmoral after the publication of the photographs from the south of France. As the Duchess was about to drive away from the castle, Beatrice started shouting, 'I don't want to go. I want to stay here with Papa.' Sarah remembered her heart sinking into her shoes. It was, she recalled, the very last thing she wanted to happen at that moment. But she remained calm. She told her daughter, 'Don't worry—Papa's going to work soon.'

Beatrice also wanted her mother, of course. She was at what Leach called the 'clinging' stage, and when Sarah took them to see Andrew she always had to go too.

Again according to Leach, children of that young age 'usually refuse to believe in the fact or the permanency of the separation.' On that score, however, Sarah was adamant. No entreaties by the Queen could persuade her to reconsider her marital situation.

'I can't live a lie,' she explained. 'He is my friend. I love him. But I can't go back.' The pressures of being a member of the Royal Family had finally proved too much for her.

She is equally single-minded, though, in her determination to remain on friendly terms with Andrew, who remained remarkably supportive towards her throughout the tribulations of the separation, even when the intimate photographs of Sarah on holiday in the south of France with her financial advisor John Bryan were published.

For a long time Andrew hoped for a reconciliation. He kept the marital home just as she had left it. On his side of the bed, piled on a bedside table, were all his books, papers and personal things, and on her side, nothing. Eventually Andrew was forced to admit Sarah was not coming back. But he refused ever to believe she had had an affair and still holds out hope that they could be a family again.

There have been plenty of dramas in Sarah's life, but whatever personal turmoil she has experienced she has remained composed in front of her children.

'My children are my world,' she told me. 'They are the only thing in my life that is absolutely one hundred per cent safe and loving and wonderful. They are my everything.'

Bibliography

The Kents – Audrey Whiting, Hutchinson, 1985.

The Duke – Tim Heald, Hodder & Stoughton, 1991.

My Young Friends – Valerie Garner & Janyne Fincher, Weidenfeld & Nicholson, 1989.

Elizabeth II – Douglas Keay, Century, 1991

Princess Margaret – Christopher Warwick, Weidenfeld & Nicholson, 1983.

George & Marina – Christopher Warwick, Weidenfeld & Nicholson, 1988.

George V's Children – John Van Der Kiste, Alan Sutton, 1991.

The Royal Baby Book – Phoebe Hichens, Octopus Books, 1984.

The Royal Baby Album – Diana Thomas, Arlington Books, 1984.

Diana: Her True Story – Andrew Morton, Michael O'Mara, 1992.

The Princess A to Z – Penelope Leach, 1983.

To Be a King – Dermot Morrah, Hutchinson, 1968.

Dinner at Buckingham Palace – Charles Oliver, Prentice-Hall, 1972.

Katherine, Duchess of Kent – Valerie Garner, Weidenfeld and Nicholson, 1991.

Charles – Anthony Holden, Weidenfeld & Nicholson, 1988.

The Last Kaiser – Tyler Whittle, Heinemann, 1977.

King George V – Kenneth Rose, Weidenfeld & Nicholson, 1983.

The Rise and Fall of the British Nanny – Jonathan Gathorne-Hardy, Hodder and Stoughton, 1972.

Bibliography

The Real Charles – Alan Hamilton, Collins, 1988.

By Royal Invitation – Ingrid Seward and Unity Hall, Sidgwick & Jackson, 1988.

Royalty Revealed – Ingrid Seward and Unity Hall, Sidgwick & Jackson, 1989.

Diana – Ingrid Seward, Weidenfeld & Nicholson, 1987.

William of Gloucester, Pioneer Prince – edited by Giles St Aubyn, Frederick Muller Ltd, 1977.

Prince Henry of Gloucester – Noble Frankland, Weidenfeld & Nicholson, 1977.

The Royal Baby Nursery & Fashion Handbook – Sue James, Orbis, 1984.

HRH Prince Andrew – Anwar Hussein, Hamlyn, 1978.

Prince Charles: Horseman – Michael Clayton, Stanley Paul, 1987.

Charles – Penny Junor, Sidgwick & Jackson, 1987.

Elizabeth II – Douglas Keay, Random Century, 1991.

Royal Children – Nicholas Courtney, Dent, 1982.

Riding Through My Life – HRH The Princess Royal with Ivor Herbert, Pelham Books, 1991.

HRH Princess Margaret – Nigel Dempster, Quartet, 1981.

Anne, The Princess Royal – Brian Hoey, Grafton, 1989.

Princess Alexandra – Paul James, Weidenfeld & Nicholson, 1992.

Prince Andrew – Graham and Heather Fisher, WH Allen, 1981.

Cecil Beaton: The Royal Portraits – Cecil Beaton and Roy Strong, Thames & Hudson, 1988.

The Good Schools Guide – Harpers & Queen, 1986.

Memories of 90 Years – Princess Alice, Duchess of Gloucester, Collins & Brown, 1991.

Sarah, HRH The Duchess of York – Ingrid Seward, HarperCollins, 1991.

Acknowledgements

Looking through the archive files of Camera Press one day I found a collection of the most beautiful photographs of royal children – most of them never published before – and decided I wanted to write a book about the royal children of this century. As the summer of 1992 came to its sad conclusion I was left wondering what went wrong. Why were these children seemingly incapable of forming a happy relationship? Just how difficult is it to bring up a child in the rarefied atmosphere of royalty? In my quest for the truth I have spoken to many members of the royal family and many of their friends. In particular, I would like to thank HRH Prince Michael of Kent who regaled me with tales of his schooldays and HRH Princess Michael of Kent who told me with great humour and frankness how she loathed nappy changing and pushing prams and had always managed to employ someone better than herself to do it. I would also like to thank the Duchess of York, whom I have known for many years. I have enjoyed her company and that of her sweet (and beautifully behaved) children on several occasions. Both she and Marina Mowatt, who was extremely helpful, are now outside the royal circle and can look on in a partisan manner. Eileen Parker's observations on the early life of Prince Charles and Princess Anne were invaluable. Many other people also helped, but wish to remain nameless for no other reason than that they do not want media attention drawn so themselves.

I would also like to thank those at Buckingham Palace and in the archives at Windsor Castle, especially Oliver Everett, for

269

Acknowledgements

allowing me access to Queen Mary's photograph albums and the letters of George V to his children. And, finally, a special thanks to Richard Cheeseman of Camera Press who spent so many painstaking hours helping me with picture research.

Index

Index